William Henry Green

The Hebrew Feasts

In their Relation to Recent Critical Hypotheses Concerning the Pentateuch

William Henry Green

The Hebrew Feasts
In their Relation to Recent Critical Hypotheses Concerning the Pentateuch

ISBN/EAN: 9783743386419

Manufactured in Europe, USA, Canada, Australia, Japa

Cover: Foto ©Thomas Meinert / pixelio.de

Manufactured and distributed by brebook publishing software (www.brebook.com)

William Henry Green

The Hebrew Feasts

THE HEBREW FEASTS.

BOOKS BY PROFESSOR GREEN.

The Argument of the Book of Job Unfolded. 12mo, $1.75.

"That ancient composition, so marvellous in beauty and so rich in philosophy, is here treated in a thoroughly analytical manner, and new depths and grander proportions of the divine original portrayed. It is a book to stimulate research."—*Methodist Recorder.*

Moses and the Prophets. 12mo, cloth, $..00.

"It has impressed me as one of the most thorough and conclusive pieces of apologetics that has been composed for a long time. The critic confines himself to the positions laid down by Smith, and, without being diverted by any side issues or bringing in any other views of other theorists, replies to those positions in a style that carries conviction."—*Professor W. G. T. Shedd, D.D.*

THEIR RELATION TO

RECENT CRITICAL HYPOTHESES

CONCERNING

THE PENTATEUCH.

BY

WILLIAM HENRY GREEN,
Professor in Princeton Theological Seminary.

NEW YORK:
HURST & COMPANY, Publishers,
122 Nassau Street.

THROUGH the liberality of the Hon. J. Warren Merrill, A.M., three courses of lectures upon topics selected by the Faculty of the Newton Theological Institution have been delivered to the students during the last three years by teachers connected with other seminaries. In each of the first two courses different topics were discussed by several eminent lecturers. The series now published is the only full course yet given by a single lecturer upon one theme. It is hoped that in process of time there will be many other volumes of " Newton Lectures " offered to the Christian public.

ALVAH HOVEY,
President Newton Theological Institution.

NEWTON CENTRE, *Aug.* 5, 1885.

PREFACE.

THE new departure in Old Testament Criticism represented by Reuss, Wellhausen and Kuenen rests upon the conception that the religious institutions of Israel, as these are exhibited in the Pentateuch, are not the product of one mind or of one age, but are the growth of successive ages; that the laws in which they are enacted, and which have been commonly attributed to Moses, are really composite, and are divisible into distinct strata, which are referable to widely separated periods, and that the growth of these institutions can be traced in the laws which ordain them from their primitive simplicity to those more complicated forms which they ultimately assume. And it is further claimed that this result, which is reached by an analysis of the laws, is verified by the statements of the history, provided the history itself is first subjected to proper critical treatment, and its earlier and later elements are correctly discriminated. Wellhausen's "Prolegomena to the History of Israel," which has recently been issued in an English dress, is a most elaborate attempt to establish his revolutionary ideas by appeals to the legislation and the history in regard to the Place of Worship, the Sacrifices, the Sacred Feasts, and the Priesthood. The purpose of these lectures, delivered at Newton Theological Institution at the request of its honored Faculty, and now published at their instance, is to test this critical hypothesis by an examination of the Hebrew Feasts. Two reasons led to the selection of this point for more particular discussion. First, the Feasts are alleged to be one of its main props, and to afford the clearest proof that the various Pentateuchal laws belong to different eras and represent distinct stages in the religious life of the people. And secondly, while the critical views respecting the Sanctuary, the Sacrifices, and the Priesthood have been vigorously and successfully assailed, proportionate prominence has not been given by the opponents of the hypothesis to the matter of the Feasts.

I take this opportunity to return my acknowledgments to the generous friend of sacred learning who made provision for these lectures, and to the Faculty of the institution, who honored me by the appointment to deliver them, and whose kindly courtesies made my brief stay in Newton most delightful.

W. HENRY GREEN.

PRINCETON, N. J., *August* 8, 1885.

CONTENTS.

I. THE WELLHAUSEN HYPOTHESIS IN GENERAL.
Page 11.

Its originators, 11; the previous Literary Analysis, its grounds and results, 12; its fallacies and defects, 14; the new method and its proposed test, 16; the three Codes, 17; their characteristics and the periods to which they are assigned, 18; variance with Scriptural statements, 27; causes of its popularity, 28; the Codes do not belong to distinct periods, 30; their differences otherwise accounted for, 33; alleged correspondence with separate periods unfounded, 34; other falsities and fallacies, 38; not a mere question of order, but one of vital consequence, 40.

II. THE HISTORY OF OPINION RESPECTING THE HEBREW FEASTS.
Page 45.

The several feast laws, 45, form one complete and consistent scheme, 46; not an accidental conglomerate, 50; judgment of Ewald, 50; alleged discrepancies, 51; views of Rationalists, De Wette, 52; Comparative Religion, Christian Fathers, Maimonides, Marsham, Spencer, 55; Witsius, 57; F. C. Baur, 58; Literary Criticism, 61; Gramberg, 63; Von Bohlen, 65; Stähelin, 66; Hitzig, 67; Bertheau, 68; Ewald, 69; Von Lengerke, Hupfeld, 72; Knobel, 75; Dillmann, 77; Archæology, De Wette, Winer, 79; Symbolism, Bähr, 79; result of this inquiry, 80.

III. THE UNITY OF EXODUS, CHAPTERS 12, 13.
Page 83.

Critical assertions, 83; preliminary observations, 85; the narrative in Exodus the key of the whole position, 87; Eichhorn, Dillmann,

89 ; Vater, Gramberg, 90 ; George, Stähelin, Vatke, 92 ; diversity in regard to 12: 24-27, 95 ; Nöldeke, Kayser, 98 ; Wellhausen, Dillmann, 99 ; the partition factitious, 100 ; alleged inconsistencies n the laws of these chapters, 103 ; or between the laws and the narrative, 107 ; or in the narrative itself, 110 ; alleged want of connection, 114 ; repetitions, 118.

IV. THE UNITY OF EXODUS, CHAPTERS 12, 13.
(Continued.)
Page 125.

Objections from diction and style, 125 ; preliminary remarks, 126 ; alleged criteria of the Elohist and Jehovist, 127 ; legal phrases, 131 ; other Elohistic words and expressions, 133 ; month Abib, 142 ; Jehovistic expressions, 144 ; verdict of Graf, 148 ; argument from the substantial agreement of critics, 148 ; the narrative in Exodus a credible and true history, 155 ; objections answered, 159.

V. THE FEAST LAWS AND THE PASSOVER.
Page 165.

What laws are referred respectively to the Jehovist, Elohist and Deuteronomist, 165 ; relation of Ex. 23 and 34, 166 ; Lev. 23 in harmony with and related to the preceding, 171 ; Num. 28, 29, 177; Num. 9 and Deut. 16, 178 ; alleged development of the Passover, combination with the feast of Unleavened Bread, 180 ; change from agricultural to historical, 186 ; Passover not derived from offering of firstlings, 190 ; Unleavened Bread not a harvest feast, 195 ; difficulty in regard to first-fruits, 202.

VI. THE PASSOVER.—(Continued.)
Page 205.

Time of the feast, 205 ; Hitzig's notion, 206 ; change from undefined period to a fixed day, 208 ; prolongation of the term, George and Wellhausen, 210 ; Deut. 16: 7, 214 ; changes in the ritual, 217 ; roasting the flesh, 218 ; public substituted for private sacrifices, 219 ; place of celebration, 221 ; no diversity in the laws, 223 ; the history, 224; the prophets, 225 ; Josiah's Passover, 228 ; no development discoverable, 231 ; Ezekiel, 233 ; conclusion, 238.

VII. THE FEAST OF WEEKS.
Page 243.

Its names, 243 ; Wellhausen on Ex. 34 : 22, 244 ; Hitzig's view, 245; duration of the feast, 247 ; septenary cycle, 247 ; Ewald's scheme, 248 ; liable to objections, 250 ; Hupfeld's view, 253 ; improved by Riehm, 256 ; development claimed, 256 ; no added historical association, 257 ; no change in time, 258 ; " the morrow after the Sabbath," George, 260 ; Hitzig, 264 ; Kayser, Knobel, Kurtz, 265 ; Wellhausen, Dillmann, 266 ; the traditional view correct, 267 ; Kliefoth, Hupfeld, 270 ; no change in duration, 271 ; ritual, 272 ; or place of observance, 273 ; silence of the history, 273 ; George's confession, 275.

VIII. THE FEAST OF TABERNACLES.
Page 279.

Its design, 279 ; culmination of the festal series, 280 ; oftenest mentioned in the history, 281 ; alleged development, 282 ; in character and design, 284 ; in its time and duration, 286 ; the Atsereth, 291 ; mode of observance, 292 ; critical analysis of Lev. 23, Wellhausen, Kayser, 293 ; Reuss, 294 ; Dillmann, unity of the chapter, 295 ; Wellhausen's assertion of interpolations, 296 ; Neh. 8 : 15, 17, 300 ; from individual to national sacrifices, 302 ; the latter do not chill devotion, nor engender formality, 303 ; from local sanctuaries to one central place of worship, 305 ; Wellhausen's treatment of the history, 306 ; Shiloh, 308 ; Solomon's Temple, 309 ; high places, 312 ; Bethel, 313 ; only one pilgrimage feast in early times, 314 ; the Psalms know but one sanctuary, 315 ; the Prophets, 316 ; evasions, 316 ; patriarchal narratives 318 ; the ark, 319 ; fallacy of the circle, 321.

I.

THE WELLHAUSEN HYPOTHESIS IN GENERAL.

THE HEBREW FEASTS.

I.

THE WELLHAUSEN HYPOTHESIS IN GENERAL.

IT was in 1866 (just nineteen years ago) that Karl Heinrich Graf published his now famous treatise on the "Historical Books of the Old Testament." From this properly dates the hypothesis of the post-exilic origin of the Pentateuch, which has of late attracted so much attention, as further elaborated by Kuenen, Kayser, and others, and especially by Julius Wellhausen, who is now the acknowledged leader of the school. A like view had been propounded by Vatke in his "Religion of the Old Testament," and by George in his "Older Jewish Feasts" in 1835; and it is also claimed by Prof. Reuss, of Strassburg, that he had broached the same in his lectures since 1833; but at that time it gained no adherents, and was universally regarded as extravagant and paradoxical.

The way had been prepared for the new hypothesis by the literary analysis which had previously been undertaken of the Pentateuch. This took its rise from the suggestion that the remarkable alternation of divine names in successive sections in the book of Genesis is referable to distinct writers, each of whom was characterized by the constant or predominant use of one favorite term for God. It was hence assumed that Genesis was originally compiled from two or more independent treatises, into which it might again by the application of critical rules be freshly decomposed. And the same process was further carried with more or less success through the entire Pentateuch and even beyond it. This hypothesis was supposed to find abundant confirmation in the alleged fact that when the treatises now blended in the Pentateuch were properly sundered, they were found to bear all the marks of separate authorship, each being in a measure complete in itself, each having its own peculiar diction and style, its plan and purpose, its range of ideas and conception of the history and of the various actors in it, and betraying more or less distinctly the circumstances and the tendencies under which it was composed. The microscopic comparisons which were instituted between these newly discovered treatises, brought to light the most astounding and pervading divergences between them, discrepant accounts of the same transaction, variant representations of the life and manners and particularly of the religious usages of the same periods and the same men, so that it was plain that they had severally followed quite diverse traditions. The final Redactor, to whom the Pentateuch owes its present form, had evidently sought to harmonize his conflicting sources and to cover up their disagreements; but the critical process by removing his late additions left these original treatises in bald and sharp antagonism and revealed the underlying discordance in what seems to the ordinary reader a continuous and consistent narrative.

Conclusions were hence drawn unfavorable to the truthfulness and accuracy of one or other of these primary sources and perhaps of both; until the Pentateuch, from being a homogeneous record of events and institutions accredited by the authority and inspiration of Moses, was reduced to a compilation, by no one knows who, of legends gathered from diverse and contradictory sources originating no one knows how. The extent to which this destructive process was carried, varied with the taste or fancy of the critic. In general the work of demolition was carried on with an unsparing hand. And such of the divisive critics as were most disposed to reverence the Pentateuch and to defend its sacredness and its truth found the ground slipping away beneath their feet in spite of their utmost endeavors. The hypothesis proved even to the soundest and best of its adherents a steep incline down which they inevitably slid, destitute of any firm support, to lower and still lower views of this portion at least of God's inspired word.

The several ages of the various documents, from which it was held that the Pentateuch had been made up, were eagerly discussed. Conjectures ranged *ad libitum* through the centuries without reaching any clear or well-sustained result. But amid all diversities on other points it was generally agreed that Deuteronomy was the capping stone of the Pentateuchal edifice and that it must have been added at or before the time when "the book of the law" was found in the temple in the reign of Josiah.

Such in brief was the state of things in the critical world, when the new hypothesis of Reuss, Graf and Wellhausen appeared upon the scene. Symptoms of weariness and discontent had begun to manifest themselves at the dreary monotony of a literary criticism with its infinitesimal and subtle distinctions, which assumed to settle all questions of style and authorship by the mechanical application of the rule and the compass, which paraded its long drawn out lists of words and phrases the use of any one of which infallibly determined the author not merely of paragraphs or sections, but of single sentences, clauses and even words, which may thus be torn out of their connection and assigned to some foreign context and in a sense quite different from that which they must bear, where they actually appear. The arbitrary character of the whole proceeding was apparent; and no less that the assumed diversities of style were largely fictitious. That the poetic words should belong to that document to which the poetic passages were regularly assigned; that given words and phrases should not appear in passages in which there is no occasion for their employment; that different expressions should be used in relation to the same thing in different connections where the shade of thought to be conveyed is varied; that classes of words which are akin in thought or usage should be regularly found in combination; that a partition conducted on the assumption that certain words and phrases characterize one writer and accordingly all sections, paragraphs or sentences in which they appear must be assigned to him, while those containing certain other words and phrases must, with like regularity, be assigned to the other writer, should result in precisely the division which the critic has undertaken to make;—all this surely is not surprising, and requires no such extraordinary hypothesis to account for it, as the critics would have us suppose. For with all the appearance of painstaking and scientific caution and rigorous accuracy with which their reasoning is conducted, the imposing accumulation of details adduced in support of diversity of authorship is to a great extent entirely irrelevant, and of no force whatever for the purpose for which it is urged. The indefinite multiplication of airy nothings does not amount to anything substantial after all. We may be excused if we hesitate to commit ourselves without reserve to the guidance of those whose arguments are so often unreliable, or to confide implicitly in the strength and durability of a structure built so largely of hay and stubble.

A further difficulty with the literary criticism of the Pentateuch was the absence of any external criterion by which to test the truth and accuracy of its results. Its text was parcelled among the various writers who were said to have had a share in its composition, and confident assertions were made as to the period when these writers lived and the principles by which they were actuated. But there was no trace whatever of their existence apart from the literary phenomena of the Pentateuch itself, upon which all the argumentation of the critics was based. There was no extraneous proof to establish the objective reality of the critics' conclusions or to do away with the suspicion that they may only have been building castles in the air.

The new hypothesis was skilfully framed to supply these deficiencies in its predecessor. In the first place it is based upon a different method; and secondly, it offers an external test of the correctness of its results. Its method is to trace the growth of laws and institutions. The principle upon which it is based is that of development, which is founded in the nature of man and must have had the same application in Israel as among other nations. The simpler and more natural form must have preceded the more complex and recondite. Different enactments relating to the same subject belong to distinct periods of time and are to be arranged in the order of their advancement from small beginnings to more fully developed forms. The correctness of the result is to be tested by an appeal to history. The successive stages of the institutions of Israel, as these can be traced in the Pentateuchal laws, can be recognized afresh in the course of their history. They are, it is claimed, in precise correspondence with what the historians and the prophets show did actually exist at different periods among the people. The conclusions deduced from the legislation find thus their voucher in the history; and the date of any given portion of the legislation is determined by its coincidence with the state of things at some known epoch.

The so-called Mosaic law according to Wellhausen

forms the starting-point for the history of modern Judaism, but not of ancient Israel. It has been invested with undisputed authority since the Babylonish exile; but the entire history prior to that is not only at variance with its most express and solemn provisions, but is such as to render it evident that it was altogether unknown. There are three clearly distinguishable bodies of law in the Pentateuch. The first is in Exodus, ch. 20–24, and is technically called the Book of the Covenant. The second, to which Wellhausen gives the name of the Priest Code, embraces the subsequent portion of Exodus, ch. 25–40, with the exception of three chapters (32–34) relating to the affair of the golden calf, the whole of Leviticus and considerable sections of Numbers, ch. 1–10, 15–19, 25–36. The third is found in the legislative portion of the book of Deuteronomy. These three bodies of law, it is affirmed, are not the product of one legislator or of one age, but took their rise in distinct and widely separated periods.

In the dissection of the Pentateuch, which Wellhausen accepts with some modifications from the literary critics, the Book of the Covenant belongs to what is commonly termed the Jehovist document; so called because it, throughout the book of Genesis, prevailingly speaks of God by his name Jehovah. Wellhausen distinguishes it by the initials JE, to indicate its composite character, as including likewise the sections which, since Hupfeld, have been attributed to the so-called Second Elohist, a writer who uses the term Elohim for God in Genesis, but differs materially in style from the other sections using the same term. This document is of a prevailingly historical character, only inserting this brief code of laws at what the writer considers its proper historical place; and another still briefer legislative passage in Ex. 34, which seems to be closely related to the Book of the Covenant, but which Wellhausen claims was of a quite independent origin. According to the narrative in which they are found, these laws were given by God to Moses on the summit of Sinai. But the internal evidence is held to be decisive against this. It implies that the people for whom it was drawn up were engaged in agriculture. It speaks, Ex. 22 : 5, 6, of fields and vineyards and standing grain, and prescribes the restitution to be made in case of damage done to either; ver. 29 requires promptness in offering the best of their fruits and the products of their presses; 23 : 10, 11 directs that their fields should be tilled, and the fruits of their vineyards and oliveyards should be gathered for six years, but not in the seventh; ver. 16 appoints feasts at harvest and at ingathering. Hence it is inferred that these laws could not have been drawn up until Israel was settled in Canaan, and there learned the art of agriculture, the people having been nomads previously.

It is further claimed that these laws imply and sanction numerous sanctuaries in different parts of the land: that the direction, 20 : 24, 25, to erect an altar of earth or stone wherever God should record his name can not refer to the brazen altar at the tabernacle or temple, and can not be limited to one single spot; and that the same thing is implied 21 : 13, 14 in God's altar being a refuge for the unintentional manslayer, since one place of refuge would be manifestly insufficient for the whole land; as well as 22 : 30 in their giving the firstlings of their cattle to God on the eighth day, since the owner of flocks and herds could not journey to a distant sanctuary every time that a first-born lamb or calf reached its eighth day. These regulations, it is said, correspond with the state of things exhibited in the books of Judges and Samuel, and in the early part of the history of the kings. Samuel and others offered sacrifice in various parts of the land without censure and apparently without any knowledge of the existence of a law restricting sacrifice to the altar at the tabernacle.

And with this agree, it is said, the historical portions of this same Jehovist document, which record the offerings made by the patriarchs at various places, at Bethel, Beersheba and elsewhere. These are not narratives of actual fact, but stories designed to give an ancestral and even divine sanction to the sanctuaries of later days. Among the sacred spots resorted to in different parts of the land, some had been sanctuaries before the Israelites occupied Canaan, the people continuing to venerate the places which had been hallowed by the former inhabitants, only substituting the worship of Jehovah for that of Baal; other sanctuaries had been founded by the Israelites themselves since the conquest. The distinction between the more ancient and the more recent sanctuaries survived in popular remembrance, and stories of ancestral worship or of remarkable events in the lives of the patriarchs readily grew up in connection with the former.

The prophets from the days of Hosea discountenanced the abuses and idolatrous forms which were sanctioned or tolerated at these local sanctuaries. Hence they could not have been the authors of narratives designed to exalt and add lustre to such sanctuaries. These narratives and the Jehovist document, which contains them, must belong to a time when the sacred places thus linked with the patriarchs were universally reverenced, and before the better disposed began to regard them with suspicion or to denounce them as sources of corruption. The Book of the Covenant, which is incorporated in this document, must therefore antedate the period of the prophets.

The first of the Pentateuchal codes, then, the Book of the Covenant, took its rise some time after the occupation of the land of Canaan, and before the time of Hosea, Amos and Isaiah. The Deuteronomic laws, while adopting and repeating with some modifications almost everything contained in the code already spoken of, in one point present a striking contrast with it. They insist with the utmost strenuousness that all the old Canaanitish sanctuaries must be destroyed and that all sacrifices must be brought to one sole altar at the place which the LORD should choose; and that the people must not continue to do "after all the things that we do here this day, every man whatsoever is right in his own eyes," Deut. 12: 1–8. This, it is claimed, gives evidence that these laws constitute a new departure, an attempt to reform the existing state of things by abolishing the local sanctuaries, to which the people had freely resorted before, and confining the worship of God henceforth to a single sanctuary.

Now just such an attempt to centralize worship was made in the reign of Josiah. By the most active and resolute measures he put an end to the sanctuaries outside of Jerusalem, and required all worship to be strictly limited to the temple there. And he did so in confessed obedience to a book of the law then recently discovered in the temple. This book was the Deuteronomic law, and this event fixes both the time when and the circumstances under which that law originated. It was the product of the prophetic party, aided by the priests, in opposition to the hitherto prevailing popular religion. The best men of the nation had become convinced that worship could only be regulated and kept pure by being centralized. The local sanctuaries tended to foster debased and corrupting forms of worship. All attempts to purify them had proved unavailing. Hosea and Amos unsparingly denounced them, not thereby meaning to disapprove of multiplicity of sanctuaries in itself considered, but of the abuses which had gained lodgment in them. Solomon had built the temple at Jerusalem, not with any view of making it the sole place of sacrifice, much less under the constraint of any statute, requiring that there should be only one sanctuary, but to add splendor to the royal residence by rearing a magnificent sanctuary there. The worship in high places was not abolished under Solomon nor his immediate successors. The recorded attempt by Hezekiah to destroy them Wellhausen discredits, thinking it much more probable that he simply sought to destroy the images and idolatrous symbols which were found in them; inasmuch as Isaiah, who had the largest influence with the king, did not oppose the high places as such, but only the idolatry which was practiced there, and he regarded Jerusalem as sacred not because it contained the temple, but because it was the centre and seat of Jehovah's empire.

While, however, the centralization of worship had never yet been attempted nor so much as thought of, there were influences at work which tended in that direction. The temple at the capital was naturally superior in splendor and celebrity to the sanctuaries in rural districts and provincial towns. The overthrow and exile of the ten tribes, amongst whom high places principally abounded, came to be regarded as a divine declaration against them, while the signal protection accorded to Jerusalem and the disastrous overthrow of Sennacherib gave new éclat to its temple as a specially favored divine abode. The prophetic denunciations of the high places, though really directed against the corruptions which had crept in there and the perverted notions of the merit of ritual performances, further lessened their prestige and influence. The comparative purity of the worship maintained at Jerusalem, though this was not free, so Wellhausen thinks, from idolatrous taint, and the fact that it was more directly subject to a supervision which could exclude abuses that were liable to spring up in remoter or more obscure places, strengthened the attachment of the pious to the temple and led them to look with disfavor upon all other sanctuaries. While finally the inconsiderable size of the kingdom of Judah, which now alone survived, made the closing of the local sanctuaries possible as never before. Under these circumstances the restriction of worship to the temple at Jerusalem was resolved upon as a necessary reform and the only method by which idolatry could be effectually and permanently suppressed. Accordingly with this view the Deuteronomic Code was prepared, and a hearty support given by both priests and prophets to its enforcement by Josiah.

The centralization of worship, which was thus the great need of that period, is the characteristic feature of Deuteronomy, which explains all its deviations from the antecedent Book of the Covenant. Thus, while the early usage had been that every animal slain for food must first be offered in sacrifice at some sanctuary easily accessible, Deuteronomy recognizes the fact that under the new order of things it would be impossible to make a pilgrimage to the one central sanctuary at Jerusalem, on every such occasion. Hence formal permission is granted, Deut. 12 : 15, 21, to slay animals for food in all their gates, *i. e.*, at their homes in any part of the land. By closing the local sanctuaries those who had ministered in them would be deprived of their occupation and means of livelihood; hence the frequent injunctions in Deuteronomy to befriend the Levites as a needy class, 12 : 19, etc., and the explicit direction, 18 : 6–8, that Levites coming up from any part of the land to Jerusalem should have the same right to minister there as those connected with the temple

Under the old law of the Book of the Covenant, Ex. 22 : 30, the firstlings of their cattle were offered to God on the eighth day: this was practicable when there were sanctuaries in every neighborhood. But in abolishing these, Deuteronomy makes provision for the change in this respect by ordaining, 15 : 19, 20, that all firstlings should be offered year by year at the sanctuary, and permission was given, 14 : 23-26, to convert them into money at their homes with which to purchase an equivalent when they arrive at Jerusalem.

While for reasons such as have been recited, the law of Deuteronomy is assigned to the period of the struggle for centralization of worship, which culminated under Josiah, the Levitical law is attributed to a still later date, when that struggle had been successfully terminated. Instead of the urgent demand to abolish other sanctuaries and restrict worship to one only, which is found in Deuteronomy, the Priest Code everywhere takes the unity of the altar and of the sanctuary for granted, as a settled principle of the worship of Jehovah, and one which was universally acknowledged.

The success of the prophetic party under Josiah was only temporary. The attachment of the people to their ancestral sanctuaries was too strong to be uprooted at once. In succeeding reigns the high places were again restored and things returned very much to the old status. And it is doubtful whether the desired change could have been brought about had the people remained undisturbed in their own land. But the Babylonish exile by removing them from Canaan broke up all their old associations and severed them from their holy places until these were forgotten and their spell was broken. After the captivity Israel as a whole did not return, but those only who were most firmly attached to the worship of Jehovah and who were willing to be guided by the prophets. They were not properly a nation, but a religious sect. The small impoverished community which settled at or near Jerusalem had but one sanctuary to which to go. The disposition to worship in high places was completely broken and never reappeared. It was to a public assembly of these returned exiles that Ezra produced the law adapted to this state of things, formally read it, and in a solemn manner engaged them to obey it. This, then, was the origin of the Priest Code, in which the unity of the sanctuary is not, as in Deuteronomy, spoken of as an innovation upon existing usages, but as though it had been established from the beginning and even ordained by Moses in the wilderness, the figment of a Mosaic tabernacle, being simply the reflex of the temple of Solomon transported back to those early times.

As a consequence the whole character of the religion of Israel was completely changed. This was indeed a necessary result of the centralization aimed at in Deuteronomy, though it was a result neither foreseen nor desired by the authors of that law. Religion now became a matter of public ritual, an affair of the priesthood; from being the spontaneous expression of devout feeling in the varied circumstances of life, it was petrified into a monotonous round of the most minutely prescribed services. The body of the people were remote from the sanctuary and only visited it at special and stated times. The daily worship was conducted by the priests without the participation of the people, whose presence was in nowise essential to its efficacy. Sacrifice had formerly been a joyous tribute of gratitude to God for personal or domestic gifts or blessings, and a chief feature of it was a festive meal partaken of by the offerer and his family or friends. But now the individual and the household were sunk in the mass of the congregation of Israel. What was peculiar to each, gave way to what was common to all. The sacrifice instead of being a specific offering on individual occasion was presented rather on behalf of the whole people, and came to be regarded in the sombre light of an atonement for sin in which all shared. New forms of sacrifice giving special prominence to this idea, the sin-offering and the trespass-offering, which were never heard of till the time of Ezekiel, are prescribed in the Priest Code. And the idea culminated in the annual day of Atonement, which was altogether foreign to the worship of earlier times, and is an innovation later than the time of Ezekiel, and, in fact, even than that of Ezra. The sacred incense, which none but a priest could offer except at the peril of their lives, and the golden altar of incense, of which earlier history knows nothing, are also innovations of the Priest Code, which is quite in the spirit of the later Phariseeism rather than in that of ancient Israel.

The advocates of this hypothesis are at no pains to conceal the fact, which is sufficiently obvious, that it is quite at variance with the statements of the sacred writers. It is expressly declared of the three codes that they originated not in distinct and widely separated periods after the settlement in Canaan, but with Moses himself before Canaan was entered. The Book of the Covenant and the law of Deuteronomy are explicitly stated to have been written by Moses, and the Levitical law is said in each of its statutes to have been directly communicated by God to him. And the precise time and occasion, when these several laws were either orally declared or committed to writing, are given with circumstantial detail. All this, however, is set aside as mere fictitious drapery, though it has never been satisfactorily explained how successive codes of law could ever have been accepted and submitted to as genuine and authoritative enactments of Moses, and which had always been in force since his day,—and that, too, by the generation in which they had been concocted and who must have known that they had never been heard of before.

Then in the various historical books of the Old Testament, it is claimed that a distinction is to be made between the facts as they really were and the coloring which the various writers have given to them. Chronicles, which clearly represents the Levitical law as in operation throughout the whole period of the kingdom in Israel, is set aside as altogether unreliable, written in the interest of the Priest-Code and falsifying the history in order to bring it into correspondence with that Code. The author of Kings, though unacquainted, it is said, with the Priest Code, lived subsequent to the introduction of the Deuteronomic law, and has not scrupled to weave in his own opinions of its Mosaic origin, which must be disentangled from his narrative before it can be implicitly relied upon. So too the histories of Judges and Samuel, though these are paraded as the stronghold of the hypothesis, nevertheless have not come down to us in their primitive and authentic form. They have been revised and retouched, and these additions of a later age, imbued with the notions of that period, must be eliminated by critical processes before the true original shape of the narrative is reached. The history of Israel as it has been transmitted to us, has been systematically altered and falsified to further the ends of the prophetic and priestly party. It must be restored to what the modern critical instinct sees fit to regard as its true original form,—that is to say, to a form which shall correspond with the hypothesis to be maintained and from which everything has been expunged that opposes it.

The hypothesis, which has been thus briefly sketched in its outline and in the general tenor of the grounds adduced to support it, though bold and revolutionary, had such an appearance of scientific precision, and was so ingeniously shaped in correspondence with historical facts, that it gained a sudden popularity. Two additional causes likewise contributed to this result. In the first place it coincided with the current tendency to trace everywhere a gradual development by subjecting the religion of Israel to this same law. It claims that their institutions were not given to the people in completed form at the outset of their history, **but** proceeded from rude and imperfect beginnings to more and more advanced forms under historical influences which it undertakes to indicate. Their ideas and worship were slowly lifted from the level of their idolatrous and polytheistic neighbors to the elevation which they reached under the prophets, and finally passed into the stage of ritualistic formalism which characterized the Judaism of a later date. This commended it to those who saw in it a plausible means of undermining supernatural religion by doing away with the need and the reality of miraculous interventions and prophetic foresight and reducing all to a progression explicable on purely natural principles. It proved likewise acceptable to others who held fast their religious faith, but who thought that they could see the supernatural hand of God still conspicuous though working by other methods and in different lines from those which he had previously been supposed to pursue.

The other potent cause of its popularity lay in the state of critical opinion when it made its appearance. It completely outflanked the positions taken by its predecessors, and bore down upon them with irresistible force. To their uncertain and slenderly supported conjectures as to the respective ages of the successive strata, which they agreed to distinguish in the Pentateuch, it opposed sharply defined conclusions based on an imposing number of skilfully marshalled historical data. And it showed how utterly untenable was the opinion of those who referred Deuteronomy to the time of the later kings on the ground that its law restricting sacrifice to a single sanctuary could not have existed before the reign of Josiah, or at any rate that of Hezekiah, and yet quietly suffered Leviticus, with its recognition of but one sanctuary and one altar of sacrifice, to have been in existence long before. This position is self-contradictory; and Wellhausen justly directs his well-aimed and unsparing shafts of ridicule against those who "with blind faith hold fast not to the church tradition—there would be sense in that—but to a hypothesis a few decenniums old, for such is De Wette's discovery that Deuteronomy is more recent than the Priest Code."[1]

There are a few general observations, which may here be made in relation to this hypothesis of Wellhausen in a preliminary way.

1. The three Pentateuchal codes so called do not belong to distinct periods of the people's history. It is claimed for them all in the most explicit manner that they were delivered immediately by Moses himself. The account given of them is quite simple and satisfactory, and there is no sufficient reason for discrediting it. The Book of the Covenant was drawn up at Mount Sinai directly after the proclamation of the ten commandments from its summit and preparatory to the formal ratification of the covenant between Jehovah and Israel. That such a relation was established then and there and under the circumstances here recorded was the steadfast faith of Israel from that time forward; a faith which is well accredited, and is the more remarkable as the scene is altogether outside of the territory of Israel, the holy land, to

---

[1] Wellhausen's "Geschichte Israels," p. 173. This paragraph is dropped in the second edition, entitled "Prolegomena zur Geschichte Israels," 1883.

which, as the critics tell us, Jehovah and his worship were so strictly bound. No possible reason can be given why this most sacred transaction, which lay at the basis of the entire history and worship of Israel, should have been referred to this remote point in the desert, away from the sacred soil of Canaan, away from every patriarchal association, away from every spot that was venerated in the past or that was hallowed or resorted to in the present, unless that was the place where it actually occurred. That laws first issued in Jehovah's name in Canaan should be attributed to this mountain in the wilderness, with which Jehovah had no special connection before or since, is inconceivable. The sublime miracles attending the promulgation of the law are surely no reason for disputing the truth of the record; for they were certainly in place if miracles ever were. Moses, trained in the wisdom of Egypt, was plainly competent to the task of framing this simple body of statutes, which was largely intended in the first instance for the guidance of the judges who had recently been appointed to assist Moses in the settlement of controversies arising among the people. And as they expected shortly to take possession of Canaan, these laws naturally contemplated not only the immediate present, but the proximate future when they would be the owners of fields and vineyards and be engaged in agricultural pursuits.

After the covenant with Jehovah had been duly ratified, provision was next made for the maintenance of this relation by instituting ordinances of worship. A new body of regulations was accordingly demanded for this specific purpose, establishing a sanctuary, a priesthood, a ritual and sacred seasons. This was done in the Levitical law or the so-called Priest Code, which was mainly drawn up during the year that the people remained encamped at Sinai, and then added to from time to time during the subsequent journeying in the wilderness. The particularity and minuteness of its prescriptions need not surprise any one who recalls the numerous petty details with which the ritual of ancient Egypt was burdened.

Finally, when Israel had reached the borders of the promised land, and their great leader knew that he must die, he delivered those impressive farewell discourses which are found in the book of Deuteronomy, exhorting them in the most tender and earnest terms to adhere faithfully to the LORD'S service and to obey his laws. And he takes this opportunity to recapitulate them so far as was needed for the guidance of the people, with such modifications as were suggested by the experience of forty years and the altered circumstances of Israel, who were now to enter at once upon the inheritance promised to their fathers.

Each of these bodies of law has thus its distinct occasion and separate purpose, and each is appropriate to the circumstances which called it forth. They are throughout cast in the mould of the Mosaic age and of the abode in the wilderness, and their whole style and character are as different as possible from that which they must have borne if they had been produced at any subsequent period. Much of the contents, particularly of Deuteronomy and of the Levitical law, would be not only superfluous, but preposterous, if the former was produced in the time of Josiah and the latter in that of Ezra.

2. The differences between these codes are such as arise naturally from the difference of occasion and purpose already referred to, and do not by any means justify the assumption that they did not all emanate from one authority and belong to the same period of time. Most of the discrepancies alleged are purely imaginary, and are created by false interpretations of the critics themselves. And while there are a few particulars which it is difficult to harmonize, these are not more than might be expected in institutions so ancient, so foreign to our usages, and in regard to which we are so imperfectly informed. The asserted difference in regard to the unity of the sanctuary, which is the main prop of the entire hypothesis, positively does not exist. The Book of the Covenant does not sanction a plurality of altars: on the contrary it contemplates but one altar, Ex. 21 : 14, and one house of God, 23 : 19. It contains, 20 : 24 f., the most general law for the Israelitish altar, and one designed to cover all possible cases; and it is of course less explicit than the succeeding codes to which it was preliminary. It does not restrict the altar to any single locality, for Israel was marching through the wilderness and must offer worship wherever they encamped. It does not limit sacrifice to the tabernacle, for this was not yet built, and no direction had yet been given for its construction. It prescribes that an altar of earth or stone should be erected, not in every place taken at random, nor wherever they might think proper to rear an altar, but wherever God should re-

cord his name, or make his name to be remembered by any disclosure or manifestation of himself. After the erection of the tabernacle all such manifestations of God were ordinarily confined to it; so that this then became coincident with the requirement of the Levitical law that all sacrifices must be brought to the tabernacle, wherever that might be in their migrations. And when the time arrived, to which Deuteronomy looks forward, 12 : 9 f., when Israel should come to the inheritance which the LORD was giving them, and he should give them rest from all their enemies round about, then the migrations of Israel and of the house of God established in the midst of them would terminate, and the injunction to build an altar where God would record his name becomes identical in thought, and closely related even in the form of expression, with the phrase so constantly employed in Deuteronomy, "the place which Jehovah shall choose to place his name there," 12 : 5. At the same time the fact that Deuteronomy itself directs, 27 : 5, 6, the erection of an altar of stone upon Ebal in terms manifestly drawn from the earlier law in Exodus, 20 : 25, shows that extraordinary altars having immediate divine sanction were no violation of that unity of the sanctuary, upon which this book so strenuously insists. There is accordingly the most thorough agreement of the three codes in this matter, both in principle and in its application; and no such divergence, as this most extraordinary hypothesis assumes, is to be found.

3. The separate correspondence of the three codes severally with three distinct periods of the history is

likewise a chimera. It is utterly at variance with the testimony of every witness that we are able to summon, to maintain that the unity of the altar was not an accepted part of the religion of Israel until the reign of Josiah. The book of Joshua explicitly informs us that it belonged both to their creed and to their practice at the time of their first settlement in Canaan. When Joshua had completed the conquest of the land the whole congregation of the children of Israel assembled together at Shiloh and set up the Mosaic tabernacle, 18 : 1, whose exclusiveness is beyond dispute. Here Eleazar the son of Aaron was priest; and he with Joshua and the heads of the people divided the land by lot before the LORD at the door of the tabernacle of the congregation, 19 : 51. The narrative of the altar of witness erected on the east of the Jordan by the two tribes and a half and the negotiations relative thereto, ch. 22, show how criminal a departure from the faith of Israel the building of a separate altar was felt to be. We can not concede to the critics the right to set these statements aside as summarily as they do, simply because they do not square with their hypothesis.

Proceeding to the next historical book, Judges knows but one house of Jehovah, 19 : 18, that at Shiloh, 18 : 31, where the annual feast of Jehovah was celebrated, 21 : 19. The critics indeed profess to find mention made of a number of sanctuaries at Bochim, Gilgal, Kedesh, Tabor, Ophrah, Shechem, the two Mizpehs, Zorah, Bethel, Dan, and the chapel of the renegade Micah. The whole of which is pure invention; and to adopt a simile, which Wellhausen[1] him-

[1] "Geschichte Israels," p. 167. Prolegomena (Eng. Trans.), p. 161.

self employs, but with a different application, they have liberally besprinkled the chart of history with their own ideas after a fashion in which geographers sometimes indulge in maps of unexplored regions. With the exception of those which are distinctly stigmatized as idolatrous there is not one sanctuary in the whole number. The only seeming deviations from strict regularity arise from the fact that upon the extraordinary manifestations of God's presence sacrifices were at once offered upon the spot; but so far as appears they were strictly limited to the occasion that called them forth. The allegation that the stories of these theophanies originated at a later time to procure credit for sanctuaries which had been established at these various places, as well as the like assertion made respecting similar events in the lives of the patriarchs, inverts the real order of cause and effect. Places thus hallowed by divine manifestations gained a prestige which led in some instances to their subsequent selection as seats of idolatry. But the narratives of the theophanies were not generated by their being frequented as places of sacrifice, and can not of themselves be adduced in proof that they were ever put to such a use.

According to the Books of Samuel, at the close of the period of the Judges, the house of God was still in Shiloh, 1 : 24, and is expressly identified with the Mosaic tabernacle of the congregation, 2 : 22. It was resorted to by all Israel, 2 : 14, 1 : 3, as the appointed place of sacrifice, 2 : 28, 29, and contained the ark which was the symbol of the divine presence, 4 : 4. But from the time that God forsook Shiloh for the sins of the priests and people, suffering the ark to fall into the hands of the Philistines, until his habitation was fixed in Zion, Ps. 132, or more exactly until the temple was prepared for its reception, Jehovah had no dwelling-place in Israel. During this anomalous period the law of the unity of the sanctuary was necessarily in abeyance; and the people were obliged to sacrifice in high places so far as they sacrificed at all, I. Kin. 3 : 2.

But with the erection of the temple of Solomon and the depositing of the ark in its most holy place, and the coming in of the radiant cloud betokening the divine glory, the old legal status was again renewed. Thenceforward this was, as it was designed to be, 1 Kin. 8 : 16–21, the one house of God in Israel, and high places were ever after synonymous with corruption and idolatry, 11 : 7, 8, 14 : 23. Good men never sanctioned them. To this there is but one exception, which serves to confirm the rule, the altars of which Elijah speaks, 19 : 10, 14, when in the schism and apostasy of the northern kingdom the pious there were debarred from attendance at the temple. God-fearing princes sought to remove the high places, with only partial success, until Hezekiah, who suppressed them during his reign. His ungodly son and grandson, Manasseh and Amon, restored them, but Josiah abolished them afresh. The law of the unity of the sanctuary instead of originating in the reign of the last-named king, was the law of Israel's history from the beginning, only passing under eclipse at one degenerate period in the lifetime of Samuel and of Saul, when the ark of the Lord became an object of dread instead of joyful confidence, and Israel was for a season without the symbol of Jehovah's presence or the privileges of his sanctuary. There never was but one ark of the covenant: the presence of that ark in the sanctuary made it Jehovah's dwelling: and there could be no other.

This same conclusion is further confirmed by the unanimous voice of Psalmists and of Prophets. They uniformly speak of Zion as God's earthly dwelling-place, never of any other. Not a solitary passage can be adduced from any one of them which refers to other places of sacrifice than Zion, except in the language of rebuke and denunciation. The attempt to foist upon different periods of Israel's history a diversity of views in relation to God's true sanctuary is a signal failure. It is in the face of the teaching of every book in the Bible.

It will be sufficient at present to refer briefly to certain other palpable falsities in the methods or results of Wellhausen's hypothesis.

He infers the non-existence of a statute from a neglect or disobedience which warrants no such conclusion; and he claims that it must have originated at the time when it is brought into new prominence or is more fully enforced than before; a method of reasoning which might equally be made to prove that Luther invented the New Testament. He also infers the non-existence of laws and institutions from the simple circumstance of their not being mentioned or referred to in the history, even though there was no occasion for such mention, and no reason to expect it; and the fact of their being so well known and constantly observed may itself account for the omission of what might safely be taken for granted, so that any special reference to it seemed unnecessary Or must a historian of America be perpetually referring to the fact of the observance of the fourth of July or the use of the Gregorian calendar?

He undertakes to establish the hypothesis by its correspondence with the history: and in order to do this he first adjusts the sources of history themselves by critical processes in which he assumes the very thing to be proved, and denies the validity and genuineness of every passage that controverts it; thus proving his point by the fallacy of the circle.

He requires us to suppose that forged codes of laws were at two different times successfully imposed upon the people as the genuine productions of Moses, and this though they were at variance with laws previously in force and regarded as his, and though the serious changes which they introduced were hostile to the interests of numerous and powerful classes.

He asks us to believe further that three conflicting codes of laws, the more recent of which had in each case displaced its predecessor, came in some mysterious way to be regarded as of equal validity, and were all blended together as one harmonious body of law, in which no discrepancies were suspected, all being accepted as alike Mosaic and canonical, and all faithfully obeyed notwithstanding the increased burdens thus assumed.

He would have us think that the people of Israel have been from the beginning utterly mistaken as to their own institutions and written records, and that these have throughout been systematically falsified without any suspicion of the fact ever being awakened; that their entire history is a gigantic fabrication, which was accepted as consistent and true until a few years ago, when he and his compeers detected and exposed the cheat.

It has sometimes been said that this hypothesis does not affect the Christian faith in any vital way. It leaves the contents of the Scriptures unchanged. It is merely a question of order; whether that which has commonly been placed at the beginning, really belongs there or has its proper place at a later stage in the divine plan of guidance or instruction; whether the true order is first the law, then the psalms, then the prophets, or whether the prophets may not have preceded the law and the psalms; whether the law was all given at once in the infancy of the nation, or whether it may not have been gradually evolved as the changing necessities of Israel required. Why may not the divine authority of Deuteronomy and of the entire Pentateuch be the same, though the former was produced under Josiah and the latter reached its present form under Ezra, as though all had come, as we now have it, from the pen of Moses?

The serious aspect of the matter is that the truthfulness of the Scriptures is impugned at every step. If this hypothesis be true, the Scriptures are not what they represent themselves to be; the facts of the history are altogether different from that which they declare; their testimony is unreliable and untrustworthy. It requires great critical acumen to sift the evidence and extract the modicum of truth from the mass of fable. The inspiration and authority of the Old Testament are swept away entirely or can only be maintained in a very qualified sense. And as the New Testament is based upon the Old, how can the former be rationally defended, if its foundation in the latter is undermined and totters to its fall? How can our confidence in the Lord Jesus himself remain unshaken, if his declarations respecting Moses and his law are not to be trusted? The authors and chief promoters of the hypothesis do not disguise their hostility to supernatural religion. The denial of the truth of miracles and of prophecy is one of their primary principles, and is the cornerstone of their entire structure. The hypothesis is just an ingenious attempt to account for the Old Testament on purely naturalistic principles. The violence of the methods to which it is obliged to resort to compass this end, and the extravagant and incredible conclusions to which it leads, show how impossible is the task which it has proposed to itself.

The spirit and aims of those who urge this hypothesis do not, however, concern us at present. We have to do simply with the hypothesis itself and the arguments by which it is defended. In this brief course of lectures it will be impossible to deal thoroughly with this subject in its entire extent. It will be best to restrict our examination to a definite field; and I have selected for this purpose the sacred seasons of the Hebrews, as a theme interesting in itself and one upon which great stress has been laid in connection with this subject. It is generally agreed among the critics that the laws relating to the religious festivals of the Jews furnish one of the strongest supports for the view that the Mosaic institutions were not the product of one mind or of one age, but that they advanced from simple forms in primitive times to those which were more and more complex; and that the successive stages of the process can still be traced in the various enactments on this subject. The topic to which your attention will be requested in the subsequent lectures of this course, then, will be the annual feasts of the Hebrews in their bearing upon the latest phase of Pentateuchal criticism. In the next lecture the endeavor will be made to trace the history of critical opinion in relation to these feasts.

II.

THE HISTORY OF OPINION RESPECTING THE HEBREW FEASTS.

II.

THE HISTORY OF OPINION RESPECTING THE HEBREW FEASTS.

DR. ROBERTSON SMITH in his article on the "Bible," in the "Encyclopædia Britannica," p. 636*b*, says: "On the Passover and feast of Unleavened Bread we have at least six laws, which if not really discordant, are at least so divergent in form and conception that they can not be all from the same pen." Kuenen undertakes to determine the chronological order in which these laws must have severally followed each other, each representing the usage of the period to which it belongs. Wellhausen maintains that certain of these laws correspond with the practice indicated in the historical and prophetic books before the Babylonish exile, and he points out others which represent the practice subsequent to the exile and which he consequently infers could only have originated in the post-exilic period. These laws are nevertheless all found in the Pentateuch, where it is expressly declared that they were without exception given by Moses to Israel in the wilderness.

The passages in the books of Moses relating to the annual feasts are the following, viz.:

1. Ex. xii. 1–28, 43–51, xiii. 3–10, the narrative of the original institution of the Passover and of the

feast of Unleavened Bread, and the regulations respecting them given before leaving Egypt.

2. Ex. xxiii. 14–19, a summary account of the three annual feasts, in which pilgrimages were required, as prescribed in the Book of the Covenant ratified at Mount Sinai.

3. Ex. xxxiv. 18–26, a substantial repetition of the preceding upon the renewal of the covenant after the sin of the golden calf.

4. Lev. xxiii., an enumeration of the feasts and holy convocations to be observed in the course of the year, with the special ceremonies connected with them.

5. Num. ix. 5–14, on the occasion of the first annual repetition of the Passover a supplemental observance of it was ordained for those unclean or absent at the appointed season.

6. Num. xxviii., xxix., the public offerings required throughout the year, including those at the annual feasts.

7. Deut. xvi. 1–17, an admonition to observe the three annual feasts and to celebrate them at the sanctuary about to be divinely chosen.

The scheme of the sacred seasons set forth in these laws is consistent and complete. It is based on the primitive institution of the weekly Sabbath. This is a regularly recurring portion of time, withdrawn from ordinary worldly occupation and surrendered unto God the Creator, not as a full discharge of obligation, a payment of what is due to God, so that when this is given a man has purchased the right to the remainder of his time for his own exclusive use; but this is set apart in a special manner in recognition of the fact that all belongs to God and should be used for him. The observance of the Sabbath is a privilege as well as a duty. It is a weekly release from the curse of labor which sin has imposed, and was further to Israel a commemoration of their deliverance from the servitude and toil of Egypt, Deut. 5:15, and a participation for the time in the rest of Paradise and the rest of God and a foretaste and anticipation of the rest that remaineth for the people of God. Ps. 95: 11.

This patriarchal institution was in the Mosaic law expanded into a sabbatical system by applying the septenary division in succession to every denomination of time. The seventh month was a sacred month, marked by an accumulation of holy days, its first day being observed as a sabbath, including which there were four festive sabbaths and six additional feast days in the month. The seventh year was a sabbatical year, during which the land was to rest and lie untilled. The fiftieth year, or the year succeeding seven times seven years, was the year of Jubilee, which gave release from the burdens of impoverishment and servitude; in it the Israelite who had sold himself for debt was set free, and property that had been alienated reverted to its original owners; and all was thus restored to its primitive status.

The sense of obligation to the Creator, and rest from worldly toil, were thus provided for. Gratitude for the gifts which he bestows, both individual and national, and the expression of thankful joy in them was next to be added. This was the specific purpose of the feasts, which were accordingly appointed at those seasons when God's bounty is so richly manifested in the productions of the earth, viz., at the harvest and the vintage. The harvest, which lasted through several weeks, was, as it were, consecrated throughout by being enclosed between two festivals, Passover and the feast of Unleavened Bread at the beginning when the barley was reaped, and the feast of Weeks at its close when the wheat was harvested. The ingathering of fruits from their vineyards and their oliveyards completed the yield of the year and was followed by the most joyous feast of all, that of Tabernacles. Passover and Tabernacles were likewise commemorative of great national benefits, the former occurring at the season of the Exodus and observed in memory of the sparing of the first-born in Israel during the plague which desolated Egypt; the latter by its booths, such as were used by those engaged in the vintage, being a reminder of the march through the wilderness. At each of these three festivals every male Israelite was required to make a pilgrimage to the sanctuary and there rejoice before the LORD, bringing with him his offerings of thanksgiving.

These feasts were linked with the sabbatical series by being governed throughout by the number seven. Unleavened Bread and Tabernacles each lasted seven days, and began on the fifteenth, *i. e.*, the day after 2 x 7 days of the first and the seventh month respectively; while the feast of Weeks, which lasted but one day, was observed upon the fiftieth day, *i. e.*, the day after 7 x 7 days reckoned from the presentation of the sheaf of the first-fruits at the feast of Unleavened Bread, to which it stood in obvious and direct relation, thus encircling the entire harvest season, and bringing the festivities connected with it to a termination, while at the same time it pointed forward to the feast of Ingathering yet to come. In like manner a day observed as a sabbath was added at the end of the feast of Tabernacles, in a sort of dependence upon it, though not properly forming a part of it, which brought the festivities of the ingathering and the entire festive cycle of the year to a termination.

One other idea remained to be emphasized, that the sacred seasons might duly represent and bring out in proper prominence all the distinctive features of the religion of Israel, to whom Jehovah was not only the Creator of all and the bountiful source of all good both individual and national, but also the holy God, whose imperative demand is that his people shall be a holy people. In the sacrifices of every day, augmented every Sabbath and feast day, a symbolic expiation was offered for sin. These reached their culmination in the annual day of Atonement, whose services are not precisely to be regarded as supplementing the deficiencies of other sacrifices: but the idea of the expiation of sin already represented in the latter found in the ritual of this day its highest and most solemn expression in regard to the offences of the entire year, and in addition there was a striking representation of the thought that the sins of the people were taken away absolutely and forever. This was fixed on the tenth day of the seventh month, so that this purgation was effected just before the crowning festival of the year, that the people emancipated from the burden of guilt might with a heightened joy pay their thanksgivings to Him who crowned the year with his goodness. And it was with signal propriety that the trumpet was sounded upon the day of Atonement every fiftieth year to announce the opening of the year of Jubilee, proclaiming liberty throughout all the land, and the return of every man unto his inheritance.

The sacred seasons form thus a complete and symmetrical scheme, giving proper and balanced expression to the leading ideas of Israel's religion, and especially adjusted to their relation to God as their Creator, Benefactor and Sanctifier. It is a natural, if not necessary conclusion that this is no accidental conglomerate. It is not the long accretion of ages, a body of laws and usages aggregated in the course of time under varying and contingent circumstances. It is just the consistent unfolding of one definite scheme of thought, and as such bears the stamp of one reflecting and constructive mind, by which it has been carefully elaborated and adjusted into correspondence with certain dominant ideas. The judgment of Ewald[1] upon this subject is the more instructive, since no critic ever had less bias in favor of traditional opinions. He rejected as determinedly as any the Mosaic authorship of the Pentateuch. He alleged that "only a few scattered and mutilated fragments of the life and laws of Moses survive": and he only referred to Moses "such of the ancient institutions of the Hebrews as are of so unusual and remarkable a character that they must have

[1] "Zeitschrift für die Kunde des Morgenlandes," Vol. III., pp 411, 434.

proceeded from the exalted genius of one man." But this test of itself convinced him that the sacred seasons of the Jews originated with Moses. "You behold," he says, "a structure simple, lofty, perfect. All proceeds as it were from one spirit, and represents one idea, and is carried into effect by what resembles counters exactly matched strung upon one cord. And it is no mean praise that prior merely natural feasts are wisely not abolished nor contemptuously cast aside, but restored and filled with new vigor and invested with a higher meaning. And while other ancient nations have a multitude of festivals with no obvious connection, these are few, but linked together, illumined with one light, and relating to one supreme end (every one a Sabbath of Jehovah). Whoever has a thorough knowledge of these festivals, will be persuaded that they have not arisen by slow degrees from the blind impulse of external nature, nor from the history of the people, but are the product of a lofty genius."

Other critics, however, have been of a different mind, as appears from instances already recited. It has been confidently affirmed that there are variations in the laws above enumerated, which amount to serious and irreconcilable discrepancies. These differences affect the number of the feasts, the names they bore, the design of their institution, the times when they were held, the place at which they were celebrated, the accompanying sacrifices which were offered, and in general the characteristic usages connected with their observance. It has been maintained that a careful comparison of these laws will disclose the fact that they can not all have proceeded from a common source; that they do not even belong to any one age, least of all to the Mosaic; that they severally represent notions which were entertained and customs which prevailed at widely separated periods; that the origin and history of these institutions can here be traced through successive ages and through the different phases which they assumed from time to time, from the simplicity and rudeness of their early beginnings to the elaborate complexity and completeness which they ultimately attained; and that the facts as thus deduced from a thorough sifting of these passages themselves and a comparison of them with the course of Israel's history, are very different from the view which is superficially yielded by them, and which is traditionally entertained by those who believe these laws to have emanated from Moses.

Critical opinions upon this subject have passed through several successive phases in the course of the present century which it may be worth while here briefly to review. The first serious assault upon the genuineness of the laws respecting the sacred feasts attributed to Moses was made in the first decade of this century, in the year 1806. This was by De Wette,[1] then privat-docent in Jena, and was quite in the spirit of the prevailing rationalism, the confessed offspring of the English deism of the preceding century. This maiden publication is marked by a shallowness and a bitterness from which DeWette himself afterward receded. It is pervaded by the idea that positive religious institutions are the invention of fraud

[1] "Beiträge zur Einleitung in das Alte Testament," I., p. 290 ff.

and priestcraft, and not only dismisses as puerile the notion of their divine appointment, but has no conception even of their being the outgrowth and expression of man's religious nature. He seems to consider the whole case settled by such flippant suggestions as that Moses and the Israelites could never have held feasts and sacrificial meals amid the privations of the desert; and as to founding them for the future he had something of more consequence to think of than such "useless and unimportant matters." Moses might have arranged for a sacrificial meal before leaving Egypt, that the people might have enough to eat, but he could not have expected the departure or he would have arranged for provision by the way. He further points out what he considers inconsistencies in the narrative sufficient to condemn it. The Passover is at one time represented as a protective against the plague of slaying the first-born, and at another as having an entirely different design, that of being a memorial of this event. As to the former, Moses could not have foreseen the plague and the blood would have proved unavailing. As to the latter, it is senseless to imagine that a memorial feast was instituted during or even prior to the occurrence of that which was to be commemorated. They were directed, Ex. 12 : 11, to eat the Passover in haste, ready for instant departure; and yet, ver. 39, they were taken by surprise at the order to leave and had not leavened their bread or prepared their food. They were bidden to eat unleavened bread, 12 : 8, before the hasty flight which occasioned it. And Moses could not in all the haste and confusion of leaving Egypt have planned for the future observance of the feast in Canaan.

The Passover, he concludes, was originally a domestic or family institution. It was subsequently observed at the various sanctuaries or high places dedicated to Jehovah throughout the land. The command to celebrate the Passover and other feasts at one central sanctuary was first given in Deuteronomy (ch. 16), which was a forgery of the reign of Josiah. 2 Kings 23 : 22, informs us that it had not been so kept before, and ver. 9 that the priests of the high places had eaten it, not at Jerusalem, but with their brethren. Upon which it is only necessary to observe here, that this passage in Kings, notwithstanding the use so persistently made of it by modern critics, neither states nor implies that Josiah's Passover was the first that had been exclusively celebrated in Jerusalem. It simply means that this Passover was observed in more exact compliance with the Mosaic prescriptions and was more universally attended than at any time since the days of the judges. And the statement, ver. 9, respecting the priests of the high places has no reference to the Passover whatever; it simply declares that in consequence of the irregularities of the worship in which they had previously ministered, they were not suffered to approach the altar at Jerusalem, though they shared the consecrated provision with their brethren.

It is a relief to pass from a captious rationalism to the more earnest spirit of Dr. F. C. Baur,[1] of Tübin-

[1] Two articles in the "Studien und Kritiken," for 1832. On the original Signification of the feast of the Passover and the rite

gen, who seeks to comprehend and appreciate the Hebrew institutions by studying them in connection with parallel observances in other religions. A new interest had been awakened in the symbolism and mythology of ancient nations by the researches of Creuzer and others, who had traced their different beliefs and forms of worship to their determining causes in the religious nature and necessities of man, variously modified by their natural surroundings and their race traditions. And it was obvious to suggest the application of like principles to the ceremonial of the Jews. The comparative treatment of the Old Testament was not indeed altogether new. Several of the early Christian fathers remark upon the resemblance between the rites of Jewish and of heathen worship, and explain it by a divine accommodation to human weakness. The people accustomed to these usages could not be induced to abandon them at once; hence they were retained by the Most High in his own worship in a modified form that they might be the more readily attracted from the service of idols to that of the true God. The Jewish philosopher Maimonides adopts the same view. This aspect of the case was copiously discussed and illustrated by an immense amount of classical learning in the last quarter of the seventeenth century by Sir John Marsham[1] and Dr. John Spencer, dean of Ely.[2]

of Circumcision; and The Hebrew Sabbath and the national Feasts of the Mosaic Cultus.

[1] "Canon Chronicus" (London, 1672; Leipsic, 1676, pp. 192 ff.

[2] "De Legibus Hebraeorum Ritualibus," Cambridge, 1685, pp. 257 ff., 598 ff.

They urge that the institutions of Moses were partly borrowed from and partly established in opposition to those current in Egypt, and make special application to the feasts as well as to other religious observances in detail. Marsham calls attention to the fact that ancient nations generally united cessation from labor with the celebration of their religious festivals; and that according to the testimony of early writers the Egyptians were the first to establish temples, feasts and sacrifices, and that in particular their feasts were older than the time of Moses. Spencer maintains that a lamb was slain at the annual Passover and oxen were sacrificed in the course of the festival, because these animals were deemed sacred by the Egyptians, appealing to the words of Tacitus that "the Jews sacrifice the ram in contempt of Ammon, and the ox which the Egyptians call Apis." The Israelites were hence to learn that these were no divinities, since they could be treated so contemptuously. The lamb was to be set apart four days in anticipation of this service, that thus they might reject the Egyptian superstition deliberately and solemnly. Its blood was to be smeared upon the exterior door-posts that it might be conspicuous to all. This was to be done not by priests, but by every father of a family, that all might testify their abhorrence of a worship so degrading. It was not to be eaten raw, but roasted with fire, and partaken of quietly within doors; no bone was to be broken and no one was to go out at the door of his house until the morning, in opposition to the Bacchanalia, in which the devotees roamed abroad, in their wild frenzy de vouring their victims raw and tearing them limb from limb. Moreover, the feasts were instituted among the Hebrews as a counter attraction to those existing among the Gentiles, not because they were pleasing to God or suited to his worship, but because they were adapted to the childish tastes of the Israelites. Passover, Pentecost and Tabernacles were appointed at the times of first-fruits, harvest and ingathering, when feasts were universally observed among other nations, that Israel might thus be more readily induced to observe these festivals which were instituted in order to remind them of God's special benefits to their nation.

Hermann Witsius,[1] the distinguished professor at Leyden, entered the lists in opposition to these views, maintaining that while the Israelites did repeatedly fall into the superstitions and idolatries of surrounding nations, yet in rites approved of God there was much less agreement than had been claimed between the Egyptians and Hebrews. Where they did agree, it was mostly in matters common to them with other cultivated nations, and which were derived by all alike from the same source of either reason or tradition. Where they agree in other matters than these, the probability is that the Egyptians borrowed from the Hebrews rather than *vice versâ*. And the ceremonial institutions were not established by way of accommodation to a refractory people, but had three principal aims, viz.: to be (1) a toilsome yoke to subdue the people to submissive obedience; (2) a wall of separation from other nations; (3) figures and shadows

[1] "Aegyptiaca" (first edition 1683), Basle, 1739, pp. 18, 47, 87, 145

of spiritual things. In regard to the feasts in particular he claimed that festive days were peculiar to no one religion, but were rooted in man's social nature; and, besides, the distinction between holy days and common days was made by God himself at the beginning and thence derived to all branches of the human race, even the rudest and most barbarous. And further, that the Hebrew feasts stood in no relation whatever to those of Egypt, inasmuch as the former were fixed at definite periods of the year, while the latter according to the testimony of Geminus were held successively at every different season, since the priests from religious scruples were opposed to the insertion of intercalary days.

Both the parties to this controversy dealt too largely with externals. Too much stress was laid upon superficial resemblances. Pagan rites as well as those of Israel were symbolical; they were significant embodiments of religious ideas, which they served to awaken or express. And it was this significance which gave them character. It was no discredit to the religion of Moses and no impeachment either of its truth or its originality, that many of its outward forms resembled those of other nations, when the connection in which they stood and the whole spirit of the system to which they belonged, determined their meaning and tendency to be quite diverse, as diverse as the worship of nature is from the worship of one true living and holy God.

Baur recognizes the symbolic character of the rites with which he deals, but fails to distinguish between the widely divergent systems in which they are found or to perceive how this affects the signification of every individual part so that it is impossible to interpret the one correctly by the other.

According to his view a lamb was slain at the annual Passover because the sun was then entering the constellation Aries; not, as Spencer imagined, to put contempt upon the god Ammon, for the Egyptians themselves sacrificed rams in the spring. A consecrated animal was slain at the season when nature was unfolding into new life, to signify that life was developed out of death. The narrative of the institution of the Passover is discredited; but its original design is inferred from the statement that it was to protect the first-born in Israel from death, and that in memory of it the first-born was consecrated unto God. The first-born of men and animals was holy to Jehovah. The first-born of the flock or the herd must be sacrificed. The first-born of an ass must be slain or redeemed. The first-born of men must be redeemed. The rigorous application of the principle would have required the death of all, first-born children as well as animals. But human sacrifices were abolished as abhorrent even in most pagan nations, and in Israel they were not tolerated. The paschal lamb, like the ram offered instead of Isaac, was a substitute for the first-born and was hence called a "Passover"; it was sacrificed and the child was spared. It was offered in the opening spring. As nature passes through the death of winter to the life of spring, so man can only attain a new life by a sacrifice devoted to death. He is entering on a new period of time and the old guilt should be purged away. It was designed to expiate the past and secure all blessings in the future for the household thus consecrated, all the members of which accordingly were to partake of it, but no stranger was to eat it with them. As a family sacrifice it was more ancient than the national and civil life organized by Moses. It was, however, readily brought into connection with the exodus; the transition from the old year to the new and the protection granted to each family finding their apt parallel in Israel's passing into this new epoch of its history, and the collective salvation of the nation. The lamb was roasted as the nearest approach to the burnt-offering, which its primary signification demanded. It was eaten with bitter herbs and unleavened bread to suggest the humiliation appropriate to an expiatory service and the purity of the new period uncontaminated by the leaven of the old. They were to celebrate the Passover with their staff in their hand and their shoes on their feet, not to indicate haste, for the haste with which they were thrust out was quite unexpected; but it was to represent them as fully equipped, God's organized host, ready for active service in his cause. The analogy of the Attic Thargelia leads to the further suggestion that in consequence of the expiatory character of the service and the associations of the season, executions at that time had somewhat of a vicarious virtue. Hence the crucifixion of our Lord and the two thieves at the Passover, and the remarkable words of Caiaphas, John 11 : 49 ff., and the execution of James at the same season, Acts 12 : 2, and the threatened execution of Peter; hence also the **cust**om of releasing one prisoner to exemplify the expiation effected by the punishment of the rest, John 18 : 39. And the story of the Israelites borrowing vessels from the Egyptians is not the record of a real occurrence, but arose from mimic representations of breaches of the law, atoned for by the Passover. And then the other feasts, as the seasons roll around, not only express gratitude for the benefits of the productive year, but also for the national blessings springing from the same source and following in the wake of the deliverance from Egypt.

Suggestive as some of the remarks of Baur are, his exposition on the whole is a failure, because the Hebrew rites as manifestations of the religious life of Israel can only be correctly explained from ideas current in that system to which they belong. An interpretation drawn from the nature-worship of heathen nations will necessarily foist upon them ideas belonging to a totally different system with which the religion of Israel has no sympathy or connection. It is noteworthy, however, that freely as he deals with the original narrative, he has no difficulty in admitting these feasts to be as old as the time of Moses, or in providing a solution from his own point of view for the discrepancies urged by his predecessors.

The next mode of dealing with the feast laws is that of the literary critics, who in consequence of alleged differences in style and language, refer them severally to different authors; these are assigned respectively to distinct periods and are supposed to reflect in the enactments which they record the usage of these several periods or at least what the framers of these laws sought to bring about. Each enactment is thus regarded as independent of all the rest If one law contains a summary statement of what is more explicitly detailed in another, the former is not allowed to find its explanation in the latter, but is held to represent a simpler and more primitive stage in the development of these institutions. If one is intended for the guidance of the people generally, and consequently does not include the ceremonial which is minutely described in another prepared for the priests at the sanctuary, it is claimed that the former represents a period when no fixed ceremonial had as yet been connected with the observance, but the worshippers were left to their own free and spontaneous action, untrammeled by the rigid rules of a later date. Every diversity in the form of expression, to which a different sense can by possibility be attributed, is pressed to the utmost and held to be significant of a varying conception of the festival. And thus laws which in their natural and obvious meaning are perfectly harmonious and consistent and mutually supplementary, are isolated and set at variance and made to do duty in some scheme of the critic's own devising.

It will not be necessary here to indicate the various forms which the hypothesis of the successive formation of the Pentateuch has assumed in the hands of different critics, nor to show in detail how these have influenced their conceptions of these laws which are now before us. It will be sufficient to distinguish the hypotheses of this school of critics from those of the most recent and most revolutionary school by one clearly marked criterion. The former regard Deuteronomy as the latest book of the Pentateuch, while Graf, Reuss and Wellhausen with their followers maintain that the Levitical law, or as they denominate it the Priest Code, is later still than Deuteronomy.

Of the former class of critics, with whose methods and results we are now particularly concerned, Gramberg and Von Bohlen maintain that the Hebrew feasts are long posterior to the time of Moses; the rest affirm them to be in part, at least, pre-Mosaic, but moulded and shaped by Moses in accordance with his own religious system.

Gramberg's "Critical History of the Religious Ideas of the Old Testament" was published in 1829, in which he undertakes to give an elaborate treatment of the whole subject. His strong rationalistic bias, however, which he is at no pains to conceal, incapacitates him for any real apprehension of the religion, with which he deals in a purely formal and mechanical manner, and which he seeks to explain upon the theory of priestcraft. The various books of the Pentateuch are assigned to separate dates from the reign of David to the close of the Babylonish exile, and their institutions or enactments are compared with the statements or allusions found in the historical and prophetical books of the corresponding period. His conclusion is that worship was originally free and subject to no statutory regulations. There were no fixed feasts except such as were of a domestic nature and involved no great amount of sacrifices, such as the weekly Sabbath and the harvest festival whose recurrence was determined by the season.

Jeroboam's opposition to the worship at Jerusalem first led the priests to think of concentrating all the services of religion at this sanctuary; and with this view they invented new feasts and multiplied the rites connected with them. Subsequently the poets[1] who wrote Exodus and the rest of the Pentateuch referred these ordinances which the priests had instituted to the higher authority of Moses; and finally the poetic author of the books of Chronicles recast the history of the kingdom so as to create the impression that the Levitical ordinances were then already obeyed. The people may have had feasts in honor of Jehovah from their first settlement in Canaan: but there is no certainty that even the most important of them were Mosaic, and at any rate they were not observed in accordance with the Mosaic requirements until the days of Josiah; and all the feasts prescribed in the Pentateuch were not in existence even then. The account of the origin of the Passover given in Exodus is self-contradictory and purely mythical. It could not have been instituted in view of their expected departure from Egypt, for Pharaoh had not given them permission to leave, and this permission could not have been foreseen. Exodus was the book of the law found in the temple in the reign of Josiah: and the observance of the Passover dates from this time. The Passover, which was celebrated on a single night, and the feast of Unleavened Bread, which lasted seven days, were at first distinct; but they are blended in Leviticus and Numbers,

---

[1] These writers are called "poets," because they deal, not with facts, but with fictions of their own imagination.

which show a great advance in the development of the cultus. The feast of Weeks was plainly an invention of the priests that they might obtain an early supply of the first-fruits. Tabernacles, which in previous laws was located indefinitely at the end of the year, and was simply the feast of ingathering, came to be fixed on a particular day of the month, and to be regarded as commemorative of the march through the wilderness.

He finds no trace of the Mosaic feasts in Judges or in Samuel: the feast at Shiloh, Jud. 21:19, does not correspond with the Levitical requirements: and the yearly pilgrimage of Samuel's parents, 1 Sam. 1:3, was a voluntary act of piety. But if the silence on this subject had been as profound as he alleges, the argument from this to their non-existence is weakened by his admission of the Mosaic origin of the weekly Sabbath, though this is not mentioned from the time of Moses to that of David, 1 Chron. 23:31, or if Chronicles be discredited, to the time of Elisha, 2 Kin. 4:23. Hosea's feasts, 2:11, he says, were not those of the Mosaic law, but were shared between Jehovah and Baal. Isaiah shows the first trace of annually recurring feasts, 29:1 (Heb.), sometime in the reign of Hezekiah. The night of the holy solemnity, to which he refers, 30:29, could not have been the Passover, though it may have been the harvest-feast: if so, however, it was not observed in accordance with Mosaic requirement.

Von Bohlen[1] thinks that the Sabbath was introduced about the time of Hezekiah; and the Passover

---

[1] "Die Genesis historisch-kritisch erläutert," 1835.

in the reign of Josiah. This was borrowed from the great spring festival of the ancient world, its name denoting the passage of the sun into the vernal equinox. Tabernacles is called, Ex. 23 : 16, the feast of ingathering at the end of the year, which implies a division of time that only became current after the exile.

Stähelin, in his "Critical Investigations," published in 1835, divided the Pentateuchal laws on the score both of affinities of language and of enactments into what he calls the first and the second legislation. The former, which is substantially what has since been denominated the Priest Code, was given by Moses himself to the Israelites in the wilderness. After the people had been long settled in Canaan, this was modified into the second legislation, which embraces both Ex. 19–24, the Book of the Covenant, and Deuteronomy. The first legislation speaks of five annual feasts: the second of only three, the feast of Trumpets on the first day of the seventh month, and the annual Atonement on its tenth day having been dropped since Tabernacles also occurred in the same month, that pilgrims might not be detained too long from home. The first legislation made both the first and last days of Passover and of Tabernacles days of rest or sabbaths: the second only their seventh day, a restriction likewise introduced for the convenience of pilgrims. The first legislation forbids, the second permits to boil the paschal lamb. The first legislation enjoins holy convocations at the annual feasts, the expression being obscure and easily misunderstood; the second explicitly enjoins three yearly pilgrimages to the sanctuary, and adds the requirement that they must not appear before the LORD empty. In the second legislation, but not in the first, mention is made of "the house of the LORD." While in the first the months are simply numbered, the second legislation defines the time of the Passover as in "the month Abib."

This view of Stähelin, while apparently at the furthest remove from the hypothesis of Graf and Wellhausen, as his order of the legislative codes is the reverse of theirs, nevertheless approximates it in this, that he places the Book of the Covenant and Deuteronomy together as most closely related, instead of interposing the Levitical law between them as is done by Hitzig, Ewald and the critics of this class generally.

Hitzig[1] maintains that the feast of Unleavened Bread was originally observed for but a single day or rather night, and that on the first of Abib, in memory of the fact that they were forced out of Egypt in the night in such haste that they had not time to leaven their bread. The extension of the feast to seven days is an incongruity, subsequently introduced, when the celebration was transferred to the middle of the month and was divided into two distinct services, the Passover and Unleavened Bread. Later still these were fused, and the Unleavened Bread became a simple addendum to the Passover, which commemorated the sparing of the first-born, while the circumstance which originally occasioned the use

---

[1] "Ostern und Pfingsten," 1837. "Ostern und Pfingsten im Zweiten Dekalog," 1838.

of unleavened bread sank into the background or was lost sight of. The second of the annual feasts was in the first instance called "the feast of Harvest" and occurred at the beginning of barley harvest, barley being the earliest of the grains to ripen. Next it received the name "feast of Weeks" and was placed fifty days after the first of Abib, one day for each of the fifty weeks of the year, which brought it to the beginning of wheat harvest, in the middle of the harvest season. Finally it was transferred to the end of wheat harvest, or seven weeks reckoned from a later time of beginning than before, viz., from the time of first putting the sickle to the corn.

Leviticus gives the immediate and organic advance upon the oldest prescriptions in the Book of the Covenant. Deuteronomy is based upon both the preceding, and produces a new result from a mixture of both, among other things simplifying the law by doing away with the feast of Trumpets and day of Atonement, and the minute and burdensome ritual in the spirit of the reformatory period of Josiah. All this he has no difficulty in establishing by a judicious application of the critical knife.

One of the best replies to the vagaries of Hitzig was furnished by Bertheau,[1] who, though he began his studies under a different impression, was brought by his investigations to the conviction that the laws of the Pentateuch, and particularly those relating to the feasts, belong to one connected and consistent scheme of legislation, the product of one mind and

---

[1] "Die Sieben Gruppen Mosaischer Gesetze," 1840.

of one period, and that this can be attributed to no other than to Moses in the wilderness.

Ewald,[1] who yields to none in critical acumen, and whose hypothesis for the critical dissection of the Pentateuch is certainly as elaborate as any, was nevertheless satisfied on internal grounds that the Hebrew feasts were undoubtedly Mosaic. He contests the allegation that nothing can be certainly known of the life and institutions of Moses, and complains that critics generally have shown more zeal in discovering what can not have come from Moses, than in ascertaining what is really from him. He finds nothing written by Moses in which the feasts are orderly treated. He conceives that the feast laws, as we now have them, are from later writers; but they contain what was established or initiated by him, only modified by the relations of later times. But the comparison of these brings to light that which attests his superior genius and can only have come from him.

He traces the festivals observed by different nations to three different sources. They may be—1. Natural, based on the changing seasons of the year; these are common to almost all ancient nations. 2. Historical, commemorating past events of importance or national interest; these are found among few peoples comparatively and differ according to the genius and history of each. 3. Legislative, when some superior mind grasps the disconnected and discordant institutions that may have arisen, and infusing a new spirit into them, brings them into one complete and

---

[1] "Die Alterthümer des Volkes Israel," and his article in the "Zeitschrift für die Kunde des Morgenlandes," 1840.

harmonious system. This is the lofty height to which the sacred seasons of the Hebrews were brought by Moses.

Their great annual feasts, so far as they are of natural origin, are pre-Mosaic, and are coincident with the festivals of the vernal and autumnal equinox observed by all nations of antiquity. In the fall they expressed their joy at the ingathering of fruits by glad processions bearing fruit and branches of trees. In the spring they had a twofold service, the presentation of the first-fruits of the opening year and an expiatory rite for cleansing and security from the perils that were before them. This expiatory service was retained in the Passover, whose very name attests its antiquity. It is derived from a verb which was no longer in common use in the days of Moses; and it denotes a sacrifice offered to obtain a happy passage, not through a sea or river, but through the coming year. Its rites breathe the spirit of an earlier time, and were sanctioned by the Mosaic law on account of their venerable antiquity. It was slain by the head of each family at his own house, was to be eaten by every male, and its blood was sprinkled on the lintel and door-posts to consecrate the house, so that all the dangers of the year then beginning might be averted from the family. It was to be roasted, this being the most ancient style of cooking flesh for food; and eaten with bitter herbs, as a more suitable accompaniment of an expiatory service than what was agreeable to the taste. It was a lamb, not from antagonism to Egyptian superstition as Spencer maintains, nor, as Baur contends, because the sun was then entering the constellation Aries; for there is no evidence that the Jews knew anything of the signs of the Zodiac for centuries afterward; but because it was an animal easily procured and of proper size for the domestic meal. The use of unleavened bread at the spring festival grew out of the fact that the bread hastily prepared amidst the toils of harvest could not be leavened.

These had no historical associations prior to the time of Moses. But what he chiefly added, was the new spirit which pervaded the whole Mosaic religion and also transformed these ancient festivals. Its supreme tenet was that every individual and the whole people should dedicate themselves and all theirs to God, should be governed by his will, and should obtain their rest and refreshment in what is pure and holy. As this is hindered by the cares and distractions of life, sacred periods were instituted for this end, specimens as it were of the undisturbed serenity of the divine life, in which men might for the time be lifted to this pure and perfect state. This idea, though not wholly wanting among other people of antiquity, nowhere appears so clearly and strongly as among the Hebrews under Moses. With this view he instituted the Sabbath. The division of time into weeks was known to many ancient nations, but the Sabbath is peculiar to Israel, and was developed into the successive cycles of the Sabbatical year and the year of Jubilee. And the annual feasts were septenary periods and in various ways bear the impress of the number seven. There were two great festivals which were precisely balanced by giving to each the same three constituents, symmetrically adjusted, a fore-feast, the feast proper, and an after-feast. They were placed respectively at the full moon in the first and the seventh month, the first month, that is, in each half of the year. In each there was first a forefeast consisting of an expiation on the 10th day; in the first month the Passover lamb was selected, and, as Ewald thinks, originally slain on that day to avert all coming evil; in the seventh month, the day of Atonement, of higher intensity and retrospective, to expiate the sins of the past, not those of a family merely, but of the whole people. Then followed on the 15th the feast itself, lasting seven days—the feast of Unleavened Bread in the one case, and of Tabernacles in the other. Finally an additional day as an after-feast, the feast of Weeks at the end of harvest, and the day following Tabernacles, which concluded the festivals of the year.

Von Lengerke[1] adopts substantially the views of Ewald, making the feasts to have all been appointed and arranged by Moses, though partly based on pre-Mosaic festivals.

Hupfeld[2] discovers much diversity and many inconsistencies in the feast laws; and in none of these, even the most ancient, is the true origin and ground of these festivals correctly stated. While the festivals themselves are Mosaic, the laws, as we now have them, were committed to writing by different persons

[1] " Kenaan, Volks-und Religionsgeschichte Israels," 1844.

[2] "De vera et primitiva festorum ratione apud Hebraeos," 3 parts, issued in 1851, 1852 and 1858, respectively, with an appendix in 1865.

long after, when their real reason had been obliterated and lost; this can now only be recovered by the study of the feasts themselves. These sacred rites, which require for their proper observance a peaceful and flourishing condition of public affairs, became in the calamitous and unsettled state of things after the occupation of Canaan disturbed and obsolete beyond other institutions; so that there is almost no trace of their having been celebrated in accordance with the requirements of the law at any subsequent period of the Biblical history, whether before the Babylonish exile or after it.

There was according to Hupfeld but one agrarian feast properly speaking, that of Tabernacles or Ingathering, and one of consecration, that of Unleavened Bread. The latter was only improperly called a feast. It was a solemnity, but not a period of festive joy, like the feast of Tabernacles, which is hence often spoken of as "the feast" by way of eminence, as though it stood alone,—Lev. 23 : 39, 41, 1 Kin. 8 : 2, 65 (whence 2 Chron. 5 : 3, 7 : 8, 9), 1 Kin. 12 : 32, Ezek. 45 : 25, Neh. 8 : 14, Ps. 81 : 3. It had two preliminary antecedents, standing in the same preparatory relation to it, as the Passover to the feast of Unleavened Bread, and they rose by three gradations to the climax. There was first, at the beginning of harvest, the presentation of a sheaf of the firstfruits, with appropriate sacrifices, though the day was not kept holy. Secondly, at the close of harvest two loaves were presented with augmented sacrifices and the day was observed as a Sabbath. Finally, after the fruits were all gathered in, the feast proper was celebrated for seven days, the customary length of a sacred period, and was crowned with the closing solemnity of the eighth day.

When the calendar was changed so that the month of the Exodus became the first in the year, that of Tabernacles was counted the seventh. But from the earlier laws, Ex. 23 : 16, it appears that the year originally began with the autumnal equinox, and the feast of ingathering then occurred "in the end of the year," or as Hupfeld renders it, "after the end of the year," that is, in the first month of the new year. It was with this month also that the Sabbatical year and the year of Jubilee began, the entrance of the latter being formally announced by the blowing of trumpets throughout the land. The first day of this month, which was observed as a Sabbath, and upon which the trumpets were also to be blown, was accordingly the opening of the new year. And the day of Atonement on the tenth of the month was designed to effect, at the beginning of the year, an expiation for the sins of the past, that thus as a holy people they might be prepared for their feast of thanksgiving, and in it consecrate the produce of their land to God the giver.

Thus reckoning, the month of the Passover will be the seventh, at the middle or culmination of the year, and its services are an advance upon those held at the beginning. Passover was not at first a commemoration of the exodus. And it was not an expiatory offering, but an act of communion and of consecration. Unleavened bread was the food of priests. The father of each household performed a priestly function in slaying the lamb, which had the same significance as the ram of consecration offered for Aaron and his sons, when they were admitted to the priesthood. The sprinkling of the lintels and door-posts was with the same intent as the sprinkling of the altar and the sanctuary on the day of Atonement; it hallowed the house. The aim of the day of Atonement was negative, the removal of sin, a general expiation on behalf of the whole people, such as was common among other nations. That of the Passover was positive, sacerdotal communion with God, lifting each head of a family with his entire household to the priestly dignity, making each and all priests unto God, a service wholly unique and peculiar to Israel.

The seventh month, upon this enumeration, was characterized by the consecration both of the people and of the land to God; the devotion of the first-born, which was associated with or superseded by the Passover, and the offering of the first-fruits, in two successive acts of presentation, fifty days apart, corresponding to the two harvests of barley and of wheat. In the seventh year not the first-fruits only, but all that the land yielded was given unto God. In the fiftieth year all alienated properties and all bondmen were restored gratuitously, or rather were surrendered unto God as sovereign proprietor and lord of both the land and the people, who grants to those who hold possessions under him no right of absolute ownership, but only of temporary use.

Knobel[1] is more disposed to look to the historical statements respecting the origin of the feasts for their

[1] "Die Bücher Exodus und Leviticus" (1857), especially his preliminary remarks on Lev. ch. 23.

explanation than any of his critical predecessors, who have preferred to ignore these statements entirely. Yet even he does not venture the length of giving full credence to the Mosaic narrative. That perhaps would have been quite uncritical. The Passover, he infers from the history, was borrowed from no pre-existing custom. It was not a nature festival, celebrating the transition from winter to spring, nor an expiation offered to gain a happy transit through the year which had just begun, but a sacrifice appointed by Moses in the immediate prospect of leaving Egypt, to obtain the help and protection of their fathers' God. It may be compared with burnt-offerings sacrificed on the eve of great undertakings to obtain the divine aid in their accomplishment. As the enterprise proved successful the ordinance continued to be celebrated in memory of the heavenly assistance which had been vouchsafed to them. In later times it came to be specially associated in the minds of the people with the divine interposition in sending those plagues upon Egypt, which rendered their departure practicable, while sparing Israel from their effects: and it was hence called the Passover. At a still later time the last plague of pestilence was converted into a miraculous slaying of the first-born; and then the Passover and the sprinkling of the blood were explained with particular reference to it. But this is a departure from the truth of the history. All which shows how easy it is for a critic to believe just as much or just as little as he pleases of a historical record. The feasts of Unleavened Bread, of Harvest and of Ingathering were previously existing festivals which

Moses adopted and into which he infused a new spirit. Passover, the day of Atonement, and the Sabbath were original with Moses. In general the Elohistic legislation faithfully reproduces the institutions of Moses; the Jehovistic contains modifications of a later age. Leviticus enjoins no pilgrimages; accordingly in the early periods of the history, attendance upon the festivals was dependent on each one's free will, though pilgrimages were the prevailing practice. Later legislators, as in the Book of the Covenant and Deuteronomy, erect this custom into a law, prescribing that every male must appear at the sanctuary, three times in the year, at the great annual feasts.

Dillmann[1] concludes from his critical principles that the Book of the Covenant dates from the period of the Judges, the Levitical code from the time of Solomon, and Deuteronomy from a period later still. But although these laws, in the form in which we have them, are supposed to belong to various epochs subsequent to the Mosaic age, he nevertheless regards the feasts as Mosaic or pre-Mosaic; and to the objection drawn from the infrequent mention of them in the history, he replies that there are as many references to them as we have any right to expect in so brief a narrative. Dillmann adopts the grouping of the feasts proposed by Ewald, and agrees with him in supposing that the annual feasts were based upon the spring and autumn festivals common to all ancient nations. These were probably observed by the Israelites before the time of Moses, possibly with some of the same usages as in later times, such as the use of

[1] Art. Feste in Schenkel's "Bibel-Lexicon" (1869), Vol II., pp 265-272.

unleavened bread and sacrifice. Moses rearranged the feasts and gave them a new meaning. By converting the spring festival into a commemoration of the deliverance from Egypt, the time of its observance came to be definitely fixed, the slaying and eating of the lamb became a symbol of God's delivering grace and a means of appropriating it, and the unleavened bread was indicative of the purity of God's redeemed people. Its old relation to the change of seasons was lost sight of, except in so far as it became a feast of thankful consecration of the harvest; and as in the climate of Palestine it corresponded with the first ripening grain, its closing day was put seven weeks later when the harvest was ended, thus assuming almost the character of a separate and independent festival. The time of the autumn feast had previously fluctuated with the character of the season. But as the feast of Unleavened Bread was now established in the first month, that of Ingathering was placed in the seventh or sabbatic month, together with the day of Atonement as a suitable preparation for it, and a final day as the solemn conclusion of the festivals of the year. That but three festivals are spoken of in the Book of the Covenant and in Deuteronomy, while the Levitical law names seven, is in his judgment no discrepancy, and is not to be explained by the gradual increase in the number actually observed, but by the fact that in the one case reference is had to the three pilgrimage feasts exclusively, and in the other to additional solemnities as well.

More recently the professor[1] appears to have

[1] "Die Bücher Exodus und Leviticus" (1880). See particularly on Lev. 23.

changed his mind with regard to the Mosaic origin of the two agricultural feasts of Weeks and Tabernacles, and to have adopted the opinion that these can only have been introduced after the occupation of Canaan; and that the time of Tabernacles may at first have been regulated by the actual ingathering of the fruits, and so have varied with the locality and with the season; only it must, at least in the region about Jerusalem, have been fixed in the seventh month by or before the time of Solomon, from the express mention of it at the dedication of the temple.

This subject has further been treated from an archæological point of view, as by De Wette himself, who in his "Archæology," published in successive editions in 1814, 1830 and 1842, divides the religious institutions of Israel into pre-Mosaic, Mosaic and post-Mosaic, and classes as Mosaic all those which are ordained by the laws of the Pentateuch;—also by Winer,[1] who finds in the thorough and organic relation of the feasts to one another a voucher for their contemporaneous Mosaic origin; and who says of the critical theories upon this subject that if every one is to arrange the materials of Biblical Archæology in accordance with his own easily framed hypothesis of the composition of the books of the Bible, this science will soon be destitute of all historical basis.

The Mosaic Legislation has also been studied symbolically, and that in the most exhaustive manner by Bähr,[2] and with the like result. He finds one consist-

[1] "Biblisches Real-Wörterbuch." Third edition, 1847, Art. Feste, Pascha, etc.
[2] "Symbolik des Mosaischen Cultus," Vol. II., 1839. Second edition, Vol. I., 1874, pp. 1, 2.

ent and harmonious system of religious ideas embodied in the whole, generically distinct from those of every other people; all is pervaded by one spirit, and the outgrowth of one conception, showing that the entire ceremonial law is the product of one mind and the historical evidence is in his view yet unshaken amid all the diversity of opposing hypotheses that this is the mind of Moses.

We are thus brought in our survey of various opinions to the Wellhausen hypothesis respecting the feasts of Israel, which claims in consequence of their agricultural character that they were borrowed from the Canaanites after Israel's occupation of their country, and that by slow degrees in the course of many centuries they grew up to the completed form represented in the Pentateuchal laws.

It is sufficient now to say as the result of our inquiry into the previous treatment of this subject that this hypothesis stands opposed to the conclusion, which with a surprising degree of uniformity we have found to be reached by those who have approached its study from so many and such widely different points of view; and by those likewise who certainly can not be charged with undue deference to traditional opinions and who do not scruple in the most unceremonious manner to set aside the statements of the Pentateuch itself. For I have purposely refrained from adducing the sentiments of those who like Frederick Ranke, Hengstenberg, Hävernick, Drechsler, Welte, Baumgarten, Kurtz, F. W. Schultz, Oehler, Keil and Bachmann, accept the historical testimony of the Pentateuch as unquestionably true.

III.
THE UNITY OF EXODUS,
CHAPTERS 12, 13.

III.

THE UNITY OF EXODUS, CHAPTERS 12, 13.

IT would seem as though the inquiry into the origin and design of the Hebrew festivals should find a prompt and easy answer. We have what professes to be, and from the earliest times has been believed to be, a contemporaneous record upon this subject from the pen of the great legislator himself. It contains a narrative of the institution of the Passover at the time of Israel's departure out of Egypt and of the circumstances which led to its institution. It also records the enactments at Sinai and on the plains of Moab, in which the remaining feasts were added to the Passover and the manner of their observance was prescribed.

It is alleged, however, that neither the narrative nor the enactments are Mosaic; that they were in fact produced long posterior to the time of Moses, so long that they can yield no authentic information. The narrative may represent the current belief of the period when it was written, and the enactments set forth the usages of the time to which they belong. But the facts so minutely stated in the one can not be reasonably regarded as facts at all; and the authority of the legislator claimed for the other is altogether without foundation.

These startling assertions rest upon three propositions, which it is affirmed can be established.

1st. That the records in question can not bear the test of a searching literary analysis.

2d. That the different passages relating to this subject in the Pentateuch do not give a uniform and consistent representation of the feasts as they existed at any one time, but differ so materially that they must represent successive stages in their growth.

3d. That the same stages of development which are traceable in the laws can be discovered at successive periods of the history.

It will be necessary to give attention to these several points in their order. The one first named will occupy us on the present occasion. We proceed accordingly to inquire into the literary character of the documents with which we are dealing. The critics affirm that they are not of one tenor and style and can not all have proceeded from the same author; but that on the basis of various literary criteria they may with a good degree of certainty be assigned to distinct writers; that they are further defaced by alterations and interpolations of a more or less serious character, which are capable of being detected and removed; and that some of them are of a composite nature and are capable of being separated into their primary constituents. When this has been done all that is now inconsistent and perplexing will, it is said, become intelligible and clear: and the testimony which may be gathered from them in relation to the true origin of the Hebrew feasts will be very different from that which they appear to render in their present form.

In proceeding to examine these critical methods and results some preliminary observations should first be made.

1. The supernatural facts asserted or involved in the Mosaic record afford no good reason for a summary denial of the truth of its statements or the genuineness of its legislation. God's intervention on behalf of his oppressed people in Egypt in fulfilment of the promises made to their fathers was indeed on the grandest scale. But the occasion was worthy of the interference. If the true religion was to be established and perpetuated among the people in the midst of abounding paganism, degradation and corruption, it was fitting that its introduction should be marked by such displays of his delivering might and his divine glory, as should demonstrate the infinite superiority of Jehovah to the idols of the nations. The assumption that the miraculous is necessarily false and is to be accounted for as a legend of later times has been the guiding principle more or less openly professed of most of the critics, and with all the show of reasoning in defence of their hypotheses this has plainly been in the majority of instances the determining consideration. Such an assumption is a pure begging of the question and can not be conceded; and any superstructure built upon it is as insecure as the foundation on which it rests. The unfriendly animus of an opponent does not indeed absolve us from candidly examining what he has to adduce, and accepting any elements of truth which it may contain and any conclusions which are fairly proved. But we may be excused if we are in no haste to commit ourselves im-

plicitly to such guidance or to chase every *ignis fatuus* without knowing whither it may lead us.

2. A second observation is that confident assertion does not make up for deficiency of argument. Critics do not hesitate to take the most unwarranted liberties with well-accredited records and established historical facts. By a stroke of their pen they transform the text before them, adding to or erasing from it at pleasure to make it conform to their own preconceived notions, regulating the facts by their hypothesis instead of adapting their hypothesis to the facts. It is not without reason that Delitzsch speaks of "the omnipotence which resides in the ink of a German scholar." But baseless possibilities are not at once transformed into certainties or even probabilities because it may suit the exigencies of a critical hypothesis so to regard them.

We proceed to consider the questions raised by the critics respecting the literary form of the feast laws. This will require us to occupy ourselves, perhaps to a tedious extent, with minute questions of the form of expression and the connection of clauses and paragraphs, since this is the realm within which the discussion necessarily moves. And I hope that I may succeed in making at least the nature of the objections and the character of the defence clear to those who will favor me with their patient attention, though the subject is better suited for private study than for public discourse.

The first passage that presents itself is the narrative of the institution of the Passover in Ex., ch. 12, 13. The last plague of Egypt, the slaying of the first-born, converted Pharaoh's obstinate refusal to let the people go into the greatest urgency for their speedy departure. Israel was protected from the plague by the blood of the Passover lamb on the lintels and door-posts of their houses : and the Passover thenceforward was a memorial of this great deliverance and their being led forth from Egyptian bondage.

The history of the Exodus here recorded is the key of the whole position. If this is a bona fide record, the Passover is beyond controversy Mosaic, and owes its institution to the circumstances here recorded. It is not surprising, therefore, that this record has been most persistently and vehemently assailed, and that it has been pronounced false and mythical. It is affirmed that the Passover was not instituted to commemorate the events of the exodus, but that these are legends invented to account for an institution already existing. These events did not give rise to the Passover; but the Passover gave rise to the story of these supposed events.

Thus Wellhausen:[1] "The custom (of observing the Passover) is not barely accounted for in a historical way, but in its origin it is itself converted into a historical fact and then based on its own original. The shadow which is elsewhere cast only by an independent historical occurrence, here becomes a substance and casts itself." Or as it is tersely expressed by Dr. Robertson Smith,[2] when speaking generally of passages of this description, it is not "actual his-

[1] "Geschichte des Israels," I., p. 105. Prolegomena (English Translation), p. 102.
[2] "The Old Testament in the Jewish Church," p. 320.

tory", it is "a law in narrative form." De Wette more briefly still calls it "a juridical myth."

The account in these chapters is a continuous, closely connected and regularly unfolding narrative having all the air of truthfulness, self-consistent and suitable to the occasion described.

As the time approached for the infliction of the last plague, the LORD gave to Moses and Aaron, 12 : 1–13, detailed directions for the observance of the Passover on the fatal night, coupled with the declaration that he would pass through the land of Egypt that night and smite all the first-born both of man and beast, but would pass over those houses on which was the blood. He further adds, vs. 14–20, that this was to be commemorated in all future time by an annual feast of seven days, during which no leavened bread should be eaten and no leaven should be in their houses. Moses at once, vs. 21–27, summons the elders of the people and instructs them in regard to the Passover, informing them that it was designed to be a permanent ordinance in memory of this impending deliverance, and the people, ver. 28, did as they were enjoined.

Then follow, vs. 29–42, the infliction of the plague, the consternation of Pharaoh and the Egyptians, their forcing Israel out of the land in urgent haste, and lading them with treasures as the LORD had promised. The numbers of the people and the duration of the stay in Egypt are noted, since they were fulfilments of declarations long before made to Abraham. The mixed multitude that accompanied them

[1] "Beiträge," II., p. 198.

gave occasion, vs. 43–51, to a supplementary regulation respecting the Passover, stating the condition upon which foreigners could partake of it. The LORD further announces to Moses, 13 : 1, 2, that Israel's first-born of man and beast, so miraculously spared, were henceforth to be reckoned his. And finally Moses imparts to the people, 13 : 3–10, who had left Egypt in such haste that they were unable to leaven their bread, the divine injunction, which he had not repeated sooner, as it was designed for the future rather than the present, that when they reached Canaan they were to commemorate their departure out of Egypt by an annual feast of Unleavened Bread lasting seven days. And he completes the delivery of the messages with which he had been entrusted by telling them, vs. 11–16, of the enjoined hallowing of the first-born.

Eichhorn, one of the earliest and most ingenious advocates of the divisive hypothesis in Genesis, and to whom more than to any other it owed its sudden popularity, saw nothing suspicious in the Mosaic accounts of the Passover or of the other feasts. He appeals [1] to the fact that the writer comes back again and again to the same subject in Ex., ch. 12, 13, and that he makes supplementary additions in successive paragraphs in evidence that these passages were written on the spot, and that they have been preserved precisely in the form in which they were originally written. And Dr. Dillmann in his recent commentary, even while contending that quite distinct and

[1] "Einleitung in das Alte Testament," 3d Edit. 1803, Vol. II. p. 398.

varying accounts have been blended in these chapters, and that there have been serious displacements and interpolations, nevertheless admits[1] that "at first view they cohere admirably," such is the skill with which the final Redactor has pieced them together.

Vater,[2] writing in the interest of the fragmentary hypothesis, points out an imaginary inconsistency between Ex. 12:8, according to which the use of unleavened bread was enjoined at the first Passover, and vs. 34, 39, which trace it to a subsequent occurrence; and he suggests that several paragraphs[3] are complete in themselves, and might be omitted without creating any break in the narrative; whence it might be inferred that they were of independent origin.

Gramberg[4] discovered that two distinct narratives had been combined in these chapters, which when taken separately gave entirely different versions of the transaction. To the first narrator, or rather poet, for all is pure invention, belongs the whole of ch. 12, except vs. 14-20, the direction to observe the feast of Unleavened Bread. This, together with 13:1-16, belongs to the second poet. According to the former, the Passover was expressly limited to a single night, ver. 42, and was a sacrificial or expiatory meal, having reference to the myth of sparing the first-born, which was further symbolized by the blood

[1] "Die Bücher Exodus und Leviticus," p. 99.
[2] "Kommentar," I., pp. 32, 33 ; II., p. 447.
[3] Viz., 12 : 1-13, 14-20, 40-42, 43-49, 50-51 ; 13 : 1-16.
[4] "Religionsideen," I., pp. 271 ff.

on the door-posts. Unleavened bread was eaten with it as a purely subordinate matter, just as it was associated with other sacrifices. He finds no difficulty, therefore, in the subsequent mention by the same writer that the haste with which the Israelites had to leave Egypt, prevented their leavening their bread; and so is not obliged to avail himself of De Wette's solution,[1] that though the writer gives two divergent explanations of the use of unleavened bread at the Passover, the whole account is so inconsistent that he may easily be supposed to have contradicted himself in this instance also. Gramberg's second narrator had quite a different conception of the festival. He mentions no sacrificial lamb as belonging to it in any peculiar sense. It is with him a seven-day feast, in which unleavened bread was eaten in memory of their hasty departure out of Egypt, the first day and the seventh being marked by holy convocations and by abstinence from work. He never even seems to have suspected a difficulty, which others have found so formidable, that one passage names only the seventh day as "a feast to the LORD," 13 : 6.

The other feast laws in Exodus Gramberg parcels between the same two writers. The injunction, Ex. 23 : 15, 34 : 18, to observe "the feast of Unleavened Bread" belongs to the second; that respecting "the feast of the Passover," Ex. 23 : 18, 34 : 25, to the first. Inasmuch as these two injunctions are not directly connected, but are separated by intervening laws in both instances, he infers that the combination of the

[1] "Beiträge," II., p. 197.

Passover with the feast of Unleavened Bread had not yet taken place at the time when Exodus was issued, but belongs to the more advanced legislation of still later times.

George[1] also finds two narratives, but discriminated by a different principle; one is purely historical, the other simply legal. The first gives an account of the plague of the first-born, with only a slight allusion to the Passover in a single verse, 12 : 42. The other, when purged of interpolations, directs the observance of the Passover and states its design, but gives no description of the meal connected with it.

Stähelin[2] assigns all the legal passages without exception in Ex. 12 to the first legislation and those in ch. 13 to the second.[3] And Vatke,[4] though he reverses

[1] "Die älteren Jüdischen Feste," pp. 88 ff. His two narratives are (1) ch. 11, 12 : 29–42; (2) 12 : 1, 3–7, 12, 13, 21–28.

[2] "Studien u. Kritiken," for 1835, p. 462.

[3] Several methods of dividing these chapters as proposed by different critics may here be stated together for more convenient comparison.

Stähelin : First Legislation, Ex. 12 : 1–28, 43–51 (Mosaic).
    Second Legislation, 13 : 2–16, ch. 19–24, ch. 32–34;
    Deut. (post-Mosaic).
    Vatke, "Religion d. alt. Test." I., p. 429, note, adopts Stähelin's division, but assigns the first series to the seventh century B.C., and makes the second older, though with subsequent additions.

De Wette (Einleitung ins. A. T.):
    Elohist, Ex. 12 : 1–28, 37–51 (except 39); 13 : 1, 2.
    Jehovist, 12 : 29–36, 39; 13 : 3–16.

Knobel: Elohist, Ex. 12 : 1–23, 28, 37a, 40–51; 13 : 1, 2, 20.
    Jehovist, 12 : 24–27, 29–36, 37b–39; 13 : 3–19, 21, 22.
    This may be further decomposed into what is properly

[4] "Religion d. alt. Test.," p. 429.

THE UNITY OF EXODUS, CH. 12, 13. 93

the order of the legislations, adopts the same division. This annuls Gramberg's distinction between the writers, that one knew only of the Passover and the other

> from the Jehovist himself, and what he derived from other sources as follows :
> Jehovist (proper), 12 : 29–34, 39.
> Rechtsbuch, 12 : 24–27, 35, 36 ; 13 : 3–19, 21, 22.
> Kriegsbuch, 12 : 37 *b*, 38.

Kayser : Elohist, 12 : 1–10, 14–20, 28, 40–42, 43–51 ; 13 : 1, 2.
> Jehovist, 12 : 11–13, 21–27, 29–39 ; 13 : 3–16.
> So von Orelli in Herzog's "Encyklopædie," 2d Edition, Vol. XI., art. Passah.

Nöldeke : Grundschrift (Elohist), 12 : 1–23, (24–27),[1] 28, 37 *a*, 40, 41–51 ; 13 : 1, 2.
> Jehovist, 12 : 29–36, 39 ; 13 : 3–16.
> Redactor, 12 : 37 *b*, 38.

Schrader : Elohist, 12 : 1–23, 28, 37 *a*, 40–51 ; 13 : 1, 2, 20.
> Jehovist, 12 : 24–27, 29–36, 37 *b*–39 ; 13 : 3–16.

Dillmann : A (Elohist), 12 : 1–20, 28, 37 *a*, 40, 41, 43–50 ; 13 : 1, 2.
> B (2d Elohist), 12 : 21(?), 31–33, 37 *b*, 38, 42.
> C (Jehovist), 12 : 21(?)–27, 29, 30, 34, 35, 36, 39 ; 13 : 3–16.

Wellhausen : Q (Elohist), 12 : 1–20, 28, 37 *a*, 40, 41, 43–51 ; 13 : 1, 2.
> JE (Jehovist), 12 : (21–27),[2] 29–39, 42 ; (13 : 3–16).[3]

Vaihinger :[4] Elohist, Ex. 12 : 1–24, 28, 29, 37, 38, 40–42, 43–51 : 13 : 1–4, 20.
> Pre-Elohist, 12 : 35, 36 ; 13 : 17–19.
> Jehovist, 12 : 25–27, 30–36, 39 ; 13 : 5–9, 10–16, 21, 22.

Amid this diversity it will be perceived that there is a general agreement in referring to the

> Elohist, Ex. 12 : 1–20, 43–50 ; 13 : 1, 2.
> Jehovist, 13 : 3–16.

This seems to be necessary, if any plausible division whatever is to be made.

[1] Later addition.
[2] Later addition to Jehovist, or appendage of unknown origin to Elohist.
[3] Later addition by Deuteronomic reviser.
[4] In Herzog's "Encyklopædie," 1st Edit., art. Pascha.

only of the feast of Unleavened Bread, for the first law embraces both. But the two laws differ nevertheless. In naming the month of the festival one calls it, 13 : 4, "the month Abib"; the other designates it simply by its number as "the first month," 12 : 18, which according to Vatke and Wellhausen is a very significant circumstance, implying a change in the calendar and in the time of beginning the year, which took place after the Babylonish exile. They further clash in their provisions; one law requires a holy convocation and abstinence from work on both the first and seventh days of Unleavened Bread; the other upon the seventh day only, the civil disturbances of the period making it necessary to lighten the burdens imposed upon worshippers. Or as Dr. Dillmann still further exaggerates the discrepancy by urging the technical sense of the term used, rest from toil is not the thing required on the seventh day at all, but a pilgrimage to the sanctuary: whence he infers that while one law prescribes attendance at the sanctuary during the entire seven days, the other limits it to the seventh day alone, the Passover having first been observed by each family apart at their own homes; and a different usage still is represented in Deut. 16 : 7, which insists upon the Passover being eaten at the sanctuary, but allows the worshippers to return home on the following day, which was the first of Unleavened Bread. A further difference between the two laws, in Ex. 12 and 13, is found in the fact that while both enjoin the eating of unleavened bread for seven days, one enforces it upon the penalty of being "cut off from Israel," 12 : 15, of which the other, less rigorous, makes no mention.

The supplemental law of the Passover, vs. 43-49, is by Stähelin as by most critics assigned to the author of the preceding regulations in the same chapter, regardless of the inconsistencies which others have pointed out, viz., that one required the whole lamb to be eaten in one house, 12:46, while the other allowed two neighboring families to share it between them, ver. 4; that one was issued in Egypt, ver. 1, while the terms of the other imply settlement in Canaan, vs. 48, 49.

The majority of critics, however, differ from Stähelin, who saw no divergence between the two passages relating to the first-born in ch. 13, and consequently attributed them both to the same writer. The prevalent fashion is to divide them between distinct writers, assigning one to the so-called Elohist the other to the Jehovist, or as Wellhausen prefers to designate them, Q and JE. This allows opportunity for insisting upon a fresh discrepancy, viz., that one claims all the first-born in Israel for Jehovah without exception, 13:2; but the other, vs. 12, 13, makes the firstlings of sacrificial animals unqualifiedly his, while first-born children must be redeemed, and the option is allowed to redeem the firstlings of unclean animals or to kill them.

There is not a little diversity among the critics in their method of dealing with 12:24-27, the explanation to be given to children of the meaning of the Passover, which, as Wellhausen says, is allied to the Jehovist in phrase and diction, and to the Elohist in contents, a joint relation to both, which might tempt the unsophisticated to suspect that possibly the Elohist and the Jehovist were one and the same person after all. Schrader gives these verses to the Jehovist, and thus gains what is thought to be a better connection for ver. 28 by attaching it directly to ver. 23; but as the Jehovist could not explain what he had previously said nothing about, this makes it necessary to assume that he had before given a law of the Passover, which has been altogether omitted from our present text. Knobel rids himself of the troublesome verses by assigning them to the "Rechtsbuch," a *tertium quid*, which other critics pronounce a figment of his own imagination. Nöldeke thinks them a later addition to the Elohist, but not belonging to his work in its original form. Kayser, Wellhausen and Dillmann attach these verses to those immediately preceding, vs. 21–23, thus giving them their natural connection as an explanation of the rite which Moses had just enjoined, and obviating the necessity of assuming that a similar injunction had been omitted from the text. This whole passage, vs. 21–27, is then by Kayser assigned to the Jehovist. The consequence of which is, that ver. 28 of the Elohist document connects directly with ver. 20, and the children of Israel are represented as doing what the LORD had commanded Moses and Aaron, without having themselves been informed what it was. And it has the further consequence of leaving these verses as an impediment in the way of another junction which the critics are anxious to form. Ch. 12:29 records the actual infliction of the last plague, the smiting of the first-born throughout the land of Egypt. Ch. 11:4–8 contains the announcement of this plague by Moses to Pharaoh. Now if all that intervenes could be taken out of the way as an insertion from another source, the threatening and its execution would be brought together; the passage thus excluded would not be missed; the narrative not only proceeds without interruption, but the connection is positively improved by removing what is thus shown to be a foreign element, and a new point is scored in favor of the hypothesis that diverse sources have here been blended; on the assumption, that is, that no writer can introduce a digression or a parenthesis.

Dillmann takes a step toward effecting this result by assuming a partial transposition in the text of the Jehovist, to whom he also refers this passage. He queries, however, whether ver. 21 may not be drawn from another source, since it says that Moses called for "the elders," whereas, ver. 27, it was "the people" whom he addressed. But this interchange of the elders with the people, whose permanent representatives they were, plainly did not trouble the Redactor, and it is too frequent and familiar both in the Pentateuch and elsewhere[1] to require the application of the critical knife. He also queries whether the Redactor has not conformed the expressions in vs. 22 b, 23 to vs. 7, 12, 13: and certainly they are very suspiciously alike to be referred to quite independent writers.

Wellhausen here attains his end by throwing this troublesome passage out altogether, still undecided

---

[1] See Ex. 4: 29-31; 19: 7, 8. Deut. 5: 23. 1 Sam. 8: 4, 7, etc. 2 Sam. 5: 1, 3; 17: 4, 14, 15; 19: 11, 14. 1 Kin. 21: 11. 2 Kin. 23: 1, 2. 1 Chron. 11: 1, 3.

whether it is an appendage of unknown origin to Q, a later addition to JE. And he is also in perplexity about the similar passage, 13:3-6, on account of resemblance to the style of Deuteronomy; that is, to be sure, easily accounted for if Moses wrote them both. But as the Jehovist could not have quoted from a book written centuries after his time, this must have been inserted here by a Deuteronomic reviser.

Upon Nöldeke's division of these chapters the term "Passover" is used only by the Elohist; and he remarks that its occurrence in the Pentateuch is limited to the Elohist and to Deuteronomy with the single exception of Ex. 34:25, where it is either a later addition or has been retained from the diction of an earlier law. And from this avoidance of the term, which is created purely by his own critical process, he infers that the word "Passover" was not in common use in the northern kingdom. According to the Jehovist Pharaoh lets the people go to have their feast in the wilderness; according to the Elohist they had celebrated it already before leaving Egypt.

Kayser shifts the lines of division and finds that the Jehovist bases both the Passover and Unleavened Bread on occurrences connected with the Exodus, while the laws for these feasts as given by the Elohist are general and irrespective of any historical occasion. The Elohist fixes the day upon which the lamb was to be selected, and that on which it should be eaten. The Jehovist directs that it should be in the month Abib without specifying the day. The Elohist ordains in the general that all the first-born must be hallowed to Jehovah without defining how or when. The Jehovist gives a reason for the law, which indicates that the sacrifice or redemption of the first-born should take place at the Passover. And there are breaks in both the Elohist and Jehovist, which require the assumption of omissions from the text.

Wellhausen runs a still different line of separation and with an altered result. Q, or the Elohist, bases the celebration on the fact that Israel was spared by the destroying angel. This idea is wholly foreign to JE, the Jehovist, as well as to his sources J and E, the Jahvist and the other Elohist. They never imagined the possibility of the plague falling upon Israel. It is to them a necessary postulate, not suspended on any condition whatever, that Jehovah will make a distinction between Egypt and his own people. They lay all the emphasis upon the fatal stroke itself. It is this, and not releasing Israel from its effects, which is to be commemorated. In the Elohist the feast was appointed with a view to the exodus; in the Jehovist the exodus is for the sake of celebrating the feast. In the Elohist the blood was to be put upon the doorposts once for a definite purpose in Egypt; in the Jehovist it is a standing rite to be annually repeated. The infliction of the last plague and Moses' announcement of it to Pharaoh are put in immediate conjunction and both assigned to the Jehovist, but there is an irreconcilable variance between the different parts of the narrative; for he partly follows one of his sources, J, and partly the other, E.

Dillmann finds use for all three of his sources in these chapters, for A (the Elohist), B (the other Elohist), and C (the Jehovist); and he gives R (the

Redactor) plenty to do in the way of transposition and modification. He agrees precisely with Wellhausen in the verses and parts of verses assigned to the Elohist; but differs in the partition of the remainder, whence there results a number of new discrepancies. The Jehovist says nothing of selecting the lamb four days in advance, but appears to imply that the people were to go at once and kill it as soon as they received the order; no fixed age is prescribed for the lamb, and no particular quality; nothing is said of a Passover meal. Hyssop is to be used in the ritual, of which the Elohist makes no mention. The Elohist represents this ordinance as then first instituted by Moses; the Jehovist calls it "the Passover" when he first speaks of it, implying that it was known and observed before. The Jehovist speaks of a destroying angel; according to the Elohist God inflicted the plague himself.

It would seem accordingly that there is no difficulty in partitioning these chapters among different writers, each of whom shall represent the facts in a manner peculiar to himself. Indeed this can be done very variously and almost without limit, as the critics themselves have been at pains to illustrate. All that it is necessary to do is to sunder a closely connected passage, and insist that each separate portion shall be rigorously interpreted by itself not only with no regard to its context, but if possible at variance with it. The LORD gives to Moses directions respecting the Passover, Unleavened Bread and the first-born. Moses repeats these to the people. And this is absolutely made a basis for the allegation that two separate laws are here combined respecting these various matters. The Elohist records what the LORD said to Moses; the Jehovist what Moses said to the people. It might have been supposed, that as one of these necessarily implies the other, the natural inference would have been unity of authorship rather than diversity of writers.

But it is said that the law, as declared by Moses to the people, differs so seriously from that which is spoken by the LORD to Moses in both form and substance, that they are manifestly separate laws in every case. This allegation is at variance with the principles of the reigning critical hypothesis itself. It savors rather of the old fragmentary hypothesis, according to which the Pentateuch was a jumble of unrelated and mutually inconsistent paragraphs. But the present race of critics suppose that the Pentateuch owed its existing form to a Redactor, who has put together what he thought to be a self-consistent narrative, and meant to be so regarded. And if he is charged at times with attempting to harmonize accounts, which in their separate form and primary sense were really diverse, this nevertheless shows his belief in their consistency. He certainly intended his readers to understand that the law delivered by Moses to the people was identical with that which Moses had himself received from the mouth of God. Unless, therefore, he was destitute either of honesty or of sense there can not be the utter contrariety here which the critics profess to discover; and this may be affirmed with the greater confidence, as the critics disagree to such an extent among themselves as to the points in which this contrariety appears. In repeated instances one detects glaring inconsistencies in what another quietly ignores, or dismisses as of small account. It surely will not be insisted upon that the writer must load his narrative with the tediousness of identical repetition, whenever Moses is made the medium of divine communication to the people. Why may he not, in repeating the words of Moses, abridge what has already been presented to his readers with sufficient fulness as the utterance of God, or on the other hand enlarge more fully in the former what has been briefly stated in the latter? He had a right to presume that these would be regarded as mutually supplementary, and each would be interpreted by the other. And if the entire passage be regarded in its connection with the fairness and candor that should be accorded to any ordinary writer, the discrepancies will totally disappear.

We are entitled, therefore, to exclude from the list of alleged discrepancies mere differences in the fulness of statement where there is no positive variance, but one passage simply omits details which are mentioned in the other, and which are not repeated for the reason that a single reference to them was deemed sufficient, such as designating the Passover lamb in advance, the use of hyssop in sprinkling its blood, and the mode in which the flesh of the lamb was to be prepared and eaten. But we are told that conflicting statements are made in these chapters; that there are inconsistencies in the laws themselves, that the laws are inconsistent with the historical narrative, and that the narrative is not consistent with itself; and that the simplest explanation of these inconsistencies is that there are here blended the separate accounts of distinct writers. Let us see.

George and Gramberg tell us that the directions respecting Unleavened Bread, 12 : 15–20 and 13 : 3–10, contain no allusion to the Passover, and the writer seems to have no knowledge of any such ordinance. But this silence is not surprising, as it had been sufficiently spoken of in the preceding section; and fixing the fourteenth day of the month at even, 12 : 18, as the time to begin eating unleavened bread is a plain reference to the use of it at the Passover; and all critics now allow that the paragraphs relating to the Passover and to Unleavened Bread in ch. 12, are both from the same writer. Hupfeld and Wellhausen make a much more startling assertion, however, if it could be established. It is that the feast of Unleavened Bread and the hallowing of the first-born in ch. 13, take the place of the Passover and Unleavened Bread in ch. 12, as the annual commemoration of the smiting of the first-born and the exodus. One law directs that a lamb should be annually slain and eaten; the other ordains that not one lamb only, but all the firstlings from both their flocks and their herds should, year by year, be offered to God in memory of this great deliverance, which indicates a totally different practice, and one which corresponds rather with the law in Deut. 16 : 2. But the divisive hypothesis itself warrants no such conclusion. The Elohist in these chapters puts the hallowing of the first-born in connection with the exodus, as well as the Passover and Unleavened Bread; he does so with equal distinctness elsewhere, Num. 3 : 13, 8 : 17. The offering of the first-born is not a substitute for the Passover, but additional to it; and hence they are so often combined in the subsequent laws of the Pentateuch, Ex. 22 : 29 f., 23 : 15, 34 : 18–20, Deut. 15 : 19 f., 16 : 1. And so it is according to the general voice of the critics in the Jehovist likewise.

Hupfeld finds a difficulty in Ex. 12 : 16, according to which the first day of Unleavened Bread is to be observed as a Sabbath by abstinence from work and a holy convocation, and in Lev. 23 : 11, comp. ver. 7, it is expressly called a Sabbath. Yet on that day they were to put away leaven from their houses, prepare unleavened bread and slay the passover, and they did in fact leave Egypt. But the very passage appealed to shows that it was not a strict Sabbath, for they are explicitly allowed to prepare their food, which was forbidden on the Sabbath, Ex. 16 : 23 ff., 35 : 2 f. Besides, sacred actions belonging to the ritual and enjoined in the law were lawful upon the Sabbath. Part of what is here objected to was to be performed the day before in preparation for the Passover. And as the feast of Unleavened Bread was only intended to be observed in Canaan and had not yet been made known to the people, when they were forced out of Egypt, this compulsory march was surely no violation of the statute.

A more plausible ground of objection is that 12 : 16 directs a holy convocation upon the first and seventh days of Unleavened Bread, while 13 : 6 only distinguishes the seventh day as a feast of the LORD. Two points are raised here; one, that the first passage singles out two days of the seven for special observance; the other, that the terms used to describe this observance are different in the two cases. One directs that "there shall be a holy convocation and no manner of work shall be done"; the other, that there "shall be a feast to the LORD." Hupfeld thinks that these are identical in meaning, the former defining how the feast required in the latter is to be observed. Dillmann insists that they are quite diverse in signification; that in its constant usage the word "feast" in Hebrew denotes a pilgrimage festival, and that the specific thing required is that worshippers should make their pilgrimage to the sanctuary, which is quite independent of a holy convocation that might be held, though none were expected or required to be present from a distance. If this distinction be insisted on, then instead of exaggerating the difficulty, as seems to be thought by Dillmann, it neutralizes it altogether. For there is not the slightest collision or interference in the two injunctions. If two days are appointed for holy convocation and pilgrims from a distance are only required to be present at one, the regulations are in perfect harmony. In fact Dillmann himself interprets Deut. 16:7, 8, as enjoining this very thing.

If, however, with Hupfeld we suppose the expressions to be substantially identical in meaning, no difficulty is created by the mention of the seventh day alone in the verse above cited. The first day had already been singled out in the same identical paragraph but three verses before, and the stress of the whole observance put upon that day. The reason of the institution lay in it. "Remember this day in which ye came out from Egypt." This was the very thing to be commemorated. Here all the sacredness centered, which flowed over into the succeeding days, and formed them into a seven-day festival. A lower grade of sacredness attached to the days that followed, though leavened bread was forbidden throughout the entire week, which ended, as it began, with a day of marked solemnity. It should further be observed that this direction was given by Moses to the people at the close of the first day of the sacred week. Legislating for future years, he says, Remember this day of signal divine deliverance, eat unleavened bread for seven days and observe the seventh. How any one can imagine that such a command passes over the first day as inferior in dignity or to be less sacredly kept than the seventh it is difficult to understand. And it is precisely the same with the parallel passage in Deut. 16: 1, 3, 8.

The suggestion that 12:19 imposes this observance alike upon strangers and those born in the land upon pain of death, whereas vs. 43–49 debar every uncircumcised stranger from keeping it, scarcely deserves mention. For the regulations relate to different matters entirely. One refers to eating unleavened bread; the other to the paschal lamb. Leaven, the symbol of corruption, was at this holy season to be banished from their land. The celebration of so signal a divine interposition demanded the putting far away of the leaven of malice and wickedness; and the stranger who was among them was bound by the same law. But to the special act of communion denoted by participation of the lamb none but the circumcised could be admitted.

It is further alleged that the laws are inconsistent with the narrative in which they are found. But this is as untrue as the allegation already examined that the enactments are inconsistent with one another. It is said that the confusion and haste of leaving Egypt was no fit time for appointing such an observance. But the cavil overlooks entirely the nature and design of the ordinance. The sprinkled blood assured their deliverance; partaking of the lamb was an act of communion with God, which pledged to them his presence and powerful aid. It was just what they then most of all needed to be assured of in the perils of that night of terror and death, and in the fatigues, privations and dangers that were to follow, that they were under almighty safe-conduct and that He who commissioned the angel of death was their protector and guide, and would surely bring them to the land promised to their fathers.

It is also objected that although it had been announced, 11:4 ff., that the plague inflicted that night would break the obstinacy of Pharaoh and set them free, and they were directed, 12:11, to eat the Passover in haste, with their loins girt and staff in hand, yet the order to leave Egypt was so unexpected that they had not even prepared the necessary food, vs. 34, 39. But apart from any tardiness that may have been due to lingering incredulity in regard to a hope so often deferred, the people may not have understood from the midnight plague, nor from the symbolic readiness for departure in the ritual of the Passover, that they were then in actual fact to leave instantaneously. Moses himself seems not to have ex pected to go until the next morning, ver. 22. The graphic details are perfectly true to nature. The terrible consternation of Pharaoh and the Egyptians wrought a sudden revolution in their minds toward the Israelites, whom they now forced out of the country with an urgent haste, which they had not anticipated and for which they were not prepared.

The critics complain that direction was given, 12 : 8, to eat unleavened bread with the first Passover, and, ver. 15, to institute the feast of Unleavened Bread, when yet the use of unleavened bread is traced, vs. 34, 39, to a subsequent and unforeseen occurrence, the haste with which they were obliged to leave Egypt. But the difficulty is purely imaginary. It is assumed without reason that the historical incident is narrated for the purpose of accounting for the use of unleavened bread at this annual festival; which is not at all the case. The feast of Unleavened Bread was not instituted to commemorate the inconvenience of being obliged to eat their bread at that juncture without leaven, which considered in this light was wholly insignificant. The incident derives all its meaning from the feast already ordained, though not yet enjoined upon the people. The exclusion of leaven from the Passover as from other offerings is due to its being regarded as the symbol of corruption. Unleavened bread alone had the purity befitting a sacred transaction. Israel partaking of a feast of Unleavened Bread was thus sealed as a pure people, freed from their old corruption and entering upon a new career in the LORD'S service. By the apparently casual circumstance here recorded Israel was in the providence of God obliged at this time to eat that bread of purity, which the commemorative feast would in future years require. Unleavened bread being thus associated with the very circumstances of the exodus, became in every way a reminder of the great deliverance wrought and of the obligations which it involved. So that it is not even necessary with Dillmann to assume that the passage recording the institution of this feast, 12 : 14–20, has been transposed by the Redactor from its true position after the exodus had actually taken place; for which he pleads the past tense of the verb, 12 : 17, "this self-same day have I brought your armies out of the land of Egypt"; where, however, the tense is the same as when God says to Abraham before Isaac was born, Gen. 15 : 18, "Unto thy seed have I given this land."

But it is said that a commemorative service could not be ordained before the event to be commemorated had occurred. It is obvious to refer to the analogous instance of the Lord's Supper. And further, in its original observance the Passover was not a commemoration, but a preservative against the coming plague. The sneering suggestions that the blood on the door-posts was put there to enable the LORD to distinguish the houses of the Israelites, and that it would be no protection from a pestilence, only show how utterly this most appropriate and significant transaction has been misconceived. The whole symbolic ceremonial with its expiation by the blood of sprinkling is open to the same ignorant condemnation.

The direction "not to go out of the door of their house till the morning," 12 : 22, comp. ver. 10, rests, we are told, upon a different conception of the time of the exodus from vs. 31, 42, according to which they went out of Egypt by night. As both the Elohist passages, Ex. 12 : 17, 41, 51, Num. 33 : 3, and those assigned to the Jehovist, Ex. 13 : 4, speak of the day of the Exodus and refer it to the morrow after the Passover, Dillmann concludes that this nocturnal exit must belong to a third writer, the other Elohist. But we find both the Jehovist, 11 : 4, 5, 12 : 29, and the Elohist, 12 : 12, combining in the statement that the first-born were smitten in the night; while in Num. 3 : 13, 8 : 17, which by common critical consent belongs likewise to the Elohist, he speaks of "the day" in which the Lord smote all the first-born in Egypt. If "night" and "day" can in this instance be interchanged without requiring the assumption of a different writer, why not in the other parallel instance likewise? So that we have little difficulty in assuming that "day" may be used in an indefinite sense for the time of an event irrespective of the hour of its occurrence,—or in a wide sense so as to be inclusive of the night,—or that the undefined period when night is passing into day may be indifferently spoken of as either.

But it is further affirmed that the narrative is not only inconsistent with the laws here recorded, but with itself. Hupfeld points out what he considers a serious discrepancy in respect to time. In 11 : 4 ff. Moses announces to Pharaoh that at midnight all the first-born in the land of Egypt shall die: this must therefore, have been on the 14th day of the month, the plague of the first-born having been inflicted in the following night. And yet in the succeeding chapter the LORD directs what is to be done on the 10th of the month, 12 : 3 ; at the same time and in the same continuous context he says, " I will pass through the land of Egypt this night," ver. 12, and further goes on to say, " in this self-same day have I brought your armies out of the land of Egypt," ver. 17, as though it was the day after the plague, and the exodus was already accomplished. Here, it is said, there is an utter confusion of time. The 10th, 14th and 15th days of the month are all jumbled together in the most inexplicable manner.

But if the interpreter will only use a little common sense, he will find that there is no confusion whatever, but a perfectly clear and orderly arrangement. In the chapters preceding the twelfth there is a continuous account of the plagues with which the LORD had smitten Egypt in terrible succession. The writer proceeds with his narrative, not interrupting it with extraneous matter, until he reaches Moses' announcement to Pharaoh of the last decisive stroke, which would set Israel free. Here he pauses to introduce the Passover, which played so important a part in saving Israel from the destruction of that fatal night, which symbolized in the most impressive way their new character and new relation to Jehovah, and which was to be the standing memorial in all future time of their deliverance from Egyptian bondage, the birthday of their national existence, and their consecration to Jehovah as his people. In order to give a connected view of this great national and divinely appointed institution, he goes back a few days to the original direction given by the LORD to Moses on the 10th day of the month, which he could not have mentioned before without breaking the unity of his previous narrative, and dealing with the subject of the Passover in a disjointed and fragmentary way. When in the course of what the LORD then said to Moses, he speaks of passing through Egypt "this night" to smite the first-born, the night referred to belongs not to the day on which he is speaking, but that of which he is speaking, the 14th day, mentioned just before, on the evening of which the Passover was to be slain, and it is the day, which then began according to the Jewish mode of reckoning, in which he speaks of bringing the armies of Israel out of Egypt.

This also relieves George's objection that Moses announces to Pharaoh God's purpose to smite the first-born, 11:4, whereas the LORD does not himself reveal it to Moses until the following chapter, 12:12; this chapter, however, dates back at least four days before ch. 11. Besides it does not appear that 12:12 was the first disclosure of God's purpose to Moses, comp. 4:23. It is here introduced not for the sake of informing him of the fact, but as the reason for the institution of the Passover.

According to 10:28, 29, Moses was not to see Pharaoh's face again; and yet after that, 12:31, he called for Moses and Aaron and bade them go forth with the children of Israel; the simple explanation of which is that by a familiar usage of language, the king is said to do himself what he did through the instrumentality of others. And the principle is the same when the smiting of the first-born is attributed to the LORD, 11 : 4, 12 : 12, 29, and also to the destroying angel, 12 : 23, whose agency he employed. It is also urged that 12 : 31–33 contains a representation peculiar to the Jehovist, and in which he differs in a marked manner from the Elohist. According to these verses Pharaoh grants to Moses all that he had asked, viz., that they might go forth to hold a feast unto the LORD; and the Egyptians and Pharaoh are urgent upon the people to have them leave. Whereas, according to the Elohist, Moses had from the first demanded that Pharaoh should let the people go unconditionally, 7 : 2; and the LORD himself would lead them out in spite of Pharaoh's continued refusal, 7 : 4, 5. But there is no such diversity as is here pretended. In order that Pharaoh's unreasonable obstinacy might be set in the strongest light, the only demand made upon him is that he should let the people go three days' journey into the wilderness that they might sacrifice to the LORD. There is not a single passage in which the request is put in any different form. The phrase "let my people go," 7 : 14, 8 : 2, 9 : 2, etc., alternates in Jehovah passages with the fuller phrase, "let my people go that they may serve me," 7 : 16, 8 : 1, 9 : 1, etc. And there is no reason for understanding it differently in the only two passages in which the critics assign it to the Elohist, 7 : 2, 11 : 10. And if Pharaoh and the Egyptians drove Israel out contrary to their native inclination and under a divine constraint, how does this differ from the declaration, 7 : 4, that he would lay his hand upon Egypt and

8

bring forth his people? The two are not only perfectly consistent, but the divine purpose was effected by compelling Pharaoh to co-operate in its accomplishment.[1]

As the result of this examination, I think it may be unhesitatingly affirmed that the discrepancies alleged in these chapters are mere captious criticism, and afford no ground for the assumption of diversity of authors, much less for contesting the truth and accuracy of the record.

But it is further claimed that there is such a want of connection, such evident dislocations and abrupt transitions as show that these chapters could not have been originally written as they now stand. The present condition of the text can only be attributed to a Redactor who has pieced together into one narrative what were originally separate histories by different writers.

Thus it is urged that 12:14 does not connect with what immediately precedes. It speaks of "this day" being a memorial, when no day had been referred to, but only the night of the plague. Kayser, therefore, throws out vs. 11-13 and connects it directly with ver. 10. Hupfeld proposes to substitute ver. 42 in its place; he then puts ver. 15 after 19, and ver. 17 after 20, and transposes the entire paragraph, vs. 14-20, thus rearranged so as to stand at the end of the chapter after ver. 41. Dillmann complains of the isolation of ver. 42, but admits that the pronouns show that it does not belong after ver. 13, where Hupfeld would place it. He gives it to the other

[1] See Bachmann, "Festgesetze," p. 63.

Elohist, without being able to find any connection for it there. He does not approve of Hupfeld's transpositions in the body of vs. 14–20, but locates the entire paragraph after ver. 41, supposing it to have been occasioned by Israel having to leave Egypt without leavening their bread, vs. 34, 39. This fact, however, is only mentioned by the Jehovist, as Dillmann partitions the verses; which makes it necessary to assume that the Elohist had said the very same thing, only his account has not been preserved.

But really these critics give themselves a needless amount of trouble for very small reason. The "day" spoken of in ver. 14 is the one of which the night of the plague, which had just been alluded to, formed a part in the ordinary Jewish reckoning. And the allegation is doubtless in the main correct that the feast, which in this verse they are required to keep, is the seven days of Unleavened Bread, which the writer thus links to what he had before said of the Passover; though the confident affirmation that the Passover could not properly be called "a feast" is refuted by Ex. 34:25, comp. also the Hebrew form of the parallel passage Ex. 23:18, and Isa. 30:29. In ver. 42, Dillmann adopts Wellhausen's conceit that "a night to be observed" should be rendered "a night of watching," this sense being forced upon a word that nowhere else occurs, for the sake of thus creating a new conception of the mode of celebrating the night, different from all that preceded, and different it may be added from all the rest of Scripture, for Isa. 30:29 affords it no justification. Deut. 16:1, with its plain allusion to this verse, is sufficient to show that the common rendering is correct, and instead of its standing "isolated," it really gathers up in one emphatic utterance the spirit of all that precedes it. The night, of which it speaks, is included in the day of the foregoing verse; and that memorable day and night have been ringing through the entire chapter.

It has been argued that the introductory verse of ch. 12 sounds like an entirely new beginning, as though what follows was an independent paragraph, standing in no relation to anything before it. It marks the transition to a new topic, but is nevertheless a link of connection with the preceding. In summing up the narrative of the antecedent plagues, 11:9, 10, the LORD had declared his purpose to multiply his wonders in the land of Egypt. In direct continuation the writer proceeds to declare what the LORD had further done "in the land of Egypt" in fulfilment of this design. This objection properly has its place only in the old exploded fragmentary hypothesis, which regarded every title, or subscription to any section, as evidence of its separate and independent existence. The documentary hypothesis now in vogue is obliged to regard them more correctly as indicating convenient subdivisions of the subject matter and introduced for the sake of clearness, but no proof of any lack of continuity.

It is further contended that there are several paragraphs in these chapters which are but loosely connected with the general thread of discourse, and may be sundered from it without being missed, and whose removal will really improve the connection by restoring a continuity which they only obstruct. Such passages, it is claimed, are clearly interpolations and can not have belonged to the text as at first written; they indicate that narratives originally distinct have been blended together in the existing text. Thus George points out that 12:1-28 sunders the declaration of God's purpose to slay the first-born from its execution. It is, therefore, an interpolation, and in the course of it other interpolations occur, as ver. 2, vs. 8-11, and vs. 14-20; vs. 43-50 are similarly condemned. Wellhausen throws out as later additions 12:21-27, 13:3-16.

Every parenthetic statement, every digression for the sake of introducing what was not precisely in the line of previous remarks, however important in its bearing upon it, is unhesitatingly rejected as an interpolation. No writing was ever produced that could not be torn to pieces by such treatment. Passages can be sundered from the most closely concatenated discourse without the reader being aware of the omission. These chapters are clearly continuous; they pursue one constant aim. Nothing is irrelevant to the main theme. There is no lack of coherence in the several parts. Every paragraph and sentence adds something to the completeness of the view which the writer is presenting, and contributes to the general effect of the whole. The critics impute this to the skill of the Redactor, or final editor, who has selected his materials and put them together with admirable adroitness. But if he has really done what they attribute to him, he has performed the most marvellous feat in all literary history. He has taken two or more writings prepared quite independently of each other, on different plans and with different aims and tendencies, and preserving the identical language of each unchanged, he has fitted them together like a choice piece of mosaic, producing what has all the appearance of one self-consistent, indivisible record, and was universally so regarded until under the critical microscope its infinitesimal seams and sutures were detected. According to Dillmann he drew ver. 28 from A; 29, 30 from C; 31-33 from B; 34-36 from C; 37*a* from A; 37*b*, 38 from B; 39 from C; 40, 41 from A; 42 from B; and out of all this patchwork he has wrought a seemingly continuous fabric. The wonder is that a writer who was capable of performing a task like this should have imposed such needless trammels upon himself, and have worked in such a purely mechanical way, instead of doing what could have been done with much less labor and with a more satisfactory result, recasting the materials furnished by his sources in the mould of his own thoughts and bringing forth a narrative of his own.

It is further asserted that there are repetitions in these chapters, which justify the assumption that distinct narratives have here been combined, and parallel accounts of the same transactions have been retained from each. Thus apart from the supplementary law of the Passover, 12 : 43-49, which the critics themselves recognize as such, there are here two passages that contain directions about the Passover, two about Unleavened Bread, and two about consecrating the firstborn. But these are not superfluous repetitions in any case. God first gives the law to Moses, which Moses afterward repeats to the people. Neither of these would be complete without the other. No one surely but a critic who has a hypothesis to support would dream of rending them asunder, and assigning them to distinct documents. Ch. 12 : 35, 36, is not a needless repetition of what had already been said, 11 : 2, 3; the latter is the divine direction, which, when the proper time arrived, the people obeyed with a result which had already been foretold, 3 : 21, 22, each passage having its own special appropriateness in its place. And the evident reference of one to the other and their close verbal correspondence proves rather that they are of the same origin, and that they belong to the same continuous record. Ch. 12 : 51 repeats the last clause of ver. 41, but it is for the sake of resuming the narrative after a brief digression, just as is done, 6 : 28–30, comp. vs. 10–12.

In the simple style of Hebrew narrative it is not unusual for the writer to dwell upon matters of special interest, recurring to them and restating them that his readers may be more impressed by their magnitude and their consequence. It hence results that in connection with the recital of stupendous events like the flood, the plagues of Egypt, the crossing of the Jordan, and the exodus, there is an amount of repetition, of which the critics are not slow to avail themselves, that they may make out the show of a double narrative. But if the Redactor could introduce so many repetitions, why might not the original writer? The fact is that repetitions are found in each of the so-called documents taken singly, such as are elsewhere made the pretext for division. There are instances of this even in these chapters.

Ch. 12 : 19 repeats what had already been stated in ver. 15; and ver. 17 what had been said in ver. 14; though all belong to the Elohist.

But with all the liberties taken of sundering what plainly belongs together, and though passages are pressed into the service as duplicates which are not such, still serious gaps remain in the alleged documents. Thus the smiting of the first-born is threatened in the Elohist, 12 : 12, 23, but this document contains no record of its having been performed. It passes at once from the observance of the Passover, ver. 28, to the unexplained statement, ver. 37, " The children of Israel journeyed from Rameses to Succoth," with no intimation of what had happened in the interval. Yet from Num. 3 : 13, 8 : 17, 33 : 4, passages belonging to the Elohist, it is plain that the smiting of the first-born had been mentioned before; but that mention is only found in the Jehovist. Kayser insists that 12 : 37 a is indispensable to the Jehovist; but the majority of the critics are agreed from the reference to it in Num. 33 : 5, that it must belong to the Elohist. If this be so, then the Jehovist speaks, ver. 39, of Israel having brought forth their dough out of Egypt, without any previous intimation of their having left the country themselves; and he speaks incidentally, 13 : 17, of Pharaoh having let the people go, with no prior mention that he had done so. And upon Kayser's own division the Jehovist explains, 12 : 11, how the Passover is to be eaten without any intimation of what the Passover was or any direction to prepare it.

We have now reviewed what the critics have to

say in favor of parcelling these chapters among different writers, so far as that is based upon an analysis of the chapters themselves, the connection of thought and the relation of the several parts. We have found that by sundering them on different lines of division, they could bring out very various representations of what these assumed writers severally contained; which simply proves that the part is not equal to the whole, and that different portions of a narrative taken separately do not contain the same identical things. The alleged discrepancies in the laws, as well as those which are alleged in the narrative, and those which are said to exist between the laws and the narrative, prove upon examination to admit of ready reconciliation. The charge of a lack of connection between the parts, such as might imply dislocation or interpolation, turns out to be groundless. The repetitions, real or pretended, give no such indication of parallel narratives as might awaken the suspicion that different accounts have been blended. I think it may be safely said, notwithstanding the persistence and ingenuity with which these points are urged by the critics, that they do not severally or collectively yield any support to the divisive hypothesis, so far as these chapters are concerned. I shall not refer in confirmation of this opinion to those who while eminent in critical learning have sturdily defended the old-fashioned views of the authority, inspiration and genuineness of the Old Testament Scriptures, lest they might be thought partial in their judgments in this matter. But I may refer to scholars who are certainly competent to judge in a question of this sort, and who, themselves adherents of the divisive hypothesis, can not be suspected of any undue leaning to traditional opinions. Thus Winer[1] says, "The origin of the feast is certainly veiled in the dress of the miraculous, Ex. 12 : 12 f., 29 ff.," which to him of course means the incredible; but he adds: "I can not find actual contradictions or a double narrative in that chapter." And Bertheau[2] says, "The entire 12th chapter of Exodus gives a connected narrative; nowhere is there the slightest trace of disorder; nowhere anything that can justify the suspicion that any one verse stands out of relation to the whole."

[1] "Biblisches Realwörterbuch," 1848, art. Pascha, II., p. 197.
[2] "Die sieben Gruppen Mosaischer Gesetze," p. 58.

IV.
THE UNITY OF EXODUS,
CHAPTERS 12, 13,—(Continued).

IV.

THE UNITY OF EXODUS, CHAPTERS 12, 13, (CONTINUED).

WE have considered the question of the unity of Exodus, chapters 12, 13, so far as this is related to the contents of these chapters. After patiently listening to all that the critics have to allege from this quarter, we have discovered no reason for suspecting a diversity of writers. To all appearance they form one coherent and consistent narrative, such as might be supposed to come from one mind and from one pen. It is written with one evident design that is steadfastly adhered to throughout, and to which all the parts in their measure contribute. All is skilfully arranged, and the whole develops regularly from first to last. There is unity of purpose and plan, and unity of execution; and so far as can be judged from this point of view, we must infer unity of authorship.

The unity of these chapters has likewise been assailed, however, from another side, that of diction and style. It is said that there are such differences in the use of words and phrases in different sections of these chapters as betray the characteristic habits of distinct writers. It will be necessary consequently to examine what is alleged upon this point before we can reach a settled conclusion.

Before proceeding to do this, two preliminary remarks should be made.

1. The burden of proof lies wholly upon those critics who affirm diversity of authorship. The antecedent presumption is all decidedly the other way. These chapters form a component part of a book which has from the beginning been uniformly ascribed to one writer. They are certainly one so far that they have a common theme, which is consistently and consecutively treated. The most minute and searching examination has failed to detect anything inconsistent with this conclusion. If, now, it is contended that the diction and the phraseology of these chapters establish diversity of authorship, the proof demanded should be clear and strong on the one hand in proportion to the counter-evidence which has already been adduced, and which is to be overcome, and on the other to the ambiguity and doubt which is apt to overhang this species of proof. There is nothing about which experts will differ more seriously than the identity of handwriting, unless the case is so evident as to be beyond dispute. And so with identity of style, unless the indications are of the clearest sort. They who have the longest and most intimate familiarity with an author, may often be in doubt whether a given passage is from his pen, if it is to be judged of from style alone, unless it exhibits some marked eccentricities or peculiarities of manner. The difficulty is of course enhanced when the question concerns an author in a foreign tongue and belonging to a distant age, from which we have few literary remains. There is great and palpable danger of drawing wrong

conclusions from plausible appearances, which are to be accounted for in another way. The issue, however, is a simple one. There is no evidence of diversity of authorship, unless it is found in differences of style and language. Are these differences of such a nature, and withal so clear and unambiguous that they warrant the setting aside of all the accumulated evidences of their unity?

My 2d observation is, that the discussion must at present be limited to the chapters before us. We can not in the time now at our disposal undertake to range over the entire question of the unity of the Pentateuch and the possible existence of two Elohists, a Jehovist, a Deuteronomist and a Redactor, together with those other minor characters that the varied exigencies of the divisive hypothesis in different hands have summoned to its service. We confine our attention simply to these two chapters and the application of the methods and results of the divisive criticism to them. We are not now dealing with the hypothesis on the whole, except in so far as it is complicated with this particular passage. And as we do not mean to draw any conclusion beyond that which our premises warrant, we shall not pronounce upon the hypothesis at large, except in so far as the maxim holds, *Ex uno disce omnes*.

Knobel, who has shown the most extraordinary and painstaking diligence in accumulating and tabulating the criteria of authorship, has drawn out most formidable lists of words and phrases, alleged to be severally peculiar to the Elohist and the Jehovist. Dillmann, who follows in the same line, points out twenty or more in the Elohist sections of these chapters and quite a number in the Jehovist sections, as indicative respectively of these two classes of sections elsewhere.

The first impression produced by such an exhibit is that this matter is altogether overdone and the search has been quite too successful. It is out of all reasonable probability that so many distinct criteria of style should be heaped together in so small a compass. A more sparing display of evidences would have been really more impressive. Shiploads of yellow earth are not so plausible a counterfeit of gold as though the material were less abundant. The words here gathered up are the proper ones to express the thought which the writer has to convey, and for which in many cases it might be difficult to substitute any other. They belong to the common stock of the language, of which no one writer has the monopoly. That a particular writer has used one or more of these words before, is not necessarily a proof that another passage containing them is from him, nor need it create any prejudice against his authorship of a particular passage that it does not chance to contain them. This whole critical process tacitly assumes that the same writer must constantly use the same words that he has used before and no others. And this test is applied in a purely mechanical manner, and in disregard of the fact that modified forms of speech are not invariably suggestive of distinct authorship; they may indicate a difference in the shade of thought intended; and some variety of expression must be allowed to a writer who has any facility in the use of language.

In estimating the conclusiveness of this critical reasoning for the purpose for which it is adduced, it should further be considered that whatever positive and constructive force there may be in the arguments employed, is equally available in defending the unity of the whole. It is only their negative and more intangible and inconclusive side which even seems to lie against it. So far as the long lists of words and phrases gathered up as characteristic of one or other of the alleged documents tend to establish a mutual relation or common authorship of the particular sections which compose it, they serve a valuable purpose for him who maintains the common authorship of both, for the whole includes its parts. The only thing in the argumentation of the critics that need be disputed in the interest of unity, is the hasty and unwarranted conclusion which they draw from the absence of certain words from one class of sections that are found in the other class. And this is clearly invalid, provided the fact can be reasonably explained on other grounds than diversity of authorship.

The delusive character of these critical lists of words appears from the readiness with which such lists can be made out of any length where they have no possible significance. If two paragraphs be selected at random in the writings of any author, there will inevitably be words in each which are not in the other. Let this be assumed to be evidence that they are the productions of different writers, and that the words and phrases peculiar to each are characteristic of these writers severally. Then from these paragraphs as a starting-point let the examination be extended in succession to other paragraphs and sections of the same author, and these be assigned to one or other of these writers according as they do or do not contain the characteristic expressions already determined upon for each, the list of peculiar terms and phrases growing as the work proceeds. You have here the whole process by which the divisive hypothesis was originated. While proceeding cautiously step by step and with the most scrupulous regard apparently to scientific exactness, the authors of the hypothesis have themselves created the very phenomena to which they point as triumphantly establishing it. The division has been made on a given assumption, and why should it be thought extraordinary, if when completed it accords with that assumption? Particular words and phrases are made the criterion for determining what belongs to a given writer. Every paragraph, sentence and even clause containing any of these is in consequence successively assigned to this writer; and when the process is complete, the critic claims that as a demonstration which is after all only his own work. The partition corresponds with the hypothesis simply because it was made by the hypothesis. Whatever plausibility the latter possesses is due not to its resting on a solid basis of fact, but to the extraordinary ingenuity with which it has been devised and executed. If by persistent pains and incessant correction the critics should finally succeed in making it entirely self-consistent, what independent evidence is there after all of its truth?

We pass now to the consideration of the particular

words and phrases in the chapters before us, which are held to be indicative of different hypothetical writers.

A number of those that are credited to the Elohist are adduced in the following passage extracted from Nöldeke:[1] "The ritual of the Passover is here introduced in the first instance, indeed, only for the Israelites at their exodus; but as Abraham receives the law of circumcision in the first instance, which is then immediately extended to all his descendants, so too it is here. We have accordingly the second example of legal language, which prevails further on in the ritual laws, comp., *e.g.*, בֵּין הָעַרְבַּיִם (between the evenings), Ex. 12:6; לְדֹרֹתֵיכֶם חֻקַּת עוֹלָם (in your generations an ordinance forever), vs. 14, 17, so Gen. 17:7; מִקְרָא קֹדֶשׁ (holy convocation), ver. 16 · וְנִכְרְתָה הַנֶּפֶשׁ הַהִיא (that soul shall be cut off), ver. 19; Gen. 17:14, etc. It should specially be mentioned that here in the first law concerning religion given to the entire people, the expression עֵדָה, 'congregation' (all the congregation of Israel), occurs for the first time, which thenceforward becomes for the Grundschrift (Elohist) a standing designation of the assembled people, whilst he very seldom uses the simple הָעָם (people, but see Num. 33:17; Ex. 17:1)." To which may be added from Dillmann's lists the following additional legal phrases, all which are in the Pentateuch restricted exclusively to legal sections, viz., בְּכֹל מוֹשְׁבֹתֵיכֶם (in all your habitations), Ex. 12:20; so 35:3; Lev. 3:17, 7:26, 23:3, 14, 21, 31; Num. 35:29; בֶּן־נֵכָר (stranger), Ex. 12:43; sc

---

[1] "Untersuchungen," p. 41.

132 THE UNITY OF EXODUS, CH. 12, 13.

Gen. 17 : 12, 27 ; Lev. 22 : 25 ; מִקְנַת־כֶּסֶף (bought for money), ver. 44 ; so Gen. 17 : 12, 13, 23, 27 ; אֶזְרַח הָאָרֶץ (born in the land), vs. 19, 48, 49, and occurring several times in Leviticus and Numbers. But inasmuch as these words and phrases are peculiar to the ritual law, and the whole of that law is assigned to the Elohist, what else could be expected than that they should occur only in the Elohist sections and never in those of the Jehovist? If these words and such as these can be pleaded in evidence of diversity of authorship, then it would not be difficult to prove upon the same principles that no legislator can write anything except law. We might take Mr. Gladstone's bills for the pacification of Ireland, for the extension of suffrage and other measures introduced during his administration, and discovering in them large numbers of legal terms and phrases which are nowhere to be found in his "Studies on Homer and the Homeric Age," demonstrate with as much cogency as there is in the critical argument which we are now examining, that this latter work has been falsely ascribed to the distinguished prime minister. If the uniform absence of these words from every paragraph of the Elohist himself which is not devoted to ceremonial legislation does not prevent them from being reckoned his, what is there peculiar in the fact that they are likewise absent from all the paragraphs of the Jehovist, to whom no ceremonial legislation is assigned? We may, therefore, dismiss this class of words entirely as having no bearing whatever upon the question, whether the so-called Jehovist sections of these chapters are by another hand than the Elohist sections; and only remark in passing that in some instances it is only by the smallest possible loophole that admissions are evaded which are at variance with the hypothesis. Thus the Elohist, 12 : 14, speaks of the Passover as "an ordinance forever," and this expression is reckoned among those which are peculiar to his style; the Jehovist, indeed, ver. 24, calls it "an ordinance to thee and to thy sons forever," but this it is claimed is such a deviation from the preceding that it can not be regarded as identical.

Of the other words which Dillmann reckons peculiar to the Elohist there occur in 12 : 4 a verb and a noun of kindred signification. The former תכסו (make your count) only occurs this once in the whole Old Testament. The noun מכסה (number) occurs but once elsewhere, and that in the ritual law, Lev. 27 : 23. Another derivative is found in but a single passage, Num. 31 : 28, 37-41, and that in a ritual connection, where it is applied to the "tribute" paid to the sanctuary from the spoils of war. These are certainly removed by the infrequency of their occurrence from the category of favorite expressions, and hence afford no indication of the writer's habitual style. Moreover, their exclusive connection with the ritual law prevents us from looking for them in the Jehovist sections. A prepositional phrase in the same verse, 12 : 4, לפי (according to), is also classed as Elohistic. This occurs in the whole Pentateuch in this sense eight times,[1] four of which only are outside

[1] Gen. 47 : 12; Ex. 12 : 4, 16 : 16, 18; Lev. 25 : 16, 27 : 16; Num. 9 : 17, 26 : 54.

of legal sections. Knobel is alone in assigning the first of these, Gen. 47:12, to the Elohist; Hupfeld, Schrader, Nöldeke, Kayser and Dillmann agree that the verse is not his. The second and third, Ex. 16:16, 18, are not his either, according to Wellhausen. So that if we admit the authority of this latter critic the phrase in question belongs to the Elohist but once out of the four times that it is found in any other than a legal section. We can hardly accept this, therefore, as a distinctive criterion of his style. Again we are pointed to נפש, (soul), in the sense of "person," vs. 4, 15, 16, 19; but this is not peculiar to the Elohist, for the Jehovist so uses it, Gen. 2:7, and according to Schrader and Kayser in Josh. 10:28 ff., 11:11 likewise; and there is a general agreement also that Gen. 14:21 does not belong to the Elohist. Another criterion is שפטים (judgments) which occurs in all in the Pentateuch four times,[1] and always in relation to the inflictions divinely sent upon Egypt, and this is the only word which is used in this precise sense in the Pentateuch; משפטים, which is of frequent occurrence, and is rendered by the same English equivalent, is not used in these books in the sense of a divine infliction, but of a judicial sentence or an ordinance. Most of the critics claim שפטים in each of these four cases for the Elohist; but Kayser assigns one, Ex. 12:12, to the Jehovist. As the thought is not expressed in other Jehovist sections, there is no occasion for the use of the word. It is further reckoned a peculiarity of the Elohist that he applies the term צבאות (armies) to the Is

[1] Ex. 6:6, 7:4, 12:12; Num. 33:4.

raelites, Ex. 12:17, 41, 51; so 6:26, 7:4, and elsewhere. But the Jehovist also uses this word in application to the Philistine army, Gen. 26:26, and Gen. 21:22, 32 is not Elohistic; that it does not chance to be found in a Jehovist section in application to Israel must be purely accidental, since he uses other military terms in relation to them, showing that he regarded them as an army, *e.g.*, 13:18 (Schrader) harnessed, or prepared for war, 14:19, 20 (Kayser) camp. It is claimed that באדם ובבהמה (of man and of beast), Ex. 13:2, is an Elohistic expression, but the Jehovist combines the same terms, though with a different preposition, Ex. 9:25, 13:15, and the Elohist also adopts this latter form, 12:12.

Two expressions are yet to be mentioned, upon which the critics lay great stress, claiming them with confidence, and as it might at first sight appear, with some plausibility, as characteristic of the Elohist. One is עצם idiomatically used in the sense of "selfsame," Ex. 12:17, 41, 51; and the other כן עשו in the pleonastic declaration "they did as the LORD commanded; so did they," vs. 28, 50. The former unique expression occurs nine times[1] besides in the Pentateuch, uniformly in Elohist passages; it also occurs once in an Elohist passage in Joshua (5:11) and nowhere in any subsequent book of the Old Testament with the exception of four times in Ezekiel,[2] whose priestly familiarity with the law shows itself so freely in the adoption of its language, and even the

[1] Gen. 7:13, 17:23, 26; Lev. 23:14, 21, 28, 29, 30; Deut. 32:48.
[2] Ezek. 2:3, 24:2 *bis*, 40:1.

revival of its obsolete words and phrases. It is an emphatic form of speech, which was but sparingly used and limited, as a brief inspection will show, to important epochs whose exact time is thus signalized. It marks two momentous days in the history, that on which Noah entered into the ark, Gen. 7:13, and that on which Moses, the leader and legislator of Israel, went up Mount Nebo to die, Deut. 32:48. It is used twice in connection with the original institution of circumcision in the family of Abraham, Gen. 17:23, 26; three times in the chapters before us of the day that the LORD brought Israel out of Egypt, and five times in Lev. 23, the chapter ordaining the sacred festivals, to mark severally the day on which the sheaf of the first-fruits was presented in the Passover week, ver. 14, (which is emphasized afresh on the observance of the first Passover in Canaan, Josh. 5:11); also the day on which the two wave loaves were brought at the feast of Weeks, ver. 21; and with triple repetition the great day of Atonement, vs. 28–30. If now all the emphatic moments calling for the use of this phrase have by the critics been given to the Elohist, it might not seem surprising if the Jehovist had not employed it at all. And yet it is found once in an admitted Jehovist section, Josh. 10:27,[1] showing that it can have place in these sections as well as the others, if there is occasion for its employment. This word consequently affords no ground of discrimination and no plea for division.

The other Elohist expression above referred to ac-

[1] Schrader and Kayser assign this verse to the Jehovist: Knobel to his Kriegsbuch.

cords, it is said, with his formal, precise and repetitious style. It occurs eleven times[1] in the Pentateuch, and in a slightly modified form twice more; and in every single instance it is referred by the critics to the Elohist. It is not once found in a Jehovist section. The impression which such a statement is calculated to produce, is not a little diminished, however, when we inquire a little further into the actual state of the case.

1. This expression is not to be regarded as unmeaning tautology and dismissed as the mere habit of a diffuse and repetitious writer. In the vast majority of instances in which attention is drawn to the correspondence of action with the divine command, the Elohist himself uses a briefer formula; often simply "as the LORD commanded,"[2] or "they did as the LORD commanded,"[3] or "they did so as the LORD commanded,"[4] or "as the LORD commanded, so they did."[5] The larger and fuller form, "they did according to all that the LORD commanded them, so did

[1] Gen. 6:22; Ex. 7:6, 12:28, 50, 39:32, 43, 40:16; Num. 1:54, 8:20, 17:11; and with a slight modification, Num. 2:34, 5:4.

[2] Gen. 7:16, 21:4; Ex. 16:34, 39:1, 5, 7, 21, 26, 29, 31, 40:19, 21, 23, 25, 27, 29, 32; Lev. 8:9, 13, 17, 21, 29, 9:10; Num. 1:19, 2:33, 3:42, 51, 4:49, 15:36, 20:9, 31:7, 41, 47; Josh. 21:8. Not in Elohist sections, Gen. 7:9; Ex. 34:4; Josh. 10:40.

[3] Lev. 8:4, 16:34; Num. 20:27, 27:22, 31:31; Deut. 34:9, and with a slight modification Ex. 38:22, Lev. 8:36, Jehovist Gen. 7:5. Knobel assigns Lev. 24:23 to his Kriegsbuch, others give it to the Elohist.

[4] Ex. 7:10, 20; Num. 8:3.

[5] Ex. 39:42; Num. 8:22, 9:5, 36:10; Josh. 14:5. Jehovist, or according to Knobel, the Kriegsbuch, Josh. 11:15.

they," is in the highest measure emphatic. It is reserved for the weightiest matters and for commands of the utmost consequence, which were obeyed in the most punctual and scrupulous manner. There is but one example of it in the entire book of Genesis. It is in relation to the exactness with which Noah followed the divine directions in his preparations for the flood. "Thus did Noah; according to all that God commanded him, so did he." It next occurs of Moses and Aaron, when they were charged to confront Pharaoh and lead the children of Israel out of Egypt, Ex. 7:6. It is alleged, however, that the Jehovist speaks much more simply, and with less formality and emphasis, when he describes Noah's obedience to the divine injunctions. He merely says, 7:5, "and Noah did according unto all that the LORD commanded him"; and if ver. 9 is really Jehovistic, for the critics are divided about it, he there expresses himself more briefly still, "as God had commanded Noah." The altered formula is no indication, however, of a diversity of writers, but rather the reverse. The first time that Noah's compliance with the divine command is referred to, it is stated in the strongest terms. But a single employment of the lengthened phrase of special emphasis was sufficient in this connection. Other statements of the same kind, less elaborately made, could then follow in their appropriate place. Thus the emphatic formula connected with the general statement in Ex. 39:32 is preceded, and that in Ex. 40:16, is followed by numerous particular statements with the briefer formula, and no one suspects a difference of authorship on this account.

2. Mention has been made of two historical occasions of great moment, respecting which the lengthened formula is employed. With these exceptions it is found exclusively in legal contexts. It occurs twice in connection with the first observance of the Passover, Ex. 12:28, 50; it is three times connected with the construction and setting up of the sacred tabernacle, Ex. 39:42, 43, 40:16; three times with arrangements respecting the camp hallowed by God's presence, Num. 1:54, 2:34, 5:4; once with the setting apart of the Levites, Num. 8:20; and once with the sanction divinely given to the Aaronic priesthood, Num. 17:11. In fact an overwhelming proportion of even the briefer formulæ relate to obedience rendered to ritual enactments. It ceases to be surprising, therefore, that the longer and more emphatic formula is absent from the Jehovist sections, inasmuch as the ritual law is all assigned to the Elohist; in fact it is but rarely that they have occasion to use any, even of the briefer formulæ.

3. The reason why the long and emphatic formula is never found in a Jehovist connection will become still more apparent when it is added that it is by rule referred to the Elohist simply on the ground of its occurrence, apart from any other reason, and even in the face of strong reasons to the contrary. A particularly clear example of this is found in Ex. 12:28, which is preceded and followed by a Jehovist context, with the former of which it is intimately united, to which it evidently refers and from which all its meaning is derived. And yet it is torn from this connection and linked with a distant Elohist paragraph solely

and avowedly because it contains the formula in question. This is one of the gross improprieties, in which the critics are constantly indulging, as though clauses and sentences could be torn from their proper connection *ad libitum* and attached to any other that the critic may please, and the altered meaning be forced upon them, which may result from the displacement. Thus in this same chapter it is proposed to transfer vs. 14–20 from its proper place so as to precede the formula in ver. 50, and make this latter refer to it instead of to the paragraph which it actually follows. And in the same way Kayser and Dillmann cut 9:35 and 10:20 away from the context in which they stand, and assign these verses thus isolated to another hypothetical writer with missing hypothetical contexts upon which they are assumed to have depended; and this for no ground whatever but the exigencies of a hypothesis which demands it. The hypothesis must rule, whatever stands in the way. If the text can not be made to square with the critical assumptions, it is easy enough to create a text that will, by means of erasures, additions and dislocations.

The whole procedure should be met by an indignant protest. If the Redactor was guilty of the unmeaning transpositions and eliminations which are attributed to him, removing sentences and clauses from their original place in the sources from which he drew, linking them with a different context so as to alter their meaning entirely, he was either a knave or a fool; and it is hopeless to undertake to disentangle the medley he has made. The fact is that these imputations on the part of the critics are wholly gratuitous. The text, according to all fair laws of honest dealing, must be interpreted as it stands, at least until some better reason can be shown for remodelling it than that an unproved critical hypothesis demands it. Otherwise all certainty of interpretation is destroyed, and the text and its meaning become the plaything of the critic's capricious fancy. A hypothesis which is obliged to resort to such violent and unauthorized measures writes its own condemnation. If the truth of the divisive hypothesis were for the moment to be conceded, and we were to assume the existence of a Redactor to whom we owe the present form of the text, nevertheless it must be insisted upon that it yields the correct sense as it now stands, saving any errors that may have arisen in its transmission. Any partition which is destructive of the plain sense of the work which he has left us, in whole or in part, is an unwarrantable impeachment of his integrity, and a substitution of the critic's own whimsical notions for the statements of that ancient authority with which he is professedly dealing. Whether the divisive hypothesis be correct or not, the position can not be surrendered that the emphatic formula in 12:28 must have the reference, which it is evidently designed to have. It then of necessity becomes part of a Jehovist paragraph, and the formula in question ceases to be a criterion for distinguishing the Elohist.

The criteria of the Elohist thus far considered lie mostly outside of the plane of the Jehovist, who offers no equivalents or substitutes for them. All that is claimed is that they are found in one class of passages and not in the other. We have seen that their absence is readily explicable on other grounds than that of diversity of writers. It is alleged, however, that there are things common to both which each invariably describes by a different term from the other. The most plausible instance of this is found in their respective mode of naming the months. As members of the religious society of the Friends are in the habit of numbering the months to which the rest of the community generally apply definite names, so it is said that among the Israelites the priestly usage was to number the months of the ecclesiastical year while definite names were applied to those of the civil year, which began at quite a different season. Of this it is said, there is evidence in the chapters before us. Chapter 12:2 intimates a change in the annual reckoning, that thenceforward a month was to stand at the beginning of the year, which had not done so previously. Now in accord with this the Elohist document or the Priest Code fixes the Passover invariably in the first month; the Jehovist as invariably in the month Abib.

In regard to this, however, it should be observed, 1, that there is no inconsistency in the same person employing both terms whether in the same or in different connections, as was done, for example, by the author of the Books of Kings, who in his account of the building and dedication of Solomon's temple mentions, 1 Kin. 6:1, the month Zif, which is the second month, verse 38, the month Bul, which is the eighth month, and 8:2, the month Ethanim, which is the seventh month.

2. Abib, as the name of a month, only occurs in connection with the Passover or feast of Unleavened Bread. It is so found three times in Exodus in passages assigned to the Jehovist, and twice in a verse of Deuteronomy, 16: 1, evidently based on the preceding. The Jehovist uses this name nowhere else, and no other month is referred to by name anywhere in the Pentateuch. Hitzig conjectured that Abib was the Hebrew form of Epiphi, the eleventh month of the Egyptian year, which, however, corresponded with our June or July rather than March or April.[1] The name in Hebrew means "green ears," and was applied to the month because it fell in the season of ripening grain. At the feast of Unleavened Bread a formal offering was made of the earliest sheaf from the first-fruits of the harvest, an association which naturally led to the use of this name in that connection.

3. It is further observable that the month is never called Abib when the day of the month is mentioned. Dillmann accordingly conjectures that Abib, Zif, Ethanim and Bul were months of the solar year and were incommensurable with lunar months which were numbered. Others are of opinion that Abib[2] was the only month bearing a name in the Mosaic period, and

[1] As the Egyptian did not correspond precisely with the solar year and according to ancient testimony, the priests refused to rectify the calendar by intercalation, it was an *annus vagus*, whose months in a given period of time made a circuit of all the seasons. Hence Hitzig infers that at one time Epiphi and Abib exactly coincided.

[2] In the nomenclature of a later period this month was called Nisan.

that this was not so much a proper name of the month, as indicative of the season of the year to which it belonged. Whatever be thought of these opinions, the fact remains that in every instance in which a specific date is given the month is numbered. Accordingly in 12:18 the time for observing the feast of Unleavened Bread is stated to be in the first month from the fourteenth day of the month until the one-and-twentieth. So in Leviticus 23 and in Numbers 28 and 29 where the several festivals of the year are recited in order and the exact time of each is given severally, the same nomenclature is maintained. But in Ex. 13:4 Moses said to the people on the day of the exodus, which, therefore, there was no occasion to specify further, "This day came ye out in the month Abib." So in Ex. 23:14, 34:18, where the period of the feast is only spoken of generally as "the time appointed of the month Abib," it was natural to use the name suggestive of the season of ripening grain, especially as the other feasts are in the same connection associated not with definite dates, but with the harvesting of the crops and the ingathering of the fruits. The same reason holds also in the case of Deut. 16:1.

It appears, therefore, that the alternation of names finds its explanation in the passages in which it occurs, and requires no assumption of the habit of different writers to account for it. The allegation that the Elohist says "land of Egypt," 12:1, etc., and the Jehovist "Egypt" simply, 12:27, etc., 13:3, etc., overlooks the Elohist passage, 12:40, and the Jehovist, 12:29, 13:15, where this is precisely reversed.

So, likewise, that מַשְׁחִית is used by the Elohist, 12:13, in the abstract sense of "destruction" and by the Jehovist, ver. 23, in the concrete sense of "destroyer" is not perfectly certain, and it would be of no sort of consequence if it were. And while עֲבֹדָה (service) is repeatedly used by the Elohist of the ritual in general, whereas the Jehovist here, 12:25, 26, 13:5, applies it to the individual rite of the Passover, it is to be borne in mind that this was all of the ritual that had up to that time been instituted. It is said to be peculiar to the Jehovist to call Egypt "the house of bondage" or "bondmen," though this occurs in all but four times in passages assigned to him, viz., twice in the chapters before us, 13:3, 14, once in the preface to the ten commandments, 20:2, and once in Joshua's farewell address, Josh. 24:17; also to speak of Canaan as "a land flowing with milk and honey," Ex. 13:5, though Nöldeke and Schrader refer one of the verses in which this phrase is found, Num. 14:8, to the Elohist, excepting only this one expression; and "the land of the Canaanites, and the Hittites and the Amorites and the Hivites and the Jebusites," 13:5, though he may also say simply "the land of the Canaanites," ver. 11. It is said that it is the Jehovist alone who speaks of the LORD as swearing, 13:5, though an oath of the LORD is in Num. 14:28 recited by the Elohist. It is said that the preposition בַּעֲבוּר (because of) is peculiar to the Jehovist, and it does not chance to occur in Elohist sections; so מָחָר in the sense of "in time to come," Ex. 13:14, though it is so used by him in but one other passage in the Pentateuch, Gen. 30:33; and גְּבוּל rendered 'quarters,' Ex. 13:7, elsewhere commonly 'borders or 'coasts,' notwithstanding the fact that it belongs to the Elohist, Gen. 23:17, Num. 33:44, and repeatedly in the course of Num. 34 and 35; זְקֵנִים (elders), 12:21, though the Elohist has it, Lev. 4:15, 9:1; וַיִּקְּדוּ וַיִּשְׁתַּחֲווּ (bowed the head and worshipped), 12:27, though according to Nöldeke and Wellhausen this does not here belong to the Jehovist, and according to Tuch and Stähelin the Elohist uses it in Gen. 43:28. Knobel includes among Jehovistic expressions רַגְלִי (footman), 12:37, and עֶרֶב (mixed multitude), ver. 38, though the former occurs but once besides in the Pentateuch, Num. 11:21, and the latter is nowhere else to be found in the Pentateuch in this sense; and even here Nöldeke attributes them to the Redactor, and Dillmann to the other Elohist.

I believe that in this long and tedious review everything has been gathered up that the critics allege in respect to the diction of these chapters. And this is absolutely all the ground there is for parcelling them between these supposititious writers. Many of the words classed as characteristic of these writers respectively are of so rare occurrence that the statement is unmeaning. In almost every instance what is declared to be peculiar to one writer is nevertheless found in passages attributed to the other. The presence or absence of words is noted in a purely mechanical way, irrespective of the question whether there was any occasion for their employment. And where different terms are employed for the same thing the reason is sought in unmeaning differences of style, when they are discriminatingly used accord-

THE UNITY OF EXODUS, CH. 12, 13. 147

ing to the requirements of the case or the shade of thought to be expressed. There is no evidence whatever of divergent styles or the various diction of distinct writers. Differences occur in the paragraphs assigned by the critics to the same writer, which would otherwise have been deemed significant, as when the Jehovist says בְּחֹזֶק יָד, 13:3, 14, 16 (by strength of hand), whereas his customary phrase is בְּיָד חֲזָקָה (by a strong hand), 6:1, 13:9. Or when he describes the limits of the last plague, 11:5, "from the first-born of Pharaoh that sitteth upon his throne unto the first-born of the maid-servant that is behind the mill,"—but in 12:29, "from the first-born of Pharaoh that sat on his throne to the first-born of the captive that was in the dungeon." Again, certain passages speak of the LORD as smiting the first-born, while others describe him in more general terms as smiting the land of Egypt or the Egyptians. The attempt has here, in fact, been made to show that there were two distinct traditions, according to one of which the plague was due to natural causes, and according to the other it was miraculously limited to the first-born. But the way is blocked by the fact that both forms of statement occur alike in the Elohist (12:12, 13), and the Jehovist (11:5, 12:23, 27, 29).

Inasmuch as the critics arrange the paragraphs to suit themselves and use the utmost license in so doing, the marvel is that they are only able after all to make out so poor a case.

Our examination has been limited to the diction of the chapters specially before us, and I think it may be fairly said that nothing has been adduced of any cogency to break the conclusion previously reached from the consideration of their contents, that they form one indivisible narrative. These chapters certainly yield no support to the divisive hypothesis. Whether it is applicable to other portions of the Pentateuch is not the question now before us; but certainly so far as we have yet been able to see, it has no application here.

It may not be out of place to adduce the verdict which Graf,[1] the founder of the most recent critical school, passes upon the prevalent mode of dissection by means of diction and style. "To base a determination of age," he says, "on bare peculiarities of language, especially in things that concern legal relations, in which the form of expression is not arbitrarily employed by the writer, is precarious. When the relationship of certain sections is assumed on perhaps insufficient criteria, and then other sections are added to them because of some similar linguistic phenomena, and from these again further and further conclusions are drawn, one easily runs the risk of moving in a vicious circle." "The reference of every section and every individual verse to its origin, which Ewald and Knobel have attempted, will certainly never be accomplished in a perfectly satisfactory and convincing way, and is often dependent on subjective opinion."

I know of but one other argument which has been urged in favor of accepting the results of the divisive criticism; and that is drawn from the agreement of the critics among themselves, not indeed as to all

---

[1] "Die Geschichtlichen Bücher," pp. 2, 3.

minute details, but as to their general conclusions. The early efforts of the critics, it is said, were tentative, and mistakes were made from which their successors have receded. But advances have been steadily made until the hypothesis now rests on a solid basis and is clearly defined in all main and essential points.

It is frankly confessed that the most eminent and in fact nearly all the critics of Germany who easily lead the van in this branch of Biblical scholarship, have declared with remarkable unanimity in favor of what has been called the analysis of the Pentateuch. And it is further confessed that there is a general agreement among them in certain leading points. But we must for the present at least decline to accept a vote of the majority as an infallible test of truth, for the following reasons:

1. That measure of agreement which exists among the divisive critics is readily accounted for without conceding the truth of the hypothesis. It is conditioned by the nature of the case and follows from the primary assumption which they hold in common. If an expedition to the North Pole is sent out by the Baffin's Bay route, it must follow a given track determined by the experience of preceding navigators. If practicable at all, it is only upon that line. But whether the expedition will after all succeed in reaching its objective point, is another matter. Any attempt to explain the movements of the planetary system by the Cartesian hypothesis of vortices would involve the necessity of accepting this hypothesis in all its details. An ingenious chess-player has solved the complicated problem of the knight and has shown

how that erratic piece can be made to touch successively every square of the board; other solutions may be feasible, but they have never yet been devised. If a military road is to be constructed across the Alps at a given point, the topography must first be ascertained and then engineering science will determine which must necessarily be the most practicable route.

The partition of the Pentateuch upon the principles of the divisive hypothesis is a definite problem, upon which the highest order of intellect, learning and ingenuity has been long and persistently employed. The labor and patient thought expended upon it have been prodigious. Every word and sentence of the Pentateuch has been studied with microscopic minuteness, the best possible groupings have been sought within the limits imposed by the hypothesis, the intricacies of the case have been threaded with the utmost care, weak points have been guarded, assailable positions as far as practicable avoided, and everything seized upon that can add to the apparent strength or plausibility of the scheme. The result is a marvellous specimen of artistic contrivance. Of course it has all the while been becoming more perfect as a hypothesis. The critics have been quick to learn by the blunders of their predecessors. No one, it may be presumed, will ever renew Vater's fragmentary hypothesis, once so fashionable. A general might as well undertake to storm a fort by marching his unsheltered army where they will be exposed to the fire of the garrison at every point and mowed down as rapidly as they can advance. As the halting-places of the documentary hypothesis revealed themselves, the attempt was made by Tuch and others to cover them by the supplementary hypothesis. But as on the scheme of Graf and Wellhausen, which has sprung into sudden popularity, the foundation has been converted into the summit of the edifice, that form of the hypothesis was summarily cast aside, and the critics have fallen back under cover of Hupfeld's discovery of the second Elohist. The hypothesis, as it now stands, with three, or if the Deuteronomist be included, four distinct writers, and a final Redactor to add, retrench, retouch and combine at pleasure, is flexible enough, one would think, to deal with anything however intractable. He who accepts the divisive hypothesis at all must follow very much in the line of those who have gone before him. He would be a bold adventurer indeed who would attempt an independent route, abandoning all the defences which have been so skilfully planned, and the combinations which have been so ingeniously arranged. The agreement of critics is simply a confession that the hypothesis can no longer be materially improved. It does not cease on that account, however, to be still purely a hypothesis.

2. The agreement of the critics is, however, far from perfect. The first five chapters of Genesis can only be divided in one way, if the change of divine names is made the basis; consequently there has been no variance there of any account except as to the limiting verse between the first and second sections, 2:4; and that constitutes an obstacle which has never been successfully removed. And so it is elsewhere. It is the still remaining differences which form the significant feature of the case. In very

many portions there is plain sailing. If the hypothesis is accepted and its principles and methods adopted, there is but one line of separation that is practicable. Over these easy places the critics march in unbroken column. But there is besides not a little rough and uneven ground, where they break their ranks and there are many stragglers. These after all supply the crucial tests. The hypothesis in many instances can not be made to fit, and each seeks his own method of bridging the chasm, or parrying the fatal thrust, or stretching the covering which in spite of every effort proves too narrow for him to wrap himself in. Wellhausen relieves himself by the expedient of successive revisions of each constituent document, in which Dillmann[1] sees nothing but evidence of his embarrassment in his being obliged to resort to it. Meanwhile Dillmann himself assumes such a subtle weaving together of documents by the Redactor as makes the entanglement hopeless. The critic who undertakes to deal with all the intricacies imposed upon him by the hypothesis consistently carried through, has to multiply his machinery to such an extent, before it will work smoothly, that it is in danger of breaking down by its own weight. The diversities still remaining among the critics sufficiently show that no one has yet succeeded in adjusting the hypothesis to the entire satisfaction even of his own associates.

3. To disinterested observers the style of argument, by which the hypothesis is defended, seems in large part inconclusive and vain. This has been

[1] "Die Bücher Exodus und Leviticus," Preface, p. vii.

sufficiently illustrated in discussing the reasons adduced to establish diversity of authorship in the chapters before us. It is not necessary to demolish the walls of a fortress throughout their whole extent in order to effect an entrance. If the hypothesis can be broken through at important salient points, this does not, to say the least, increase our confidence in its strength.

4. Nevertheless, the hypothesis has attractions to account for its present popularity. These are of different sorts, and address themselves to different classes of persons. First, they who discredit the supernatural have of course a strong bias in favor of this hypothesis. It has from the first been developed in the interest of unbelief, and it affords the readiest mode of setting aside the genuineness and authenticity of the Pentateuch. But it is also captivating to others by its bold dexterity, its plausible explanation of certain curious phenomena, its romantic bringing to light of long existing but previously unsuspected documents, whose mutual relations and tendencies and the circumstances of their origin allow free scope to the imagination; it opens new realms for investigation and offers chances for important and startling discoveries. It thus appeals strongly to those of an original and speculative turn of mind. It naturally kindles a like fervor of enthusiasm to that which was awakened by the search for the philosopher's stone and the elixir of life, the northwest passage, the missing link between brute animals and man, bridging the chasm from the inorganic to the organic, squaring the circle, inventing

a perpetual motion and other chimerical objects. It is a superb monument of the learning and ingenuity of those who devised it and have wrought upon it thus far. But we must be permitted to doubt its having solved the problem of the origin of the Pentateuch, though it has unquestionably been attended with immense incidental advantages in the thorough investigation of the Pentateuch to which it has led, and the light thrown upon its interpretation, its structure and the relations of its several parts. But it would be no strange thing if it should yet be sometime deserted by German love of novelty. And among the odd possibilities of the future, who knows but old beliefs may have a resurrection even there, and tenets long forgotten and out of mind may, when revived, have all the charm of a new and potent attraction?

The critical objections to the unity of these chapters have now all been examined and found, I think I may say, to be destitute of force. We are entitled, therefore, to regard them as being what on their face they appear to be, what they have always been believed to be, and what the intimate and harmonious relation of all their parts declares them to be, one continuous and connected narrative. There is no ground whatever for the assertion of the critics, that they are made up of two or three distinct and separable accounts from writers whose date is variously estimated as referable to any time from the age of Joshua to that of Ezra, and which were combined into their present form by a Redactor later still. The stand-point of the critics places the interpreter under the inevitable temptation to exaggerate every slight variation in the terms employed into a real variance, thus producing discrepancies of statement and differences of conception where none whatever exist. The critical division of these chapters, accordingly, is invariably associated with the idea that each writer represents a distinct tradition of the origin of the Passover, differing more or less from the other, so that no one is absolutely reliable, and the truth is to be eliminated by comparison and by weighing one against another. And by not a few the conclusion is drawn that no confidence can be reposed in either of the accounts, and the critic feels at liberty to develop his own views of the origin of the festival irrespective of any of the conflicting statements here made. But in fact this pretext for discrediting the narrative in whole or in part does not exist. Instead of conflicting accounts from distinct writers which are incapable of being harmonized, and must therefore be carefully sifted or given up entirely, we have one self-consistent record.

It only remains to be added further that this is a credible and true history and not, as many of the critics affirm, law under the guise of history. These chapters contain a record of what was really transacted at the exodus, of the circumstances under which the Passover was in fact instituted, and of the events which were afterward commemorated in its subsequent annual celebration—not mere deductions from the rite itself as it was observed in later times, whether these are conceived as inferences of the writer himself or as embodied in popular tales which had grown up in connection with this observance.

In evidence that this is the record of actual historical occurrences, appeal may be made, 1st, To the opening statement, 12 : 1, that this law was given to Moses and Aaron in the land of Egypt. Hupfeld objects to this as suspicious from its vague generality and because it is superfluous in the connection. But it is precisely in accordance with the usage of the Pentateuch to indicate the place in which its laws were given, *e.g.*, Lev. 7 : 38, 25 : 1, 26 : 46, 27 : 34, Mount Sinai; Num. 35 : 1, 36 : 13, the plains of Moab. And it was the more important that this should be noted here, because it was an exceptional case, all the rest of the ritual laws having been enacted in the wilderness, and because the significance of the ordinance rested largely on the time, place and circumstances of its original celebration. And that it must really have been instituted in Egypt, as is here stated, appears from the fact that it was observed in the first instance as a preservative against the plague of the first-born, as well as from the peculiar mode of its observance on that occasion. The whole ceremonial savors of a time when there was as yet no public sanctuary, no priesthood, no common altar. The animal was slain at home by the head of each family, and its blood sprinkled on the door-posts of the house.[1] These particulars reappear nowhere else in law or usage; and the last mentioned was performed

---

[1] Graf ("Geschichtliche Bücher," pp. 34, 35) absurdly enough seeks to explain this as a usage which grew up in the Babylonish exile, when the people were sundered from the place of the sanctuary. But it would be a gross violation of the fundamental principle of the Priest Code, of which the exile is made the birth-place.

explicitly for the purpose of protecting the household by the expiatory virtue of the slain lamb from the apprehended visit of the angel of death. The assumption that this describes the usage of a later time and transfers it back to the age of Moses and the scene of the exodus is altogether gratuitous, having no basis in any known fact. It is at variance not only with the traditional belief and practice of the Jews, but with all the later legislation on the subject, and it finds no support whatever in the regulations here given which direct the perpetuation of the ordinance, but not necessarily those particulars which for special reasons belonged only to its first observance.

2. No good reason can be given why the Passover alone of the three annual feasts should have been thus singled out and represented to have been the only one instituted in Egypt, unless this was really the case. In all subsequent laws the three feasts are mentioned together as of common obligation. In the later history the feast of Tabernacles as a feast of special gladness and of universal interest assumed superior prominence, and is more frequently spoken of. This distinction accorded to the Passover can only be due to the historical reason here assigned.

3. All the subsequent laws relating to the feasts directly connect the Passover and the feast of Unleavened Bread with the exodus. Thus, Ex. 23 : 15, "Thou shalt eat unleavened bread, as I commanded thee, in the time appointed of the month Abib; for in it thou camest out from Egypt." So in almost identical words Ex. 34 : 18. Both these passages are

expressly said to have been written by Moses, 24 : 4, 34 : 27; and the reason which they give for observing the feast of Unleavened Bread at the time appointed is that in it they came out of Egypt; and further, they explicitly refer to the command given for its observance in Ex., ch. 12, 13. George claims that the reference is to Deuteronomy; others to some law now unknown, or that the words "as I commanded thee" are an interpolation. But the only reason for suspecting an interpolation is that the critic wishes to get rid in this summary manner of an unwelcome part of the text. As the book of Exodus now stands, the reference to ch. 12, 13 is obvious. The Redactor, if there was one, certainly intended it to be so understood; the verbal allusion also is plain. This reference consequently must be admitted, unless some good reason can be given to the contrary and for suspecting either the honesty or the competency of the Redactor or both. Lev. 23 though it makes no direct allusion to this law, plainly presupposes it. A full account is here given of the ceremonies to be observed at the feasts which had not been previously described. But no description is given of the mode of observing the Passover nor of the peculiar services of the day of Atonement. The latter are omitted, because they had been fully set forth in Lev. 16; the ritual of the former is nowhere given except in Ex. 12, 13. Upon the first anniversary of their leaving Egypt the people were directed, Num. 9 : 1 ff., to keep the Passover in its appointed season "according to all the rites of it and according to all the ceremonies of it"; which implies that these rites had been before ordained. But there is no record of the fact except in these chapters, to which there are besides clear verbal references, vs. 11, 12, 14. Deut. 16:1-8 also connects the Passover with the exodus, and contains numerous verbal allusions to Ex. 12, 13; and the Deuteronomic law is expressly said to have been written by Moses, Deut. 31:9, 24. All the later laws are thus built upon the law in Ex. 12, 13, and presuppose it; the connection of the Passover with the exodus is explicitly declared, and that in laws which are distinctly said to have been written by Moses himself. Even on the principles of the divisive critics themselves this unanimous concurrence of all the sources of tradition and all the hypothetical writers and the Redactor as well in one explicit testimony must be accepted as evidence of truth, if anything whatever from the Mosaic age can be relied upon.

To this may be added the fact already shown in a former lecture that the great majority of the most eminent critics, however they differed in other respects, have seen no difficulty in maintaining the Mosaic or even pre-Mosaic origin of the feasts upon grounds altogether independent of the truth of the historical records.

It is objected, 1, that the formal declaration, 12:2, that the month of the exodus was to be reckoned the first month of the year, is evidently post-exilic, as it is based upon the change of the calendar then made. This has been maintained on directly opposite grounds. George[1] affirms that the Jewish year orig-

[1] "Die älteren Jüdischen Feste," p. 91.

inally began in the spring; but when the double mode of reckoning was introduced after the exile and the civil year began in the autumn, this verse was inserted to indicate that the ecclesiastical year differed from that in common use in holding fast to the ancient order. Wellhausen on the contrary asserts that prior to the exile the Jewish year began in the autumn, but that subsequently the spring era represented in this passage was adopted from the Babylonians. In fact neither is correct; both modes of reckoning were in use long prior to the exile, as is evinced by numerous passages.[1]

2. It is also objected that the feast of Unleavened Bread was not to be observed until they reached Canaan, 13:5, and that the terms of the law imply residence there, 12:19, 25 ff., 48, 49. But the very purpose for which they were leaving Egypt, was to take possession of Canaan, which had been promised them as their inheritance, and where they expected to be settled without delay. The laws are, therefore, framed with reference to this anticipated condition.

3. A further objection is drawn from the occurrence of words which are alleged to indicate a later age, שפטים (judgments), Ex. 12:12, and עצם in the sense of "self-same," 12:17, 41, 51, which reappear in Ezekiel, and העביר, used 13:12, of setting apart the first-born to Jehovah, but which is the technical

---

[1] The year beginning in the spring, when nature buds out anew and new enterprises can be undertaken, 2 Sam. 11:1; 1 Kin. 20:22, 26; Jer. 36:22. The year beginning in the fall, when the fruits of the previous year have been gathered in, and it is time to plough and sow for a new harvest, Ex. 23:16, 34:22; Lev. 25:9, 10, 22; 2 Kin. 22:3, comp. 23:23; Isa. 37:30.

term in common use in the period of the later kings for "passing through" the fire to Moloch, 2 Kin. 16: 3, etc. But the first two words though found in Ezekiel are evidently adopted by him not from the current usage of his time, of which there is no evidence, but from the familiar language of the ancient law; and the third word is not borrowed from the Moloch abomination, but from the dialect of common life, as when an inheritance is "made to pass," Num. 27: 7, 8, to him who receives it, or the kingdom was translated or "made to pass" from the house of Saul to that of David, 2 Sam. 3: 10. So the first-born were "made to pass" into the exclusive ownership of Jehovah.

4. Wellhausen[1] likewise objects to "the preaching tone of 13: 3–16, which is quite foreign to the older" writers, and to "the stage of religiosity, which comes out particularly in vs. 9, 10, upon which authors who tell of the patriarchs erecting stones and altars, planting sacred trees and digging wells, do not stand.' But now, precisely, when this ordinance was appointed to perpetuate the remembrance of God's most signal benefits, was the time to insist upon their keeping in ever-present memory themselves, and inculcating upon their children the lessons of the hour, comp. also Gen. 18: 19; Ex. 10: 2. The pharisaic literalism foisted upon 13: 9 is as foreign from its genuine sense as the fetichism which by an utter perversion he would impute to the Patriarchs.

5. But the final and most serious objection is, this can not be true history, for it is too closely entwined

---

[1] "Jahrbücher für Deutsche Theologie," XXI., p. 544.

with the miraculous to be separated. This after all is the secret of the settled determination of the critics to rid themselves of these chapters. A pestilence sweeping off vast numbers of the Egyptians might be admitted: and Israel might have escaped its ravages, for they dwelt in a district by themselves. But to those whose prime maxim is that the supernatural must necessarily be a myth, a pestilence which singled out the first-born in every house, is utterly inadmissible, though both the Passover and the hallowing of the first-born, 13 : 15, Num. 3 : 13, 8 : 17, combine to declare it true. To those who do not share these principles the institution of the Passover at the exodus is no more mythical than the American Revolution and Declaration of Independence are to be accounted myths based on the annual observance of the fourth of July.

V.

THE FEAST LAWS AND THE PASSOVER.

V.

THE FEAST LAWS AND THE PASSOVER.

THE unity and historical character of Ex. 12, 13 having been established, we have gained a vantage ground for the study of the other laws relating to the Passover. The various laws upon this subject, we are told, represent different periods; and by their aid it is easy to trace the history and development of this festival, from its simplest beginnings, through the various stages of its progress to its final form.

It is generally agreed among the critics that there are three principal strata in the legislation, which are referred respectively to the Jehovist, Elohist and Deuteronomist. To the Jehovist are assigned the laws in Ex. 23 and 34 which are supposed to be older codes embodied by him in his work, the former being a part of the Book of the Covenant, Ex. 21–23, and the latter being called, for a reason which we shall learn hereafter, the law of the two tables. Commonly also, as we have seen already, certain legal sections of ch. 12, 13 are ascribed to the Jehovist, but Wellhausen insists that these do not properly belong to his work, but are later additions to it. To the Elohist are attributed the rest of Ex. 12, 13, and the laws in Lev. 23, Num. 9: 1–14, Num. 28, 29. George claims for

Deuteronomy priority to all the other laws. Dillmann places it last of all. Wellhausen assigns it a central position, between the Jehovist legislation and that of the Elohist. In his view the Jehovist belongs to the period preceding the overthrow of the kingdom of the ten tribes; Deuteronomy to the reign of Josiah; the Elohist after the Babylonish exile. Critics are now, however, generally united in the opinion that Ex. 23 and 34 contain the oldest form of the feast laws and of the cultus generally. Wellhausen[1] says: "In the old days the public worship of the nation consisted essentially in the celebration of the yearly feasts, ... and accordingly the laws of worship are confined to this one point in the Jehovist and even in Deuteronomy."

The language of the two laws above referred to is nearly identical, with some remarkable variations, and the critics have been greatly puzzled to make out the relation in which they stand to each other and why both forms have been preserved. George[2] thinks that ch. 34 was framed upon the basis of ch. 23, the author only explaining or completing what was difficult or obscure. Kuenen[3] says very much to the same effect: "The author of Exodus 34 borrows from the Book of the Covenant and from a few other laws the rules which seem to him to be the most important, and makes of them a whole after his own fashion." Graf, on the other hand, thinks that ch. 23 was abbreviated from ch. 34, which previously existed in a separate

[1] "Encyclopædia Britannica," Vol. XVIII., Art. Pentateuch, p. 511
[2] "Die älteren Jüdischen Feste," p. 110.
[3] "The Religion of Israel," Vol. II., p. 8.

state. Reuss' remarks on this subject: "It is very difficult to say in what relation the so-called second decalogue (Ex. 34: 11 ff.) stands to the Book of the Covenant. It is not an integral part of it. One could not understand why it was sundered from the rest and contained repetitions. But the latter particularly seem to bring them near together in point of time." He accordingly cuts the knot by assuming that the feast laws were originally no part of the Book of the Covenant; this contained almost nothing relating to worship, and the gap was filled in a supplementary manner by an insertion from ch. 34. Wellhausen[2] again maintains that the feast laws in ch. 23 were neither borrowed from ch. 34, nor those in ch. 34 from ch. 23, but that they were originally quite independent of each other, only they have been mutually interpolated, 34:18 having been taken from 23:15, and 23:17-19 transferred from ch. 34. Hitzig,[3] whom Delitzsch[4] somewhat sharply describes as "having passed from Romish superstition to Protestant unbelief," made the astounding discovery, following out a suggestion of Goethe's, that this was another version of the ten commandments. Wellhausen[5] of course indorses this discovery; only in his free application of the critical knife, which never fails him in an emergency, it is surprising that he did not avail himself of his opportunity and strike out from this

[1] "Geschichte d. heiligen Schriften alten Bundes," I., p. 232.
[2] "Geschichte," I., p. 89.
[3] "Ostern und Pfingsten," 1838, p. 42.
Guericke's "Zeitschrift," for 1840, No. 2, p. 116.
"Jahrbücher für Deutsche Theologie," XXI., p. 554.

new-fangled decalogue the unwelcome words, "Thou shalt make thee no molten gods," which have no counterpart in ch. 23, but which, corroborated by the second commandment in Ex. 20 and Deut. 5, even apart from the story of the golden calf, confront the critics with multiplied evidence that Moses really did forbid image-worship. And then the frequent lapses of Israel into idolatry and the worship established by Jeroboam in the ten tribes afford glaring proofs of the falsity of the critical dictum that the open and continued disregard of a statute warrants the inference of its non-existence.

According to Wellhausen there are three quite independent and mutually contradictory traditions of the transactions at Sinai. One of these knows nothing of any ten commandments or tables of stone, but only of a series of laws or judgments, ch. 21–23, which Moses is directed to write. According to the second, Jehovah uttered ten commandments, ch. 20, in awful majesty in the audience of the whole people, and gave to Moses after he had been forty days in the mount two tables of stone upon which they had been written by God's own finger, but which Moses broke in descending the mountain. According to the third, Jehovah uttered the ten commandments in ch. 34,[1] which are,

---

[1] Wellhausen accordingly ("Geschichte Israels," p. 85: Prolegomena (Eng. Trans.), p. 83, and *passim*) calls Ex. 34 : 14–26 "das Zweitafelgesetz," the law of the two tables, claiming that this is one version of the law written on tables of stone. Dr. Delitzsch calls it by a slight modification "das Zweittafelgesetz," the law of the second tables, meaning the compendious law issued in connection with the second giving of the decalogue to Moses as an abridgment of the Book of the Covenant, ch. 21–23, which was issued in connection with the first proclamation of the ten commandments.

however, entirely different from those of ch. 20, and were spoken not to the people, but to Moses, who himself wrote them upon two tables of stone which he had prepared and taken with him for the purpose, and which there is no record of his having broken. All this is made out in the usual way in which the critics accomplish their marvellous feats, viz., by splitting up the narrative and ejecting as an interpolation whatever can not be made to bend to their purpose.

Under such guidance we may well despair of knowing anything of the Mosaic period or indeed of any other. If anything can be established by historical and monumental evidence, the law surely can be which was graven on stones that were still extant in the time of Solomon, and are even referred to by Jeremiah, though destined shortly to be superseded. The allegation that the laws of ch. 34 are the ten commandments, and that they were written by Moses on tables of stone, confounds what Moses is directed to write, ver. 27, with what was written on the tables, ver. 28, not by Moses, but by the LORD, as is plain from the explicit statement of ver. 1. In the clause, "he did neither eat bread nor drink water," the subject is plainly Moses. But in the following clause, "and he wrote upon the tables the words of the covenant, the ten commandments," the subject is as plainly the LORD, who had promised, "I will write upon the tables the words that were in the first tables which thou brakest." The change of subject in successive clauses, where the meaning is sufficiently obvious, is too familiar to create the slightest trouble. As Ranke shows, the denial of it leads to the most glaring incongruities, as that Melchizedek paid tithes to Abraham, Gen. 14:19, 20, that Abraham's servant hospitably entertained Laban, 24:32, and that Moses claims the prerogatives of the Almighty God, Ex. 34:9, 10.

The relation between ch. 23 and 34, in which the critics find so much mystery and perplexity, is as plain as a simple, straightforward narrative can make it. The former is a part of the Book of the Covenant, to which the people formally pledged obedience in that solemn transaction by which they became the LORD'S people and he became their God. This covenant was ruptured by the sin of the golden calf, and the tables of the law were broken. And when upon Moses' fervent intercession it was again renewed, the ten commandments were once more written by the LORD upon tables of stone, and that portion of the Book of the Covenant which concerned the people's duties toward God, was rewritten by Moses.

From the brevity of the feast laws in these chapters, and the general terms in which they are couched, it is claimed that they must be the original regulations on the subject; and that other laws, which contain more minute and extended regulations, must belong to a later period when these institutions had been developed beyond the primitive simplicity in which we here find them. But that this can not be the case is apparent upon a simple inspection. For, 1. They explicitly refer to an antecedent law, Thou shalt eat unleavened bread seven days, *as I commanded thee.* 2. This reference to a prior law is made in connection with one feast only, that of Unleavened Bread, which seems to intimate that while directions had been given in respect to it, none had yet been given respecting the two remaining feasts. 3. What is said of the other two feasts is so meagre that no one could gather from it anything as to their nature or how they were to be observed. There is also some variation in the terms applied to them; and the expressions, "feast of harvest," "feast of ingathering," seem to be descriptive epithets derived from the occasion of their observance rather than proper names of the feasts themselves. This is just such a general indefinite sort of reference as might be expected in the fundamental law of the covenant, leaving all further details to be supplied by subsequent legislation. George maintains that the previous law referred to is that in Deuteronomy; but Wellhausen confesses that it is plainly Ex. 13, though he seeks to escape the consequence of his admission by the groundless assertion that the words "as I commanded thee" are an interpolation.

The next law in order is Lev. 23. This, we are told, must belong to a much later period than the preceding; for instead of only three feasts there are now five, the feast of Trumpets and the day of Atonement having meanwhile been added; and further, there are ceremonies connected with each, of which no mention was made before. But there are no more feasts properly speaking, in this chapter than the three previously spoken of. The only appearance of an increase in the number in the ordinary English version arises from the confusion of two quite distinct words, which are indiscriminately rendered feasts. The first of these is the same that is correctly translated "seasons," Gen. 1:14; it properly denotes fixed or stated periods. The chapter which we are now considering professes to enumerate not "the feasts" simply, but all the stated periods in the year with which holy convocations were connected. It accordingly begins with the weekly Sabbath, and then procceds with the annually recurring stated times at which holy convocations were prescribed, whether pilgrimages were to be made, as at the three great festivals, or not. Upon these several occasions mention is made of the fact that an offering made by fire unto the LORD was required; but no specifications are given as to the number or character of these offerings. In Num. 28 this lack is supplied, and a detailed account given of the sacrifices to be offered every day, every Sabbath, and upon every occasion of special solemnity throughout the year. Here the critics themselves confess that these chapters are mutually supplementary; that they do not represent different stages in the development of the feasts, but the very same; and that the details respecting the sacrifices were purposely omitted in the one chapter with the view of bringing them together as we find them in the other. This is an admission that different degrees of fulness in the contents of the feast laws may be due to other causes than the lapse of time and the development of these ordinances in the interval. It may result from the purpose of the writer, the ordinance remaining unchanged. This is yielding the entire principle, which satisfactorily accounts for all the differences in the Pentateuchal laws on this subject without the need of assuming any protracted periods of growth between them.

   The fact is that the feast laws, instead of being scattered through the Pentateuch at random, as a superficial observer might imagine, or being isolated fragments of codes distinct in authorship and widely separated in point of time, are not only harmonious, but are integral parts of a well-contrived scheme: they have all been prepared with evident reference to one another and each is adjusted to its proper place in this comprehensive body of legislation; so that they stand in most intimate mutual relation, and at the same time in close and obvious relation to the context in which they are found, and to that part of the system of legislation which they respectively occupy. In the Book of the Covenant, drawn up as the preliminary basis of the union to be cemented between Jehovah and Israel, it would have been clearly out of place to introduce in detail the whole ceremonial of worship, which was subsequently established as the outgrowth and proper expression of this union. Accordingly it comprises first and mainly regulations regarding the relation of man to man, conceived in the spirit of the religion of Jehovah, and then in the briefest possible compass directions respecting firstlings and first-fruits, the Sabbath and the annual feasts, that is to say, oblations and sacred times, as the culminations of that outward and formal service in which the people's homage toward God was to manifest itself. Any fuller or more elaborate description even of these particulars would not have been appropriate or suitable here, where only an outline programme, so to speak, was called for.

From the Book of the Covenant everything leads by regular and easy steps to the next feast law in Lev. 23.[1] The ratification of the covenant brought with it as its immediate consequence that Jehovah condescended to dwell in the midst of his people. All the rest of Exodus is occupied with divine directions for the preparation of the Sacred Tabernacle, its actual construction and its erection. Then follow in Lev. 1-7 the various sacrifices and offerings which the people might bring to the Tabernacle; then ch. 8-10, the setting apart of a priesthood to offer these sacrifices. Ch. 11-16 declare what was requisite in the people that Jehovah might continue to dwell among them and they be suffered to bring their gifts to his Tabernacle, the laws of ceremonial purity which they must observe, together with the rites of cleansing in case of defilement, and finally the services of the annual day of Atonement. Then follow in the remainder of the book of Leviticus what have the appearance of miscellaneous prescriptions, but in reality are not so, since they are bound together by one common thought. They continue to urge in various lines of the ritual, of life and manners the obligations upon the people and the priests, which result from Jehovah's having fixed his habitation in the midst of them. A considerable section in this part of the book is by the critics commonly called the holiness-laws, since they are simply developments of the demand, Lev. 19:2, "Ye shall be holy; for I the LORD your God am holy." Upon this follow the laws respecting the sacred times when this holy

[1] See Ranke, "Untersuchungen," II., pp. 103 ff.

people are to present themselves before God in holy convocations. The feast laws thus stand at the end of the Levitical legislation, as they did at the end of the Book of the Covenant, the crown, the culmination of the whole, and are immediately followed, ch. 26, by the recital of the blessings to be shared by the obedient and the curses that shall be inflicted upon the disobedient.

These laws, accordingly, are in their proper place, as the fit sequel to the series of connected statutes thus hastily reviewed. And they are further precisely adapted to their place. Some of these sacred seasons had been with sufficient fulness described before, as the occasion required their introduction. The weekly Sabbath was set apart at the creation and its remembrance was freshly enjoined in the ten commandments proclaimed from the summit of Sinai. The Passover was instituted at the exodus. The day of Atonement, appointed when Nadab and Abihu met their death for unwarranted intrusion into the holy place, is added to and completes the laws of cleansing. The Sabbath, the Passover and the day of Atonement can hence be dismissed with a very few words. They are inserted for completeness in the list of times for which holy convocations are appointed; but the bulk of the chapter is occupied with ceremonial services not previously described, and especially those belonging to the two feasts which were simply mentioned in the Book of the Covenant, but no particulars given respecting them. Thus both by what it contains and by what it omits, this chapter shows itself to be an integral part of a connected system of legislation, not itself a complete, self-contained and separate law for the regulation of the feasts.

In regard to the theorizing of the critics respecting the section of Leviticus in which this chapter is found, I avail myself of the following terse and accurate statement by Dr. Dillmann :[1] " While Ewald, Nöldeke and Schrader explain the peculiar style of ch. 18–20 from the use of an older code by the Elohist, and Knobel derives ch. 17–20, parts of ch. 23, 24 and 25, and ch. 26 from his Book of Wars, Graf in ch. 18–23, 25, 26, and Kayser in ch. 17–26 sought to point out a collection of laws composed by Ezekiel, and subsequently interspersed with passages of the Elohist, in opposition to whom Nöldeke, Klostermann and Kuenen proved the impossibility of its composition by Ezekiel; whereupon Kuenen and Wellhausen declared it to be a collection formed after Ezekiel, and subsequently revised in the spirit of the Priest Code, which then Smend gives forth as current coin. For this fundamentally perverted hypothesis, built up on false critical principles, there is no ground or occasion in the contents or expressions of ch. 17–26. The truth is that in these chapters are contained in part the very oldest laws, which are not only presupposed in Ezekiel and Deuteronomy, but are also echoed in all the prophetical and other literature of the pre-exilic period." Dr. Dillmann's own hypothesis is that there were two revisions of these ancient laws, one by the Elohist, the other probably by the Jehovist, and that these were subsequently combined by the Redactor into the present text. The an-

---

[1] "Die Bücher Exodus und Leviticus," p. 533.

tiquity of the laws we accept. As the literary labors which, it is so confidently affirmed, were subsequently expended upon them, rest upon very uncertain and precarious proofs, however ingeniously and learnedly adduced, we may be excused from accepting them for the present, and be allowed to wait at least until the critics come to some common understanding on the subject.

The feast law just considered stands near the close of the Sinaitic legislation, and is almost immediately followed by the numbering of the people, the arrangement of the camp, the order of march, and the actual departure for the promised land. Then came the trespass for which they were condemned to wander forty years in the desert. At the end of the predicted term they find themselves in the plains of Moab, opposite Jericho. The people are numbered afresh, and it is found that the entire generation sentenced to die in the wilderness had passed away. Moses nominated Joshua as his successor, and laid his hands upon him. And now when they were thus upon the point of entry into Canaan a supplementary law was given, which would have had no application before, but could no longer be delayed. The fact had been stated in the preceding law that sacrifices were to be offered at the several feasts, but no specifications had been given. Num. 28, 29 supply the necessary complement by furnishing ample details upon this point.

Two laws yet remain to complete the legislation respecting the annual feasts: and these are as appropriate to the occasion on which they were delivered, and as suitable for the purpose of completing previous enactments, as those which we have already examined. The occasion for one was furnished by the first observance of the Passover after the people had left Egypt. Some persons who were ceremonially defiled, were unable to partake of it, and permission was given that they and all similarly affected in future might keep the Passover in a subsequent month, Num. 9 : 1 ff.* It has been alleged as impairing the credibility of this narrative, that it is out of its true chronological position: but this is a mistake. It is introduced not at the time of the proper, but of the secondary Passover, for the sake of which it was mentioned at all.

The remaining law, the last of the series, is found in Moses' final address to the people, Deut. 16. They were soon to be settled in Canaan and scattered in every quarter of the land. The legislator lifts his earnest and warning voice to remind them that these feasts must be kept not at their several homes, as the Passover had been in Egypt, but only at "the place which the LORD should choose to place his name there." They were about to occupy a land of idolaters, where images and altars abounded everywhere, and the unity of the sanctuary was of the utmost importance for the preservation of the worship of the one true God. Hence the urgency and repetition with which this one essential matter of sacrificing nowhere but at the place to be chosen by the LORD is pressed in the book of Deuteronomy. The law had not yet come into full and developed operation, many of its provisions being only practicable in Canaan, and many irregularities had been necessarily tolerated in the wilderness, Deut. 12 : 8 f.; but when they were securely and permanently established in the land which had been promised them, their happiness and welfare would lie in strict obedience to the law of God in this particular as in every other.

The fact that the law in Deuteronomy does not repeat the prescriptions of Leviticus and Numbers, is no indication, as the critics of the most recent school would persuade us, that it is of earlier date, and that the elaborate ceremonial which they describe was a subsequent growth. This is not a law giving full directions for the observance of the festivals. It limits itself designedly to the three pilgrimage feasts, and the main point insisted upon is the place of observance. As in regard to the plague of leprosy, Deut. 24 : 8 contents itself with a simple reference to laws previously given, so it is here. The ritual had been sufficiently set forth in other laws, which there was no need of repeating; to do so would only encumber the law now given and cover up the very design with which the subject was mentioned at all. That silence is no proof of want of knowledge is explicitly admitted by Kuenen,[1] who says in relation to another matter: "The Deuteronomist was acquainted with this custom, but for reasons sufficient for himself, does not expressly mention it." And Wellhausen[2] adds that "in Deuteronomy the most is left to existing usages, and only the one main matter is constantly emphasized that divine worship and consequently also the feasts could only be celebrated in Jerusalem."

[1] "Religion of Israel," II., p. 88.
[2] "Geschichte Israels," p. 94 ; Prolegomena (Eng. Trans.), p. 91.

And as we have seen already, no one of the feast laws is independent of the rest and complete in itself. Each has its own specific purpose to which it steadfastly adheres, and its particular place in the system to which it belongs. No one repeats the rest or supersedes them; but all are mutually supplementary, and it is from the combination of the whole that the complete view of these ordinances is obtained. The laws are thus not only in entire harmony, but indispensable to one another, each resting upon and implying the existence of the rest; so that the attempt to rend them from one another as though they were the products of distinct ages, or to assign them any other position than that which is plainly given to them in the inspired record, is unwarranted and inadmissible.

From this general view of the mutual relationship and interdependence of the feast laws we may now proceed to particulars. We are told that the development of the several feasts in their successive stages is clearly traceable in these laws.

First, it is alleged that the Passover was not originally connected with the feast of Unleavened Bread, but their combination was effected at a later period. Kuenen[1] undertakes to exhibit this by arranging the laws in the following order: 1. The Book of the Covenant, 23:15, speaks only of the feast of Unleavened Bread, and makes no mention of the Passover; the dedication of the first-born, 22:30, took place on the eighth day after birth, and could, therefore, have no connection with any of the yearly feasts. 2. Ex

[1] "Religion of Israel," II., p. 87.

13:3-10 has again the feast of Unleavened Bread without the Passover, but it is enclosed between two laws relating to the first-born which shows "very plainly the endeavor to connect the dedication of the first-born" with this festival. 3. Ex. 34:18, the feast of Unleavened Bread is connected again with the dedication of the first-born, and here for the first time mention is made of "the sacrifice of the feast of the Passover," ver. 25. 4. Deut. 16:1-8 combines the Passover and the feast of Unleavened Bread under one common name, but gives no prominence to the paschal lamb, which is left in the background beside the first-born of oxen and sheep produced during the past year, and which were eaten at sacrificial meals during the following days of the feast. 5th and finally. Ex. 12, which stands on the same platform with Lev. 23 and Num. 9 and 28, makes the Passover meal the prominent thing, and its union with the feast of Unleavened Bread is now complete. According to this scheme the feast of Unleavened Bread was originally a thing by itself and quite independent of the custom which prevailed of consecrating the firstlings of their cattle to God, whenever they were eight days old. Gradually the usage was formed of presenting the firstlings of the entire year at one particular season, that of the feast of Unleavened Bread. The service was then introduced of sacrificing a Passover lamb at the beginning of the feast; but still the firstlings which were partaken of throughout the festal week were regarded as the main thing. Finally, however, the firstlings came to be reckoned the due of the priests and were no longer eaten by the offerers; then the Passover lamb alone remained in connection with the feast of Unleavened Bread, the two being thenceforward considered one festival, which bore either name indifferently as in the New Testament.

But this interesting piece of ritual history is a sheer invention of the critic and vanishes altogether upon examination. I remark upon it—

1. The symmetry of this progressive scheme is spoiled by those critics who place Kuenen's third law prior to his first, *i. e.*, Ex. 34 before 23 ; for then "the sacrifice of the feast of the Passover" is distinctly named in the very first law as well as the feast of Unleavened Bread. But even if Kuenen's order is maintained it is unfortunate for his speculation that a phrase precisely identical in signification occurs in ch. 23 itself. Vs. 17–19 are plainly supplementary to the three preceding verses, adding some particulars respecting the observance of the feasts there enjoined. Ver. 17 thus attaches itself to ver. 14, declaring that at each of the annual feasts all the males should appear before Jehovah at his sanctuary. Ver. 19 connects with ver. 16, directing that at the feast of harvest or first-fruits, the first-fruits of the land should be brought to the house of God ; and those interpreters are probably correct in their conjecture who suppose that "seething the kid in its mother's milk" alludes to some pagan practice at the time of the ingathering. In like manner the intervening ver. 18 must relate to ver. 15, so that the words, "Thou shalt not sacrifice the blood of my sacrifice with leavened bread ; neither shall the fat of my feast remain until the morning," must be a regulation concerning the feast of Unleavened Bread. It

appears then from the language of this law itself that there belonged to this feast a bloody sacrifice, including, as the term used always implies, a sacrificial meal, and that from it leaven was to be excluded. This sacrifice is further called a feast, and its fat must not be suffered to remain until the morning. Fat is doubtless used here as sometimes elsewhere,[1] of choice rich food; and the meaning is that no part of the dainty flesh of the sacrifice must be left till the next day, Ex. 12 : 10.

Dillmann insists that the verse has no special relation to the Passover, but that its terms are to be taken in the utmost generality as a prohibition of leaven with any sacrifice and of delay in burning the fat destined for the altar at any of the feasts. But—1. This is contradicted by 34 : 25, the most ancient and reliable commentary upon its meaning, which expounds it of the Passover and its sacrificial meal. 2. Jehovah had as yet instituted in Israel no sacrifice and especially none in connection with any feast, except the Passover. 3. The words "as I commanded thee" in this law, can have no other reference, as Dillmann admits, than to Ex. 12, 13. He alleges indeed that this clause, though original in 34 : 18, is here interpolated by the Redactor, for which his only reason is that its presence in one passage can be accounted for on his critical hypothesis and in the other it can not. And so instead of accommodating his hypothesis to the facts, the facts are made to conform to his hypothesis. Wellhausen relieves the whole difficulty in the case by resorting to the *ultima ratio criticorum*

[1] Comp. Gen. 45 : 18, Deut. 32 : 14, Ps. 63 : 5, 81 : 16, Ezek. 34 : 3.

and expunging vs. 17–19, which is simply confessing that they are an obstruction of which he can not rid himself otherwise.

2. Kuenen's second law affords no more support to his theory than his first, if Knobel, Kayser, Schrader and Dillmann are correct in their critical analysis; they all connect Ex. 13 : 3–10 with the preceding explicit mention of the Passover.

3. The fact that the direction to consecrate the firstlings to the LORD stands in several of the laws in close proximity to the direction to observe the feast of Unleavened Bread does not prove that the firstlings were offered at this feast. It may be plausibly conjectured that this was the case, but it is nowhere affirmed. Deut. 15 : 20 speaks of their being eaten year by year before the LORD in the place which the LORD shall choose, but gives no intimation of the season at which this should be done. It may be supposed that it would be most convenient to do this at some one of the annual festivals; but this is not required, and nothing is definitely known about it. The conjunction in the law is sufficiently accounted for by their springing from the same root. It is upon the events of the exodus, which was commemorated in the feast of Unleavened Bread, that the law uniformly rests the sanctity of the first-born in man and beast. The combination of the Passover with the feast of Unleavened Bread is, however, quite independent of the question whether firstlings were or were not presented at this feast; for the rite of the Passover did not in any way originate from such presentation.

4. The fourth and fifth in the series of feast laws, as these are arranged by Kuenen, lend no more support to his hypothesis than those which we have already considered. In Deut. 16:1, 2, the word 'Passover' is used in a comprehensive sense, embracing along with the paschal meal proper which introduced the feast, all the sacrificial meals of the entire seven days during which it lasted. The Passover thus becomes co-extensive with the feast of Unleavened Bread itself. This has no parallel in the laws which he places last in order. In Ex. 12, Lev. 23, Num. 28 Passover and the feast of Unleavened Bread are uniformly distinguished, the former being used in the strict sense and limited to the paschal lamb on the evening preceding the feast; and in Num. 9 'Passover' plainly does not include the seven-day feast, for the children of Israel were again upon the march, 10:11, before the term of seven days after the secondary Passover had expired. The only real parallel is the later usage of 2 Chron. 35 : 7–9 and the New Testament. So that if it be insisted upon that there has been a progress in this matter it amounts to just this, that the word 'Passover' is in Deuteronomy used in a wider sense than in the other feast laws. By this test, then, of the critic's own choosing, Deuteronomy, in which this advance was made, must be later than the Levitical law or the so-called Priest Code, and the hypothesis of the new school of criticism, which reverses this order, is found wanting.

But the alleged development which has thus far engaged our attention is commonly subordinated to another, a change which is held to have taken place in the conception of the meaning and design of this feast. It is maintained that it was at first purely a nature-feast connected with the change of seasons, or as this was transfused with the spirit of the religion of Israel it was designed to express gratitude to Jehovah for the increase of the cattle and the products of the soil. But it came ultimately to have a historical and national meaning attached to it. Thus Wellhausen[1] argues that the cycle of three annual feasts must be homogeneous in character. The names given to the second and third in the Book of the Covenant, Ex. 23 : 16, are the feast of harvest and the feast of ingathering, which sufficiently define their nature and purpose. The name of the feast which heads the list is invariably not Passover, but the feast of Unleavened Bread. The second feast was separated from the first by an interval of seven weeks, which is defined, Deut. 16 : 9, as " seven weeks from such time as thou beginnest to put the sickle to the corn." The feast of Unleavened Bread is equivalent, therefore, to the beginning of harvest. This connection appears still further from the usage, Lev. 23 : 9 ff., of presenting a sheaf of the first-fruits at this feast. And thus the name of the feast becomes intelligible. Bread baked hastily or in sudden emergencies was unleavened, because there was no time for the slow process of leavening ; as when the Israelites left Egypt in haste, or Abraham prepared a quick meal for his guests or the witch of Endor for Saul. During harvest, time was not taken to leaven the meal

---

[1] "Geschichte Israels," I., p. 87. Prolegomena (Eng. Trans.), p. 85.

from the new grain, so that unleavened bread became characteristic of the season.

The offering of firstlings of cattle is based on the same general principle as that of first-fruits. Cain and Abel offering respectively the produce of their fields and their flocks represent the simplest, most natural and universal form of sacrifice; and as these recur annually they give rise to feasts. The three annual feasts belong to the one class, thanksgivings for the produce of the soil; passover to the other, thanks for the increase of their flocks. The firstfruits of barley harvest were presented at the feast of Unleavened Bread. The earliest lambs and calves of spring were ready for sacrifice at the same time, and so they came to be joined to the same festival. Neither of these took their origin from the exodus. They were not established because of any historical event, but were natural expressions of the primitive piety respectively of agricultural and pastoral life, which prompted an offering unto God from the gifts of his bounty.

The feast of Unleavened Bread, he further tells us, must have originated in Canaan, for the Israelites first learned agriculture from the Canaanites and borrowed from them the festivals connected with that mode of life, only transferring their homage from Baal to Jehovah. In regard to the sacrifice of firstlings traditions vary. In one of the oldest extant codes of law, the Book of the Covenant, which, from its agricultural presuppositions, is nevertheless subsequent to the settlement in Canaan, the feast of Unleavened Bread is ordained, but no feast of firstlings as yet existed, Ex. 22:30. The Jehovist tradition, however, gives a different version of the matter, viz., that the plea urged with Pharaoh for the exodus was that Israel might observe a feast to Jehovah in the wilderness, and for this purpose they must take their sheep and oxen with them ; so that the pastoral feast according to this authority, must have been pre-Mosaic, and was the ground of the exodus, not itself based upon it. This traditional connection came, however, in the course of time to be reversed, and the cause was transformed into the effect. It came to be supposed that the exodus was not for the sake of holding the feast, but that the feast was established with a view to the exodus. The yearly sacrifice of the first-born gave rise to the story that the first-born throughout the land of Egypt were smitten with pestilence to accomplish Israel's deliverance, and that this festival was instituted in commemoration of that event. An attempt was made also to account for a like origin of the feast of Unleavened Bread by the story of the extreme haste in which the Israelites were forced out of Egypt.

This explanation, he goes on to say, glimmers through in earlier statutes, but it is completely established in Deuteronomy, whose centralizing tendency was promoted by severing this feast from its primitive association with individual life and linking it with national experiences. Instead of each pilgrim expressing his personal gratitude to God for benefits which he had himself received, his thoughts were turned rather to those which were common to him with **his** fellow pilgrims, to God's goodness to Israel as a people. The deliverance from Egypt and the gift of Canaan conditioned all the blessings since experienced in the land of promise; and lively gratitude for the former embraced and contained within itself appreciation of the latter. Thankfulness for individual mercies was poured, as it were, into the common receptacle and served but to heighten the sense of God's goodness to Israel.

This radical transformation of the feast thus begun was carried to its last extreme in the Levitical code, which made the firstlings a perquisite of the priests. The festive meals, which they had previously afforded to the offerers, were thus summarily abolished. Instead of these offerings on individual account certain formal and prescribed sacrifices were offered in the name of the whole people, a transaction in which they did not participate, but which was purely an affair of the priests. All that was left for the people was a frugal meal upon the paschal lamb at the initiation of the service. In the words of Wellhausen,[1] the general character of the feasts "is entirely changed. They no longer rest on the seasons and the fruits of the season, and indeed have no basis in the nature of things. They are simply statutory ordinances resting on a positive divine command, which at most was issued in commemoration of some historical event. Their relation to the first-fruits and firstlings is quite gone; indeed these offerings have no longer any place in acts of worship, being transformed into a mere tax, which is holy only in name." This sounds

[1] "Encyclopædia Britannica," Vol. XVIII., Art. Pentateuch, p. 511.

like a pretty severe indictment. Let us see what it amounts to.

1. We have found reason already to dispute the original identity of the passover and the annual offering of firstlings, which is here so confidently assumed. Even if their joint presentation at the same season were to be admitted, which rests on plausible conjecture, not on positive proof, there is no ground whatever for their identification. There is no intimation anywhere that the paschal lamb or any of the animals offered at the ensuing feast were or ever had been firstlings. According to Deut. 16:2, the Passover was to be sacrificed "of the flock and the herd." This does not mean that the paschal supper, in the strict sense, might be an ox as well as a lamb. Dr. Robertson Smith[1] tells us, "The passover is a sacrifice drawn from the flock or the herd," "slain on the evening of the first day of the feast." But this is plainly inconsistent with what immediately follows in the language of the law: "Seven days shalt thou eat unleavened bread therewith." Consequently the term "Passover," as here used, can only denote, as we have before seen, sacrifices offered day by day throughout the seven days of the feast; not of course the burnt and sin offerings, Num. 28: 19 ff., presented on public account, with which no sacrificial meals were connected, but vows and free-will offerings and peace-offerings which are specifically provided for, Num. 29: 39. The same combination of lambs and bullocks at the Passover is found, 2 Chron. 35: 7–9, long after the Priest Code had been established by the

[1] "Encyclopædia Britannica," Vol. XVIII., Art. Passover, p. 343.

confession of the critics themselves, and in a book written, as they declare, wholly in its interest. Kuenen[1] explicitly owns the distinction: "It must gradually have become customary that the members of one family should eat the paschal lamb together, and that then the first-born of oxen and sheep that the past year had produced should be eaten at sacrificial meals on the following days of mazzôth. This is what the Deuteronomist found in existence."

2. The name "Passover" is of itself an insuperable obstacle to Wellhausen's hypothesis of the origin of the festival so called. He may well say,[2] "it is not clear what the name signifies," for it has absolutely no meaning as applied to a thank-offering of firstlings. Dr. Robertson Smith,[3] with characteristic ingenuity, comes to the rescue, and urges that "the corresponding verb denotes some kind of religious performance, apparently a dance, in 1 Kin. 18:26." We are to presume, then, that it was a festival, at which devotees executed a dance like that of the prophets of Baal or perchance modern dervishes. The brilliancy of this suggestion is as though one were to infer from the fact that "revolution" is derived from "revolve," that the English Revolution was so called because it was customary to carry revolvers, and therefore it could not have taken place in 1688, as has been commonly supposed, but must be assigned to some period subsequent to Col. Colt's invention in 1835.

This word פסח (passover) has given not a little em-

[1] "Religion of Israel," I., p. 93.
[2] "Geschichte," p. 89. Prolegomena (Eng. Trans.), p. 87.
[3] *Ubi supra.*

ployment to the critics, who have sought each in his own way to adapt it to his own peculiar hypothesis. Apart from the ridiculous conceit of George[1] that the writer of Ex. 12:11 intimates its derivation from חִפָּזוֹן (haste), it has been explained of passing over the Red Sea or the Jordan, or the sun passing over into the constellation Aries, or the winter passing over into spring, or shepherds with their flocks passing over from their huts and folds into the open pasture, or passing over into the hazards and perils of a new year, or some deity placated by sacrifice passing over the first-born child of a family instead of claiming it as his due. Widely various as these explanations are, they all involve the idea of an expiatory offering of some sort to atone for the past or to obtain divine protection or assistance for the future. In this excessive latitude of conjecture, the only certain guide to its signification is found in the meaning of the cognate verb, by which it is three times explained in Ex. 12:13, 23, 27, and which is employed in the same sense by Isaiah 31:5; פסח means to "pass over" in the sense of sparing, exempting from infliction.

Kuenen[2] accepts this only authorized interpretation, and affirms "that the paschal sacrifice is a substitutional sacrifice, that the animal sacrificed takes the place of the first-born son, to whom Jahveh is considered to have a right and to lay claim." And he goes on to elucidate his meaning: "Originally the father of every family on the eighth day after the birth of his first-born son offered up to Jahveh a redemption-offering, which was called פסח (passover)

[1] "Die älteren Jüdischen Feste," p. 93.   [2] Ibid., p. 92.

for the reasons just indicated: viz., it induced Jahveh to pass over or spare the child, to which he had a claim, and which, therefore, ought really to have been offered up to him. From its very nature this offering was of a private character: it was not and could not be congregational. Now it must gradually have become the custom to offer such an exemption-sacrifice annually, and in connection with this to combine it with one of the feasts that recurred annually with mazzôth."

This, however, is leaving the ground of the laws entirely. The development of the Passover, which Kuenen here propounds to us, is not traced in the line of the feast laws, but constructed altogether out of his own imagination, without even the pretence of any authority on which to base it. The same is true of all those hypotheses reviewed in a former lecture, which maintain the pre-Mosaic origin of the Passover, and connect it with the expiatory rites usual at the spring festival of ancient pagan nations. The relation assumed is purely conjectural and without evidence. Baur[1] regards the Passover as the mollified remnant of an ancient barbarous usage which originally demanded the sacrifice of the first-born child, for which a lamb was substituted, as the ram for Isaac. This view, especially in the more atrocious manner of its presentation by Nork, Ghillany and the like, is justly repelled by Wellhausen[2] in the following terms: "The view of certain scholars, mostly raiders upon Old Testament territory, that the slaying

[1] " Tübinger Zeitschrift," 1832, Heft I., pp. 49, 67.
[2] " Geschichte," p. 91. Prolegomena (Eng. Trans.), p. 88.

of the first-born child was originally the main matter in the Passover, scarcely deserves refutation. . . . There are certainly in history some attested examples of the surrender of an only or best-beloved child, but always as a voluntary and quite extraordinary deed. . . . . The sacrifice of human first-borns never was a regular and required payment in ancient times; there are no traces of such an enormous blood-tax, but very many of the superior rank accorded to the oldest sons."

In the absence of any historical testimony on the subject and in the limited extent of our information as to the religious festivals of Egypt or of any other pagan nation in the Mosaic age, it is certainly very precarious to allege that the Passover was borrowed in any of its characteristic features from any of them. If a connection be maintained between it and the spring festivals of the ancient world, it can only be in that general way in which all symbolical religions are bound together, the common points in whose ritual represent principles which have their seat in the universal nature of man; while all in the religion of Israel is transfused with its own pure and exalted spirit by being taken into the service of Jehovah, and rendered fit to express and stimulate that worship which he demands and expects from Israel.

No mention is made of any annual religious festival as observed by the patriarchs or by the children of Israel during their residence in Egypt. The first intimation of the sort is in the demand upon Pharaoh to let the people go that they may hold a feast unto Jehovah in the wilderness. While this implies that the idea of a religious feast was known to both the king and the people, doubtless from the usages of the Egyptians, it also implies that such a festival had not been observed by them before, inasmuch as it was necessary for them to leave the country for its celebration. Dillmann calls attention to the fact that Moses in his first mention of it to the people, Ex. 12:21, calls it "the Passover," as though it was something with which they were already familiar: but all the seeming force of this suggestion grows out of his critical dissection of the chapter, by which it is separated from ver. 11, where it is spoken of for the first time, and is indefinite in the Hebrew, "a Passover to Jehovah."

The feast of Unleavened Bread is declared by Wellhausen to be in its proper sense a harvest festival. This is an inference resting upon premises which do not warrant it. 1. It is nowhere affirmed or implied in the laws themselves; whereas it is explicitly affirmed in the laws of every successive period, as the critics are pleased to classify them, that it was observed in commemoration of the exodus. Thus the reason given in the Book of the Covenant, Ex. 23:15, and in what Wellhausen calls the law of the two tables, Ex. 34:18, and in Deuteronomy 16:3 for observing the feast of Unleavened Bread, is their coming forth out of the land of Egypt. And in Ex. 12, 13, which as we have seen is neither a record of conflicting traditions nor law in the guise of history, but a simple trustworthy historical record, all the circumstances of the original institution of the Passover and of the feast of Unleavened Bread, together with the first observance of the former on the night of the exodus, are stated with minute detail. The testimony is all of one purport, and there is nothing to contradict it or set it aside. The assertion [1] that the reference to the exodus in both Ex. 23 and 34 is a later addition, and not part of the original text, is made simply in the interest of a critical hypothesis, which those unwelcome words flatly contradict, and accordingly they must be gotten out of the way. Some astute critic might with equal reason draw the most formidable conclusions from the absence of all mention of the Passover or the feast of Unleavened Bread in the gospel of Mark, and when confronted by the fact that they are mentioned in repeated passages gravely insist that these must be interpolations from Matthew and Luke, inasmuch as Mark never referred to those festivals.

2. The fact that the two remaining feasts of the cycle are harvest festivals, does not make it necessary to suppose that the feast of Unleavened Bread was one also, unless there was no other ground of gratitude to Jehovah, and no other reason for his worship than his bounty shown in the annual products of the soil. Why should they praise Jehovah for giving them the fruits of the earth and not for delivering them out of Egypt and giving them the land out of which these fruits sprang? Why should this great initial benefit, which was the basis of every other, and really comprehended every other, as Wellhausen himself takes pains to show, be alone unacknowledged? It is this which is set forth as the ground of homage and obe-

[1] Wellhausen, "Geschichte," p. 89.

dience in the preface to the ten commandments, Ex. 20 : 2 ; so likewise not only in the farewell address of Joshua, Josh. 24 : 5 ff., to the authenticity of which the critics might object, but in the book of Judges, 2 : 1, 6 : 8 ff., which they reckon one of their strongholds, and in the earliest prophets, Hos. 11 : 1, 12 : 9, 13, 13 : 4 ; Am. 2 : 10, 3 : 1 ; Isa. 11 : 15, 16. When Jeroboam established his separatist worship, he sought to draw the people to his idolatrous sanctuaries at Bethel and at Dan by the appeal, "Behold, thy God, O Israel, which brought thee up out of the land of Egypt," 1 Kin. 12 : 28. If anything could kindle the enthusiastic devotion of an Israelite to Jehovah his God and the God of his fathers, it was this. There was perfect harmony in the festal cycle, which celebrated in the opening year the God who made Israel a people and gave them the land flowing with milk and honey; and then in the other festivals that followed in its course made grateful mention of his benefits bestowed upon them in that goodly land, comp. Deut. 26 : 8–10.

3. To make the feast of Unleavened Bread a harvest festival is not only not required by the symmetry of the festal cycle, but actually mars that symmetry. A feast of seven days at the beginning of harvest, and a feast of but one day at its close, when all has been reaped and stored, is surely incongruous. The order should at least have been reversed, since a livelier and more profound gratitude is to be expected of him who has been put in actual and secure possession of the divine gifts, than of him who holds them only in expectancy. And this view naturally leads

to the conclusion, actually maintained by Ewald, that the second was not an independent feast, but was a mere sequel or termination of the first, whose significance it shared; so that the three annual feasts are virtually reduced to two. But in every law bearing upon the subject, they are uniformly reckoned three distinct feasts. Thus, too, results even more clearly than before the singular anomaly that the feast designed to testify the husbandman's joy and gratitude is celebrated before the reaping has begun, whereas the nature of the case demands what universal experience attests, that the burst of joy comes when he has gathered his harvest home.

4. While the terms applied in the Book of the Covenant to the second and third members of the festal series, the feast of Harvest and the feast of Ingathering, sufficiently describe their character, the designation of the first, the feast of Unleavened Bread, stands in no special relation to the harvest, while it is eminently appropriate to a historical commemoration. A great variety of reasons have been suggested for the use of unleavened bread in the ritual in general and in this feast in particular. Philo[1] suggests that while leaven is artificial, unleavened bread is more simple and natural, as it was also the primitive food of men, and as such employed in this spring festival, which commemorates the new-born earth. George,[2] that it was the coarse barley food of the ancients, which maintained its place in the ritual, though in progressive culture leavened wheat

[1] "De Septenario," § 19.
[2] "Die älteren Jüdischen Feste," p. 225.

bread had supplanted it in common use. Redslob,[1] on the contrary, that made as it was of fine wheat flour it was the most delicate kind of bread and such as set before honored guests. Gramberg,[2] that it derived its sacredness from association with legends such as those of Abraham, Gen. 18:6; Lot, 19:3, and Gideon, Judg. 6:19. Baur,[3] that it is refraining from the bread in common use, such as they had eaten in the guilty past, and commencing anew in promise of a new and different life. Knobel, Wellhausen, Dillmann and others connect it with the harvest period, when bread is prepared hastily from the new grain without waiting for it to be leavened. But unleavened bread is nowhere mentioned as an ordinary accompaniment of the harvest. The food then eaten was parched corn, Ruth 2:14. First-fruits were offered either in the ear, Lev. 2:14, 23:10, or as leavened bread, 2:12, 23:17. Unleavened cakes were eaten in Gilgal, Josh. 5:11, not because it was the time of harvest, but of the Passover. And this would not at any rate account for its use at the paschal supper, where the unleavened bread must necessarily be of the old grain, Lev. 23:14, as in fact it may sometimes have been during the whole of the ensuing feast, at least in certain parts of the land.

The prohibition of leaven in this feast and in the altar ceremonial, Lev. 2:11, must be similarly explained. Unleavened bread was, as the Hebrew word

---

[1] "Die biblischen Angaben über Stiftung und Grund der Paschafeier," pp. 45, 46.

[2] "Religionsideen," p. 273.

[3] "Tübinger Zeitschrift," 1832, Heft I., p. 71.

denotes, pure. Leaven produces fermentation, which tends to corruption and decay; it thus became the symbol of malice and wickedness, as unleavened bread of sincerity and truth, 1 Cor. 5 : 8. Dr. Dillmann objects that if this were all, any other symbol of purity would have answered as well; so that the selection of unleavened bread is still unaccounted for. But this is readily explained by the consideration that it must be an article of food, since the thing to be expressed is communion with God in a sacred meal. And this symbolical signification is needed to account for the rigor with which all leaven was excluded from their houses and the eating of it forbidden upon pain of death, Ex. 12 : 15, 19. With this Deut. 16 : 3 is not inconsistent, where unleavened bread is called "the bread of affliction." This does not mean that, as less palatable food, it was intended as the bread of humility or penitence or to remind them of the affliction of Egypt. In that case it would, like the bitter herbs, have been limited to the paschal meal instead of being continued throughout the entire seven days of this feast of joy and gratitude. It was indeed, as this passage declares, associated with the haste with which they left Egypt, and thus with their happy escape from bondage rather than with the bondage itself.

Hupfeld[1] thinks that the sacrifice of the Passover and the unleavened bread have their parallel in the ram of consecration and the unleavened bread used in setting Aaron and his sons apart to the priesthood, Lev. 8 : 22 ff., and that it was designed as in some sort a priestly consecration of the entire people. But

[1] "De primitiva festorum ratione," Part I., pp. 23, 24.

to this it is sufficient to reply that the flesh of the ram was boiled, not roasted; and that uncircumcised foreigners as well as native Israelites were required to eat unleavened bread. Israel, atoned for by the sacrifice of the Passover and freed from the leaven of Egypt and feeding upon pure bread, was consecrated not to the priesthood, but as a holy people in communion with a holy God.

5. The sheaf of the first-fruits was to be waved before the LORD at the feast of Unleavened Bread; but if this proves it to be a harvest festival, Wellhausen's conclusion on his own principles should be precisely the reverse of that which he actually draws. This regulation is found only in Lev. 23 : 9–14, an Elohist law, which we are told is the latest stratum of the whole. In all earlier laws the reason given for the observance is the exodus from Egypt. A historical commemoration has, therefore, in the course of ages been converted into a thanksgiving for the products of the earth, not *vice versâ*, as he would persuade us. In actual fact, however, neither the ceremony nor the expression employed, Deut. 16 : 9, in allusion to it, "such time as thou beginnest to put the sickle to the corn," shows anything more than that the feast occurred in the season of harvest, though the time of its celebration was regulated not by that, but by the anniversary of the exodus.

The alleged development or degradation of the feast is, therefore, at fault in every particular. The feast was a historical commemoration from the beginning. It was instituted not in Canaan, but at the Exodus. And the Passover is not an impoverished relic of the more abundant and joyous festivities of which all partook when their tables were laden with the annual sacrifice of first-born cattle.

One word in conclusion as to these latter becoming the legal perquisites of the priests. If this marks a change, as Wellhausen avers, it is one in nowise destructive of the religious character of the transaction. They were given to Jehovah, who claimed them as his own, in grateful recognition of his rich bounty. And whether he bestowed them upon the priests, his ministers, or gave them back in large part to the offerers, makes no difference in the spirit of piety which prompted the consecration. It is a gross misrepresentation, therefore, to say that what had formerly been "acts of worship," were transformed into "a tax which is holy only in name."

A difficulty has indeed been long felt in reconciling Deut. 15 : 19, 20, according to which the firstlings of cattle were to be eaten by the owner before the LORD, and Num. 18 : 17, 18, which assigns their flesh to the priests. But they may be harmonized nevertheless, if from the animals on which he had a legal claim the priest considered himself bound to supply a table for the offerer and his friends. In regard, however, to this or any other obscurity in these ancient regulations the following sentence uttered by Wellhausen[1] in a different connection is worthy of consideration: "It is not surprising that much is obscure to us, which must have been self-evident to contemporaries."

[1] "Geschichte," p. 94. Prolegomena (Eng. Trans.), p. 91.

VI.
THE PASSOVER.
(Continued).

VI.

THE PASSOVER—(CONTINUED).

WE have examined two points in which it is claimed that a gradual development is traceable in the feast laws. We now come to a third, viz., the time at which the feast of Unleavened Bread was held. Here again it is affirmed that great and important changes occurred in the course of ages, seriously affecting the nature of this feast. In the oldest laws, viz., those of the Book of the Covenant, Ex. 23, and its reproduction, Ex. 34, the spring feast is only in general terms assigned to the month Abib, the month of green ears. Its time was not fixed by statute, but was dependent on the state of the crop. This was still the case in Deuteronomy, although according to some of the critics, the advance was here made of fixing its duration as a period of seven days. Ultimately, however, and as the result of the centralization of worship, which made it necessary that there should be definite and concerted times of pilgrimage, it was attached to given days of the month. It thus no longer took its inspiration from those agricultural conditions with which it was originally connected, but was regulated by the phases of the moon. This gave it an abstract, stereotyped, formal character, and severed it so completely from the hopes and fears of the husbandman and the joys of harvest, that a secondary festival was allowed and even made obligatory a month later, for those who by reason of defilement were unable to participate in it at the regular time.

Hitzig maintains that the feast of Unleavened Bread was originally observed on the first day of the month Abib as the commemoration of the exodus, but was subsequently transferred to the middle of the month and extended to seven days. He urges that the words "month Abib," Ex. 23:15, 34:18, Deut. 16:1, should be rendered "the new moon of Abib." In like manner he translates Ex. 13:4, "This day came ye out in the new moon of Abib," where the rendering "month" would not afford a proper parallel to "day" at the beginning of the verse; this consequently is claimed as a positive declaration that the exodus occurred, or was believed to have occurred, on the first day of the month. He draws a like inference from Ex. 12:41, "At the end of the four hundred and thirty years, even the self-same day it came to pass that all the hosts of the LORD went out from the land of Egypt." He argues from this that the day after the expiration of the four hundred and thirty years must have been new-year's day of the year following. "The self-same day" there referred to, however, is shown by the whole preceding context to have been the 14th day of the month, which is spoken of and emphasized again and again, and is uniformly represented as the day of Israel's leaving Egypt. Hitzig's view is inconsistent with all the statements as to the time of the exodus, with the constant meaning of the Hebrew word in question, which never has the sense of 'new moon' in the

Pentateuch, but always that of 'month,' and with the fact that no prominence is accorded elsewhere in the ritual to the first day of the first month, not even in Num. 28, 29, where the beginnings of the months all stand upon a par, with the single exception of the first day of the seventh month, which is distinguished above the rest. It is besides inconsistent with the terms of the laws themselves, to which appeal is made to establish it. In every instance in which the disputed expression occurs, it is added, "thou shalt eat unleavened bread seven days." This express declaration that the festival was continued through seven days, shows that it was not in the new moon, but in the month Abib. And in Ex. 23 and 34, the words "as I commanded thee" contain an express allusion to the antecedent law in Ex. 12, 13, where the day is fixed beyond peradventure. Hitzig's desperate shift to get rid of this testimony by declaring that the words "thou shalt eat unleavened bread seven days, as I commanded thee," are an interpolation, is not only arbitrary and unauthorized, but is after all of no avail, since the immediately following words, "in the time appointed of the month Abib," likewise allude to the same preceding regulation. And how this alleged interpolation came to be thrust into the middle of a sentence instead of added at the end, it might be difficult to explain.

The allegation that unleavened bread would not have been eaten for seven days to commemorate Israel's hasty flight from Egypt, is sometimes answered by appealing to the fact that the abstinence from leaven thus imposed upon them lasted for several days, and that the entire term is here commemorated. But, as we have seen already, the prohibition of leaven at this feast did not take its rise from this in itself trivial circumstance. Unleavened bread was enjoined because of its symbolical meaning. Direction had been given to institute this festival before the exodus, though as this was intended for the future rather than the present, the people were at this time only bidden to use unleavened bread at the Passover meal. The whole significance of the occurrence and the reason why it was recorded, is that the people were providentially restrained from partaking of this symbol of corruption at that critical period; they were compelled to observe a sort of feast of Unleavened Bread without intending it or being aware of its institution. The extension of the abstinence from leaven to seven days is simply its emphatic repetition during the usual festal period, thus exalting it to the dignity of a feast of the first order.

This whimsical conceit of Hitzig has found few, if any, adherents beyond its originator. The majority of critics on the contrary insist that in the older Jehovist laws, and even in that of Deuteronomy, the name of the month only is given in which the feast was to be held, but no day fixed for its observance. It was to be in the month Abib, that being the period at which barley, the earliest of the grains, began to ripen; but the precise day is undetermined, that being allowed to vary with the season. Whenever the harvest was ripe, each husbandman made his own presentation of first-fruits, and held his annual rejoicing at some neighboring sanctuary. There was thus a festal period rather than one common feast, in which all participated unitedly. The early harvest in the warm basin of the Jordan was separated by a considerable interval from that which was reaped on the high lands of Ephraim or of Galilee. And each was celebrated alike at the time of its occurrence.

But apart from the fact already demonstrated that the feast of Unleavened Bread was not properly a harvest festival and its time could not therefore have been dependent on that which it was not designed to celebrate, this fluctuating observance is inconsistent with the explicit language of all the laws relating to the subject from first to last. Ex. 23 and 34 direct that the feast should be held " in the time appointed of the month Abib; for in it thou camest out from Egypt." It was accordingly regulated by the anniversary of the exodus, and must therefore have been at not a shifting but a fixed and definite period. Ex. 13 : 3, 4, which is also claimed as belonging to the Jehovist legislation, is similarly explicit: " Remember this day in which ye came out from Egypt, ... this day came ye out in the month Abib." So, too, Deuteronomy 16, which says: " Observe the month Abib and keep the Passover unto the LORD thy God; for in the month of Abib the LORD thy God brought thee forth out of Egypt by night "; and further directs the eating of unleavened bread, " that thou mayest remember the day when thou camest forth out of the land of Egypt "; and yet again enjoins the sacrificing of the Passover, which introduced the feast, " at the season that thou camest forth out of Egypt."

THE PASSOVER.

It is, moreover, fatal to the hypothesis that Deuteronomy should describe the time of the feast in indefinite terms. Deuteronomy, the critics claim, introduced centralization of worship. Feasts that might previously be celebrated on "every threshing floor," Hos. 9 : 1, or at contiguous sanctuaries by each neighborhood or even separate household, must thenceforward be observed by the people as a whole at one common sanctuary. An essential requisite in such an arrangement is a fixed and definite time for the observance, which would be understood alike by all. The scheme would necessarily be impracticable without it. As then Deuteronomy plainly enjoins such common pilgrimages, it must have assigned to them certain and universally intelligible dates. The day on which it was to be observed must have been unambiguously settled by this reference to the well-known date of the exodus, even though its number in the month is not stated. But if this be so in Deuteronomy the similar expressions in Exodus must also have a determinate signification. All ground is thus cut off for the assumption that there was ever any variation in the time of the feast whether from year to year, or in different localities in the land.

In the so-called Elohistic laws, which according to the new departure in criticism are to be reckoned post-exilic, definite dates are given. Here, however, George and Wellhausen tell us that they find evidence of still further development. George[1] says that in Ex. 12 : 18, the feast of Unleavened Bread begins on the fourteenth day at even, and extends

[1] " Die älteren Jüdischen Feste " p. 243 f.

to the one and twentieth day at even, with which Ezek. 45 : 21 agrees. But in Lev. 23 : 5, 6, and Num. 28 : 16, 17, the Passover is observed on the fourteenth day at even, and the feast of Unleavened Bread does not commence until the fifteenth, from which time it extends seven days; thus making the continuance of the whole eight days instead of seven. This resulted, as he informs us, from the change which then took place in the diurnal mode of reckoning. Instead of estimating the day as formerly from the evening, they began with the morning. The evening of the fourteenth, on which the paschal meal was eaten, was too important to be abandoned; and consequently it imparted its sacredness to the entire day to which it belonged. And hence Josephus[1] says that the feast of Unleavened Bread continues seven days when the Passover is not included, but including the Passover it is a feast of eight days.

Wellhausen[2] also insists upon a similar prolongation of the feast, not, however, in the Elohist laws compared with one another, but compared with Deuteronomy. In Deut. 16 : 4, 8, he says that the evening of the Passover is reckoned the first day of the festal week, which is not the case in Lev. 23 : 6, Num. 28 : 17, Ex. 12 : 18, where the feast of Unleavened Bread begins on the fifteenth and ends with the twenty-first. A day is thus added to the feast, and that not an ordinary day, but one of special solemnity, this being the character which attached to the first day of the festal week; and this is further

[1] "Antiquities," iii., 10, 5, and ii., 15, 1.
[2] "Geschichte," p. 107 f. Prolegomena (Eng. Trans.), p. 104.

more the day immediately following the Passover on which Deut. 16:7 allowed the pilgrims to return home.

But these critics merely succeed in showing their eagerness to create a difficulty where none whatever exists. The circumstance, that they are not even agreed where the difficulty is, is somewhat damaging at the outset to the impression of its formidable character, which might otherwise have been made upon us. Exodus says that unleavened bread is to be eaten from the fourteenth at even for seven days, until the twenty-first at even. Leviticus and Numbers say that Passover is to be observed on the evening of the fourteenth, but that the feast of Unleavened Bread properly begins with the morning of the fifteenth and lasts seven days; it will thus extend precisely as before to the close of the twenty-first. And it is also perfectly easy to see how Josephus could under these circumstances call the feast one of eight days, inasmuch as it covers parts of eight different days, if these be reckoned to begin with the morning, whereas in strictness it lasts but seven days, counting from evening to evening, comp. Mat. 26:17. If I speak of one o'clock at night, or one o'clock in the morning, I would be understood to mean precisely the same point of time, only in the one case it would be reckoned as if it were attached to the day before, and in the other case to the day after. And if I were to arrive at Boston on one day at noon and leave the next day at the same hour, I might say that I had been there one day, which would be measuring the interval precisely, or that I had been there two days, which though somewhat inexact would be readily understood. I believe that no critic has ever found a discrepancy between Gen. 17:12, which requires a child to be circumcised when he is eight days old, and Lev. 12:3, which appoints it upon the eighth day, though by rigid calculation he would then be but seven days old. All are familiar with instances in the New Testament of this popular mode of reckoning among the Hebrews, as the three days of Christ's abode in the grave, and eight days used to denote a week, John 20:26, Luke 9:28, comp. Mat. 17:1, Mark 9:2; and some older people than children have been puzzled by the inquiry whether the year 1800 is the last of the eighteenth century, or the first of the nineteenth.

Wellhausen acted discreetly, therefore, in retreating from the position taken up by George and in owning that the passages which the latter sought to set at variance are really harmonious. But his own entrenchments are not a whit stronger. He says that "the first feast day in Deuteronomy is the day on the evening of which the Passover falls, and it is followed not by seven, but by six days, whereas in the Priest Code the observance extends from the fourteenth to the twenty-first of the month, Ex. 12:18." This is certainly a most extraordinary comment. Deut. 16:2 ff. enjoins the eating of unleavened bread seven days, then speaks of the Passover meal and adds: "Six days shalt thou eat unleavened bread; and on the seventh day shall be an עֲצֶרֶת (a solemn assembly) to the LORD thy God." From this he infers, if his words have any meaning, that unleavened bread was not eaten on the seventh day; its use terminated with the sixth, and the additional day requisite to make up the full number must be that of the Passover which preceded. Imagine a father writing to his absent son: "My boy, we wish you at home. You may leave your city restaurant and take your meals with us for the next seven days. We shall have something good to eat for six days and the seventh will be Thanksgiving day." Would any one but a German critic imagine that the old gentleman meant to say that on Thanksgiving day there would be nothing good to eat? Or would any one else have ever dreamed that on the seventh, which was one of the two great days of the feast of Unleavened Bread, unleavened bread was not to be eaten? The term עֲצֶרֶת (solemn assembly) here applied to the last day of Unleavened Bread is the same that in Lev. 23:36, and Num. 28:35 is used of the day succeeding the feast of Tabernacles, which concludes the entire festal series of the year. But there is nothing in the etymology or use of the word to justify the inference that it is a day additional to the proper festival in this instance where the contrary is expressly declared.

The permission given Deut. 16:7, "Thou shalt turn in the morning (after the Passover) and go unto thy tents," has been explained[1] to mean after the entire feast of seven days is ended; but the immediate connection appears to relate to the paschal meal proper and not to all the Passover offerings. Riehm[2] insists that the intention can not possibly be to allow

[1] So by Gerhard, quoted by Riehm.
[2] "Die Gesetzgebung Mosis im Lande Moab," p. 51.

THE PASSOVER. 215

the pilgrims to return home on the morning after the paschal lamb was eaten, and thus absent themselves from the solemn assembly ordained for the seventh day. He consequently interprets it of returning not to their homes, but to their lodgings in the city. But the phrase "go unto thy tents" need not refer to actual tents or temporary structures. It is proverbially used of a return home even with reference to solid and permanent abodes, 1 Kin. 12 : 16, 2 Chron. 10 : 16. The Passover, Deut. 16 : 7, was to be eaten in the place which the LORD shall choose, not necessarily in the court of the sanctuary, which could not contain the assembled multitudes; but in the vicinity of the sanctuary each family partook of this sacred meal in its own separate apartment.

Dillmann finds in this permission to pilgrims to return to their homes indications of a new stage in the history of the ordinance. In Ex. 13 : 6 the seventh day of Unleavened Bread is declared to be a feast to the LORD : from which he infers that at the time represented by that law the Passover was observed by each family at home as a domestic sacrifice, as it had been in Egypt; and that later in the festal week a pilgrimage was made to the sanctuary so as to spend the seventh day there. Deuteronomy, however, introduced a change by requiring the Passover to be eaten at the sanctuary; but in order that the pilgrims might not be obliged to absent themselves from home longer than before, they were suffered to leave when the Passover was ended, and were thus relieved from attendance at the solemn assembly held on the seventh day. All that is peculiar to Dr. Dillmann's view is drawn from his own imagination and is not found in the text. The utmost that can be said of it is that it would be consistent with the language of Ex. 13:6 if this verse were isolated from all others bearing on the same subject. But it is not required by that verse, and there is nothing there or elsewhere to suggest it. "The seventh day shall be a feast unto the LORD" certainly does not mean that the pilgrimage was to be made on that day, but that it was to be observed at the sanctuary with the special services and ceremonies usual at pilgrimage feasts. One of the most marked of these was a "holy convocation" or "solemn assembly"; and as this is particularly noted in other passages as belonging to this day, it is doubtless intended by the expression before us; and the great body of commentators have so understood it. When the pilgrims were to arrive at the sanctuary, or how long they were to remain, this passage does not inform us. Deuteronomy supplies this information. They must be present at the Passover, which was the keystone of the entire festival, but need not remain during the rest of the seven days.

It was doubtless in consideration of the exigencies of the harvest season that this leave was granted. The pilgrims might or might not avail themselves of it. Devotion would prompt them to remain during the entire sacred term. But attendance at the holy convocations at the sanctuary was not in every case obligatory on those who resided at a distance. As they were not required to be present on the seventh day, neither were they on the first beyond attendance at the Passover in the evening with which it began.

There is no inconsistency, therefore, in their being allowed to return home on the first day of Unleavened Bread, although a holy convocation was then held; and it involved no violation of the sacredness of the day, which was not observed with the strictness of the weekly Sabbath. That the first day is not in express terms named as a day of holy convocation in Ex. 13 or Deut. 16, we have before seen, involves no discrepancy with Ex. 12:16, Lev. 23:7, 8, Num. 28:18, 25. Supreme stress is clearly laid upon the initial day as the one to be commemorated and the pivotal point of the entire celebration, the ground and basis of the whole; and as Dillmann[1] justly says: "That the first also was a chief day, is self-evident."

It is further claimed that the ritual of the Passover underwent changes in the course of time. The common opinion has been that several of the rites prescribed on its first observance in Egypt were peculiar to that occasion, and were due only to the special circumstances of the case. The slaying of the lamb by the head of each family at his own house, the sprinkling of the door-posts and lintels, and probably also the posture in which they partook of the lamb, with their loins girded, their shoes on their feet and their staff in their hand, were of this temporary character. They never recur again. God had not yet established his sanctuary in the midst of his people, and the Aaronic priesthood was not yet instituted. At a later time the Passover followed the usages of other sacrifices; the animal was slain at the altar; and the priests sprinkled the blood, 2 Chron. 30:16 f., 35:11.

[1] "Die Bücher Exodus und Leviticus," p. 581.

Dillmann very needlessly presses the letter of Ex. 12:24 in reference not merely to the ordinance as such, but to all the details before described. The complete change of circumstances necessarily led to a corresponding modification in the mode of observance.

Wellhausen[1] finds a significant change in the directions respecting the flesh of the lamb. The ancient, and even in later times, the general custom, he says, was to boil meat. The word בשל (boil) occurs very frequently, but צלה (roast) is comparatively rare. The flesh of sacrifices was always boiled. But the better class of people came to prefer their meat roasted. And so the sons of Eli demanded of the worshippers, "Give flesh to roast for the priest; for he will not have sodden flesh of thee, but raw," 1 Sam. 2:15. Now in Deut. 16:7, they were not bidden to "roast" it, as it is rendered in the authorized version. The word used is בשל, the same that is employed, Ex. 12:9, in the prohibition, "not sodden at all with water." According to the former passage it was to be boiled; according to the latter it must not be boiled, but roasted. Boiling had passed out of fashion, and roasting had come into vogue. But unfortunately for this view of the case, 2 Chron. 35:13 also uses this very word בשל of the preparation of the Passover, though Chronicles is always represented as such a stickler for the Priest Code, in which roasting was so rigorously prescribed. It uses this word, moreover, both of roasting and of boiling, uniting in the same sentence בשל with fire, and בשל in pots, showing

[1] "Geschichte," p. 70. Prolegomena (Eng. Trans.), p. 68.

that the word has neither the specific sense of boiling or roasting, but the general meaning "to cook" in any mode. Exodus gives specific directions that the lamb must not be boiled, but roasted. Deuteronomy simply speaks of cooking it, without particularizing the mode, assuming that the proper style of preparation was known, and that no further explanation was necessary.

It is further charged that the Levitical law alters the whole character of the festal celebrations by the substitution of public sacrifices for those which had previously been offered on individual account. Thus Wellhausen:[1] "The celebration proper is exhausted in prescribed public sacrifices. There were offered day by day at the Passover, besides the continual burnt-offering, two bullocks, one ram, seven lambs as a burnt-offering, and a he-goat as a sin-offering. Additional free-will offerings of individuals are not excluded, but they are subordinate. Elsewhere both in the older practice, 1 Sam. 1:4 ff., and in the law, Ex. 23:18, the feast-offering was always associated with a meal, and was hence a private sacrifice. Deuteronomy directs that the poor and needy classes should be invited to these sacrificial entertainments. This is an advance which stands much nearer the old sacrificial idea of communion between God and men than those solitary general church sacrifices."

The transition here affirmed from private to public sacrifices is altogether imaginary. Both subsisted side by side from the beginning to the end. The apparent development on which Wellhausen insists, is

[1] "Geschichte," p. 102. Prolegomena (Eng. Trans), p. 99.

simply created by the critical assumption which rends asunder laws, that form related parts of one connected system of legislation. Deuteronomy does not repeat the ritual of Leviticus and Numbers, for that had been detailed sufficiently in its proper place. It steadfastly adheres to its own purpose and aim. Wellhausen himself says, "In Deuteronomy almost everything is left to existing usage, and only the one main matter insisted on, that divine worship, and consequently the feasts too, must be celebrated only in Jerusalem." With this view of the design of the book no presumption arises against the existence of the scheme of festal offerings enjoined in Num. 28, that no allusion is made to it in Deuteronomy. There was no occasion to make such allusion. This book concerns itself with the offerings which the people themselves were to bring for themselves as individuals and as families rather than with those which the priests were to offer in the name of the congregation. And that Leviticus and Numbers do not exclude the private offerings of the people is explicitly declared, Num. 29: 39: "These things ye shall do unto the LORD in your set feasts beside your vows and your free-will offerings, for your burnt-offerings and for your meat-offerings, and for your drink-offerings, and for your peace - offerings": and again in similar terms, Lev. 23: 38. This too is somewhat ungraciously admitted by Wellhausen, his admission being qualified by the gratuitous assertion that these latter are subordinate to the public sacrifices. There is no subordination about it. The one was a matter

---

[1] "Geschichte Israels," p. 94. Prolegomena (Eng. Trans.), p. 91.

of statute, and full specifications are consequently given. The other was wholly left to the devout feelings of the offerer, upon which no restriction whatever was laid. The spontaneous piety which he represents as characteristic of the early stages of Israel's religion received no check from the ritual legislation, which afforded it free vent at all times. The public offerings did not come in subsequently to crowd out those that had formerly been presented by individuals. They were the framework and support of the edifice of Israel's worship, which was filled in, completed and beautified, made habitable and precious in the eyes of the LORD by the numberless acts of piety and devotion of the thronging worshippers.

There is still one other respect in which the critics claim to be able to trace a development in the feasts, viz., the place of their celebration. The earlier laws, it is held, bind them to no one locality. They were celebrated everywhere. Each neighborhood had its shrine and its annual festivities. The larger places doubtless had more showy sanctuaries, and they attracted larger crowds of pilgrims and from remoter parts. Some sanctuaries may have been frequented more at one season, others at another. The worshipper thus resorted to the sanctuary whenever the occasion arose that called forth his homage. The first sheaf gathered from his ground could be offered to the LORD as soon as it was reaped, and immediate expression could be given to the gratitude which the sense of God's bounty awakened within him.

But Deuteronomy brought with it a momentous change. Abuses had sprung up at the local sanctuaries which brought them into disrepute, and the prophetic party resolved upon the centralization of worship as the only available remedy. They gave utterance to their ideas in the Deuteronomic code, by which they sought to suppress all sacrificial worship except at one central sanctuary. It was therein ordained that all sacrifices and all feasts should thenceforth be limited to the place that the LORD should choose, by which is plainly meant the temple at Jerusalem. The feasts thus removed to a distance from the residences of the people, were necessarily separated from their natural occasions and became formal, stereotyped and statutory ordinances instead of free and joyous expressions of the religious life, elicited by the fresh experience of God's ever-recurring bounty. The iteration with which Deut. 16 insists upon sacrificing the Passover in the place which the LORD should choose to place his name there, shows it to be a new requirement which it was apprehended that it would be difficult to enforce. In Leviticus and Numbers, on the other hand, no further solicitude was felt on this subject. Not a word is said respecting the place of observance. It is taken for granted that the feasts can be observed only at the sacred tabernacle. This seemed too obvious to call for remark or injunction. These laws accordingly emanate from a period when the struggle represented in Deuteronomy was at an end, and had terminated in favor of the central sanctuary. All local sanctuaries had been suppressed, or the attachment of the people to them had been overcome, and the temple in Jerusalem had no longer a rival.

But the alleged diversity of laws on this subject has no existence. The legislation of the Pentateuch in all its parts allows but one sanctuary. The Book of the Covenant, Ex. 23 : 19, and its reproduction, 34 : 26, ordain that the first of the first-fruits should be brought "into the house of the LORD thy God," one definite place. And 20 : 24, to which the critics so confidently appeal as sanctioning a multiplicity of altars, does not contemplate contemporaneous rival sanctuaries, but only successive spots at which God would reveal himself to his people, while they were still without a settled habitation. When the covenant had been ratified, and God condescended to take up his abode in the midst of his people, the tabernacle was thenceforward the only place of acceptable sacrificial worship; and the Levitical code bases itself upon this idea. In the great lawgiver's final address to the people, he speaks no longer in the brief and formal language of a statute, but in that of earnest exhortation and admonition, warning them of the danger and the sin of defection from Jehovah, and urging them to strict and faithful adherence to the laws which he had given. Foreseeing the dangers that would arise from their being ensnared into attendance at the idolatrous temples of the Canaanites, he directs his utmost urgency to this source of their most immediate peril, reiterating his cautions upon this point again and again, and especially enjoining it upon them to present all their sacrifices and observe all their feasts at the place which the LORD would choose, after he had given them rest in the land which they were going in to possess. There is thus perfect harmony throughout all the laws on this subject; the same spirit pervades the whole; and there is but one uniform requirement.

Finally, the critics make their appeal to the history. There, we are told, the same successive stages which they find indicated in the laws, can be recognized afresh in the recorded development of these institutions, as set forth in the historical books and the books of the prophets. This, it is claimed, supplies the ultimate and decisive test, demonstrating the correctness of the results arrived at by the investigation of the laws, inasmuch as these are seen to match precisely with the condition of things exhibited in the actual life of the people at distinct and determinate epochs.

In Wellhausen's review of the history, he has much to say of the gradual rise of feasts from the presentation of first-fruits, and of their annual observance at neighborhood sanctuaries, and the growth of larger sanctuaries toward the close of the period of the judges, and of the people resorting at different seasons to different sanctuaries, and of the increasing influence of great royal temples; but the whole thing is spun out of his own brain. It is as purely fictitious as an astronomical map would be of the other side of the moon. The only pretence of any historical evidence is found in a jumble of defections from the worship of Jehovah, which historians and prophets combine to denounce as such, but which our critic adduces as the genuine outgrowth of Israel's religion. He might as well gather the sentiments and practices of confessed outlaws and of vicious classes, and deduce from these the recognized statutes or the prevailing standard of public morality at different periods of a nation's history.

But even thus his testimonies are few and far between. A pagan festival at Shechem, mentioned in the book of Judges, 9:27, and Jeroboam's idolatrous feast at Bethel, established in open and avowed opposition to the worship at Jerusalem, of which we learn in 1 Kin. 12:32, a passage which, from his point of view, he pronounces unreliable, are positively the only instances which he is able to adduce from the entire range of the historical books to confirm his confidently reiterated assertions that religious festivals were held elsewhere than at one legitimate sanctuary. If now his interpretation of the facts is correct, and the annual feasts were as freely observed, as he imagines, at numerous sacred localities, and yet this fact nowhere comes out in the history, what are we to think of the critical principle which underlies all his reasoning that the silence of a historian respecting an occurrence discredits its reality? If throughout every period of the history down to the reign of Josiah, these annual festivities were held at so many distinct places without any trace of it being preserved in any one of the historical books, why should the absence of any more explicit statements than we possess in these same histories respecting the observance of the Levitical ritual in its details be urged in proof of its non-existence?

In the paucity of authorities the degraded festivals denounced by Hosea as feasts of Baal and of which Amos speaks with loathing and abhorrence, are eagerly caught up as evidences. These excrescences which the prophets would pare away, these nuisances which they would abate, are held up before us by the critics not in their contrast with the purer worship maintained at the seat of the divine abode, which they attest and illustrate as spurious coin does the genuine and unadulterated, but as forms and manifestations of the religion of Jehovah. These aberrations from the ancient faith and from the pure worship of their fathers, of which Hosea and Amos speak in terms of unmitigated rebuke and indignation, afford the only proof that is forthcoming, that the Mosaic law, restricting the annual festivals to the one sanctuary where God had recorded his name, was not in existence. Not one passage can be adduced from the entire Old Testament to show that the Passover, or either of the other annual feasts or any national anniversary whatever was celebrated anywhere but at Shiloh or Jerusalem.

The allusions to the annual festivals by Isaiah are scanty and incidental and yet sufficient to show their existence in his time. The regular festive cycle is plainly referred to, Isa. 29 : 1, which should be translated, "Add ye year to year; let the feasts run their round." In 1 : 13 he brings together quite a number of technical terms connected with festive celebrations, some of which are peculiar to the Levitical law which the critics would persuade us is post-exilic; thus "the calling of assemblies," or holy convocation, as Ex. 12 : 16, Lev. 23, Num. 28; spoken of again, 4 : 5, in connection with Mount Zion; "the solemn meeting" or solemn assembly, as Lev. 23 : 36, Num. 29 : 35, Deut. 16 : 8; spoken of likewise by his older contemporary, Joel 1 : 14, 2 : 15, who connects it with Zion, and its idolatrous counterpart in the kingdom of Israel is referred to 2 Kin. 10 : 20, Amos 5 : 21, and "the appointed feasts." Isaiah calls Zion, 33 : 20, "the city of our solemnities," using here, as in the expression last cited, the word employed in Lev. 23 to denote both the three pilgrimage feasts and the other annual festivals. And he affords us a glimpse of the impressive spectacle presented on these sacred occasions in 30 : 29, which should be translated, "Your song shall be as in the night of consecrating a feast, as when one goeth with a pipe to come into the mountain of Jehovah." This solemn march in festive procession with joyful music to the temple has its counterpart in Ps. 42 : 4, where the Psalmist says: "I passed by with the throng, and marched with them to the house of God with the voice of joy and praise, a multitude keeping the feast." Gramberg[1] is in doubt whether Isaiah here alludes to the Passover, since Exodus says nothing of glad songs accompanied by the flute, and whether he has not rather in mind the autumn feast of ingathering, which was celebrated in later times by illuminations and glad festivities like the Dionysia, or feasts of Bacchus. Wellhausen correctly identifies the feast here spoken of with what he and Dillmann translate "the night of watching," Ex. 12 : 42, but the majority of commentators "the night of observance" or celebration, that is to say, the feast observed at night, the Passover. And though Isaiah does not actually use the name, he unmistakably alludes to it a few verses

---

[1] "Religionsideen," p. 284.

later, 31 : 5, "The LORD of hosts will defend Jerusalem; .... passing over he will preserve it," which likewise shows the meaning that he attached to the name of the festival; whence it may fairly be inferred that it was to him not a harvest feast, but a historical commemoration of a great deliverance. Wellhausen calls attention to the fact that it is a prophet of Jerusalem who thus speaks of the festal cycle, and who ties the observance of the feasts to Zion. But we look in vain for testimony of a different nature from any other quarter. There is not a word in any writing in the Old Testament to intimate that they ever were observed in whole or in part in any other locality than that of the tabernacle or temple.

The first celebration of the Passover of which Wellhausen finds any record is that in the eighteenth year of king Josiah, 2 Kin. 23 : 21, 22, which he tells us was kept in accordance with the requirements of Deuteronomy and not those of Ex. 12. If he means anything more than that the lamb was now slain at the temple and its blood sprinkled on the altar instead of on the door-posts and lintel, we may well ask him where he obtained his information. All that is said of the mode of observance is contained in this single verse: "And the king commanded all the people, saying, Keep the Passover unto the LORD your God, as it is written in this book of the covenant." The terms of the king's command seem to be drawn from Deut. 16 : 1 (though see Ex. 12 : 48). And the critics claim with some plausibility that the reformation of Josiah took its impulse and shape from the book of Deuteronomy.[1] But as the book of Kings gives no account of the ritual observed in this instance, this question is of no consequence to us at present.

Great stress is, however, laid upon the statement in ver. 22, " Surely there was not holden such a Passover from the days of the judges that judged Israel, nor in all the days of the kings of Israel, nor of the kings of Judah." This is interpreted to mean that this was the first Passover ever held in accordance with Deuteronomic law. Previously there had only been local celebrations, each neighborhood or district observing it in their own particular sanctuary. Now for the first time these were superseded and there was one celebration for the whole people. Wellhausen's idea is that the feast of Tabernacles may have been observed as a national festival in Jerusalem at an earlier period, perhaps from the time of Solomon; but that the Passover had never reached this distinction. And the peculiarity of Josiah's Passover was that it too was now made national. But—1. This is importing a meaning into the text which is not there. This verse not only suggests no contrast with previous local celebrations, but there is not a line in the entire Old Testament to intimate that such a thing had ever been known as local celebrations of the Passover. 2. This is scarcely consistent with the passages above cited from Isaiah, which plainly declare the celebration of the Passover at Jerusalem. 3. If 2 Chron. 30 is to be believed,

[1] See " The Old Testament in the Jewish Church," by Dr. Robertson Smith, p. 425.

there had been a national observance of the Passover in the reign of Hezekiah, which although repudiated by some, ver. 10, had yet not had its equal since the period of the schism, ver. 26. 4. The verse before us, even as interpreted by Wellhausen, necessarily implies that such national celebrations of the Passover at the sanctuary had taken place in the time of the judges, when as we learn from 1 Sam. 2 : 14, all Israel resorted to the tabernacle at Shiloh. 5. The natural suggestion of the verse is that the distinction of Josiah's Passover lay not in its being national as opposed to neighborhood celebrations, but in the universality of the attendance as opposed to the coming up of a part only of the people. This evidently lies in the words, "all the days of the kings of Israel and of the kings of Judah," that is to say, the whole duration of the schism, in which the ten tribes were debarred from attendance at Jerusalem, comp. the paraphrase of this verse in 2 Chron. 35 : 18. And the writer would have us understand that the enthusiastic eagerness with which the whole population now flocked from every part of the land to engage in this sacred service even exceeded that of the days of David and Solomon.

According to Wellhausen this is the first mention of the Passover in any of the historical books. As he attributes no weight to the testimony either of Joshua or Chronicles, he gives no credence to the Passover at Gilgal, Josh. 5 : 10, nor to that of Solomon, 2 Chron. 8 : 13, nor to that of Hezekiah, 2 Chron. 30. Redslob[1] will not even allow the his-

---

[1] "Stiftung und Grund der Paschafeier," p. 33.

torical character of the Passover of Josiah, and says: "It is plain to see that the passage, 2 Kings 23 : 21-23, which gives an account of the Passover observed by him, is interpolated here by a different hand from another source." But accepting Wellhausen's view of the case, how comes it to pass that though three pilgrimage feasts are enjoined in what he considers the very oldest codes of law, Ex. 23 and 34, the first of the series is nowhere mentioned in the history until the reign of Josiah? Whatever explanation he may propose of this circumstance, the conclusion is not to be evaded on his own premises, that the existence of a statute is not discredited by an omission on the part of the sacred historian to record its observance.

Another consideration which forces itself upon us is that he has utterly failed to verify in the history the development of the festival, which he claimed to have discovered in the feast laws in even so much as a single particular. The Passover is twice spoken of after the time of Josiah, viz.: by Ezekiel, 45 : 21-24, and as observed by the returned exiles, Ezra 6 : 19 ff. The comparison of these cases with one another and with the accounts given in Chronicles of the celebration of the Passover, in which it is held that the writer reflects the usage of his own day rather than that of the period which he is describing, might appear at first sight to favor the idea of progressive changes in certain respects. The critics affirm, as we have seen, that the earliest Passover laws do not fix it at a definite date. It was observed in the first month, but the precise time may have varied from year to year with the character of the season and the forwardness of the harvest. But after it was transferred to the capital of the nation, and concert of action became necessary on the part of pilgrims, the Priest Code fixed it upon the fourteenth day of the month. In seeming correspondence with this the day of Josiah's Passover is not named in 2 Kin. 23 : 21, 22 ; but it is given as the fourteenth day of the first month in Ezekiel and Ezra, and so in the account given in Chronicles of Josiah's Passover, 2 Chron. 35 : 1 ; while Hezekiah's Passover, 30 : 15, was on the fourteenth day of the second month, as allowed, Num. 9 : 11, when there had been any absolute hindrance at the proper season.

But the slightest examination will show that any inference from these premises would be invalid. For, 1. In the brief allusion to the Passover in 2 Kin. 23, not even the month is named, though this is fixed in all the oldest codes, so called, Ex. 23, 34, and Deut. 16. 2. The statement in 1 Kin. 12 : 32, 33, that Jeroboam ordained his feast on "the fifteenth day of the eighth month, even in the month which he had devised of his own heart," implies that he had changed the month, but not the day; and that the fifteenth was the proper day for Judah's feast of the seventh month, 1 Kin. 8 : 2, and for a festal observance in general ; which raises the presumption that the feast of the first month was also observed on the same day of the month. 3. If the Asaph named in the title of Ps. 81 as its author, was the seer and contemporary of David, 1 Chron. 16 : 7, 2 Chron. 29 : 30, we have here explicit testimony as to the time of the observance of the Passover at that period. Though explained by some authorities of the feast of Tabernacles, the evident allusion to the plague of the first-born, and the exodus as the occasion of the festival, determine it to be the Passover, ver. 3-5. "Blow the trumpet in the month, in the full moon for the day of our feast. For this is a statute for Israel, a law of the God of Jacob. This he ordained in Joseph for a testimony, when he went out over the land of Egypt," *i. e.*, to inflict that plague which set Israel free. And even though the Psalm be of later date, of which, however, there is no clear evidence, it still suggests a reason that was equally cogent from the beginning, for assigning the great pilgrimage feasts to the fifteenth of the month, viz., that this was the time of the full moon. This commended itself as the most appropriate time, not from any superstitious or pagan association, but on account of the brightness of the nights it was far more favorable for journeying.

But here we are confronted with those mysterious chapters in the latter part of the prophecy of Ezekiel, his vision of the temple rebuilt, the ritual restored, and the land distributed again among the tribes. This, we are told, is actually the first draught of the Levitical law. We see it in the process of formation. Ezekiel, from the part of a prophet, proceeds to exercise the function of a legislator in regard to the sanctuary and the ceremonial, for which his priestly origin and perhaps priestly experience had fitted him. Smend[1] tells us that "the decisive importance of this section for the criticism of the Pentateuch was

[1] "Der Prophet Ezechiel," p. 312.

first recognized by George and Vatke. It has rightly been called the key of the Old Testament. In fact it is only intelligible as an intermediate link between Deuteronomy and the Priest Code, and it thence follows that the latter is exilic or post-exilic. This intermediate position it holds not merely logically, but historically. The transformation here takes place before our eyes of ancient into modern Israel; that is, in this case of Deuteronomy into the Priest Code." And he undertakes to exhibit in detail the evidence that the ritual prescriptions of Ezekiel must have preceded those of the Levitical law; but his entire argument is based on his own prepossessions, and loses all its force if these are not first taken for granted.

He tells us that "Ezekiel's feast legislation is absolutely inexplicable, if he was acquainted with the Priest Code; on the contrary, the latter is built upon Ezekiel's enactments." In inquiring whether this is so, we shall first avail ourselves of Smend's clear presentation of their distinctive features. Ezekiel, 45: 18 ff., divides the year into two equal parts, and begins each with an expiatory sacrifice, offered on the first day of the first and seventh[1] months respectively. Each is followed a fortnight later by a seven-day feast, Passover, and the autumnal festival. No mention is made of the feast of Weeks, which occurs in every other feast law; nor of the eighth day of Tabernacles; nor of sacrificial meals that are so prominent in Deuteronomy; but only of sacrifices offered in the

[1] This is based on the supposition of an error in the text of ver. 20, where for "seventh day of the month," read "first day of the seventh month."

name of the whole people, such as are prescribed in the Levitical code, but differing throughout in details. The same offerings are to be presented at each feast, a bullock for a sin-offering for the prince and people of the land, and daily during each term of seven days seven bullocks and seven rams for a burnt-offering, and a kid of the goats for a sin-offering. Instead of this Num. 28 prescribes for each day of the Passover two bullocks, one ram, and seven lambs for a burnt-offering and one goat for a sin-offering; and at Tabernacles from thirteen to seven bullocks, two rams and fourteen lambs for a burnt-offering and one goat for a sin-offering. Ezekiel also says nothing of the presentation of the sheaf and the loaves of the first-fruits with their accompanying offerings or the dwelling in booths at Tabernacles.

This, it is claimed, is a wholly new departure, and involves a radically different conception of the feasts from that of the older legislation, where festive meals and offerings on private account are the main thing. Ezekiel, like the Priest Code, has no interest except in the public sacrifices, while yet in the details of his prescriptions he deviates from the Priest Code in every particular. Why, it is asked, did not Ezekiel simply repeat the directions of the Priest Code, if he was acquainted with it, since it accomplished precisely the transformation of the festivals which he was seeking to effect? Why depart from it perpetually in details which were quite unimportant and without any assignable reason, while in principle he agrees with it throughout? Smend infers that Ezekiel could not have been acquainted with the Priest Code; in fact that it was not yet in existence. Ezekiel initiated a movement, which was further carried out in the Priest Code. This latter is simply the scheme of Ezekiel elaborated and modified.

But this reasoning assumes the very thing at issue. The alleged change in the mode of observing the feasts, from joyous sacrificial meals to formal, stereotyped and statutory sacrifices in the name of the people, is a pure fiction. We have seen already that the Levitical law does not exclude free-will offerings and festive meals, and that Deuteronomy does not exclude the public sacrifices; that these laws are mutually supplementary, and presuppose each other. Though Ezekiel says nothing of the feast of Weeks, Smend claims that he did not intend to set aside the pilgrimages which Deuteronomy ordained for that day. There is indeed no paschal lamb; but Smend imagines him to mean that the firstlings should be eaten at festive meals. He might as well say the same of Lev. 23 and Num. 28, which likewise say nothing of the paschal lamb, for the very sufficient reason that it had been already ordained in Ex. 12. Why does Ezekiel place the Passover on the fourteenth, while the other feast was on the fifteenth, but for the service of the paschal lamb which is presupposed as too much a matter of course to require special mention? Ezekiel's scheme is simpler and less intricate, particularly as regards the sacrificial animals, than that of the Levitical law; but who shall say on this ground which is the primary and which the secondary draught? A reviser may simplify as well as elaborate. The alphabet is far less complicated than hieroglyphics. Ezekiel certainly showed a disposition to simplify in reducing the old cycle of three feasts to two; why may he not have done the same in the festal ceremonial?

But why, it is asked, did Ezekiel deviate so constantly from the Levitical law and in such petty details for no imaginable reason? It is as easy to reverse the question, and quite as difficult to answer it; why should the Priest Code differ in this petty manner from Ezekiel after he had ordained the law on the express authority of the LORD God? Ezekiel's whole sketch is ideal. It was not literally obeyed in a single particular. The temple was not rebuilt by his directions. The ceremonial was not restored as he prescribed. The land was not divided agreeably to his injunctions. This non-compliance on the part of those who honored him as a prophet of the LORD, shows that they understood his words not as commands which they were to obey, but as an idealized picture of the future which the LORD would bring to pass. It was no more designed to guide in the work of reconstruction than Jeremiah 31 : 38–40 was to be followed in rebuilding the walls of Jerusalem, or than Zechariah 2 : 4 enjoined their demolition. The departures from Levitical law above referred to may have been designed on the one hand to intimate that the ceremonial was not a finality and forever unalterable; and, on the other hand, like plain impossibilities, that are also incorporated in his scheme to suggest that they were not intended to be obeyed, so long, at least, as the Mosaic law held sway. There never could be any hesitation about the proper answer to the question whether their obedience was due to the vision of Ezekiel or to the statutes of Moses. The latter was law; the former was a picture of the future, which in many respects may have been perplexing, but it was not for the guidance of their conduct.

We have looked in every quarter for the promised evidence of a historical development of the feast of the Passover, and have not been able to discover it. Dr. Delitzsch,[1] who advocates the progressive development of the feasts to a certain extent, nevertheless uses the following language: " In the reconstruction of the course of development we are thrown entirely upon the Pentateuch; the historical books give us no certain disclosures; for actual practice has at no time slavishly bound itself to the letter of the law, and consequently no sufficient proof of the existence or non-existence of legal norms can be drawn from the history."

We have now canvassed the whole ground covered by the critics in relation to the Passover. We have minutely examined all the discrepancies and contrarieties which they allege in the history of its institution in Ex. 12, 13; and all the proofs adduced to show that two or more accounts are there blended, whose conflicting representations render them untrustworthy. But we found nothing to militate either against the unity of authorship or the truthfulness of the record. We have carefully examined the mutual relations of the several feast laws to one another and

[1] Riehm's "Handwörterbuch des Biblischen Alterthums." Art. Passah, p. 1142.

to the general body of the legislation in which they are imbedded, and have found that, instead of being distinct and isolated laws, conflicting in their provisions and representing different stages in the development of the ordinance, they are quite harmonious, and, in fact, presuppose and supplement each other. We have examined in succession the various particulars in which the growth of the Passover is said to be traceable in the laws, the original separateness, and subsequent combination of the Passover and the feast of Unleavened Bread, the change from a feast of first-fruits and firstlings to a historical commemoration, from a movable feast regulated by the changing time of harvest to its establishment on a fixed day of the month, the alleged modifications in the ritual, and particularly the change from voluntary offerings of an individual and domestic nature to public sacrifices prescribed with unvarying uniformity, and from a neighborhood festival to its celebration at the national capital; and we have found no evidence of such development in any one direction. There is none discoverable in the laws, there is none discoverable in the history; and even the mysterious vision of Ezekiel leaves the subject where it found it. In the absence then of any good reason for departing from the old and well-attested belief upon this subject, we have a right to conclude that the Passover was from the beginning precisely what is recorded in the history of its institution, and what it is defined to be in the several Mosaic statutes.

VII.
THE FEAST OF WEEKS.

VII.

THE FEAST OF WEEKS.

THE second feast in the Hebrew cycle is called in Ex. 23 : 16 'the feast of Harvest.' It occurred at the end of harvest as the feast of Unleavened Bread did at the beginning, and was observed in acknowledgment of God's bounty shown in the ripened grain. In Ex. 34 : 22, Deut. 16 : 10, it is denominated 'the feast of Weeks,' since it was seven weeks after the Passover; in Num. 28 : 26 'the day of the first-fruits' because of the presentation on that day at the sanctuary of bread made from the first-fruits of the wheat harvest. It is more familiarly known among us by its Greek name 'Pentecost' (fifty), which it bore because of the interval of fifty days from the preceding feast. In the New Testament it is associated with the outpouring of the Holy Spirit and the first ingathering into the Christian Church, the first-fruits of the great harvest of Redemption.

This feast was also called by the Jews עצרת or solemn assembly. Josephus, who mentions this fact (Antiq. III., 10, 6), betrays the most astonishing ignorance of Hebrew by saying that the word means 'fifty,' though it has not the slightest resemblance to that numeral.

THE FEAST OF WEEKS.

Wellhausen,[1] with more ingenuity than good sense, makes a different application of the name 'feast of Weeks' in Ex. 34:22. According to his critical hypothesis, ver. 18, which speaks of the feast of Unleavened Bread, is not an original part of the text in which it stands, but has been transferred from 23:15. Excluding this, he finds all three of the feasts mentioned together in ver. 22,[2] "the feast of Weeks, of the firstfruits of wheat harvest, and the feast of Ingathering." The feast of Weeks he takes to be a common name for the first and second festivals, or rather for the entire joyful period of harvest embraced between them, though only celebrated in a festive manner at its two extremities. The suggestion that the text requires correction, because vs. 19–21 interrupt the connection as they stand at present, however plausible at first sight, is not decisive. The injunction to observe the three annual feasts instead of being given continuously as in 23:15, 16, and as might naturally be expected, is interrupted by the insertion of another subject. They are first bidden to keep the feast of Unleavened Bread, ver. 18. Then comes a law for the sanctification of the first-born, vs. 19, 20, and of the Sabbath day, ver. 21. And after that follows the command to observe the two remaining feasts, ver. 22. Their dislocation, it is said, is the work of some ignorant interpolator, who, not perceiving that all the feasts are named in ver. 22, undertook to remedy the

---

[1] "Geschichte," p. 89.

[2] In "Jahrbücher für Deutsche Theologie," 1876, p. 554, he treats ver. 18 as genuine, and throws ver. 22 out of the text. But a critic may be allowed sometimes to change his mind.

supposed omission by inserting, ver. 18, a special order to observe the feast of Unleavened Bread. But the consecration of the first-born was by a very natural association connected with the feast of Unleavened Bread, since both are alike traced to the last plague of Egypt, and hence they are similarly placed together in other laws. And that the law of the Sabbath is introduced by a like association is evident from the reason here given for its observance. "In ploughing-time and in harvest thou shalt rest." It is a digression, to be sure, but such a digression as is easily explained. And if ver. 18 were an interpolation, it would still remain to be accounted for, that it was not inserted in immediate connection with the other feasts, but at such a remove from it; and this would be as difficult to explain as that it should have been originally written as it now is.

Hitzig[1] makes some very remarkable deductions from this difference of names, and some slight differences in the forms of expression relative to this feast. In Ex. 23 : 16 it is called "the feast of Harvest, the first-fruits of thy labors, which thou hast sown in thy field." Now as barley was the first to mature of all the grains sown in the field, he infers that the feast here stands at the beginning of barley harvest, while the feast of Unleavened Bread according to his hypothesis, spoken of in a former lecture, was observed at the new moon of Abib, or on the first day of that month. In Ex. 34 : 22 it is called "the feast of Weeks, of the first-fruits of wheat harvest," and accordingly had been shifted from the first harvesting of barley

[1] "Ostern und Pfingsten im Zweiten Dekalog," 1838.

to that of wheat, which came later; the designation 'feast of Weeks' is interpreted to mean as many days as there are weeks in the lunar year, *i. e.*, fifty days reckoned from the preceding feast, which still stood on the first day of Abib. In Deut. 16:9, 10, the seven weeks to this feast are no longer reckoned from the first of Abib, but from "such time as thou beginnest to put the sickle to the corn," which brings it later still and puts the feast where it subsequently remained, at the end of wheat harvest.

But the word 'first-fruits' בכורים here used does not denote the very first grains that were reaped, and thus imply that the festival came at the beginning of the reaping instead of at the end. The time for grateful joy and thanksgiving is naturally at the termination of harvest, when the crop has been successfully stored, rather than at the outset when many contingencies are still possible to cloud the prospect. This appears further from the analogy of the succeeding feast, that of Ingathering, which was celebrated after the fruits had been collected. This same word בכורים (first-fruits) is, Lev. 23:17, applied to the wave loaves presented before the LORD after the harvest was over, and is different from that used of the sheaf of first-fruits (ראשית), ver. 10. If accordingly this festival belonged at the end of harvest, Ex. 23:16 can not limit it to the harvest of barley; for it terminates in the middle of the harvest period, and the anomaly would result of a harvest festival with no relation to the wheat, the chief of all the grains, which then would not have been gathered until after the feast. "Thy labors which thou hast sown in thy field" can not be limited to barley, but must embrace wheat as well; so that the celebration must have been in reference to the entire harvest and have stood at its close. The time assigned to this feast in Ex. 23 and 34 and Deut. 16 is, therefore, identical, notwithstanding the slight variations in the form of expression, and the weeks in Ex. 34 are to be reckoned in the same manner as in Deut. 16, where it is more precisely defined.

The feast of Weeks lasted but a single day, while each of the other feasts continued seven days. It is not to be inferred from this that all were originally limited to one day, but that from the special interest attached to the Passover and Tabernacles, they were afterward prolonged: just as mention is made that, both at the dedication of Solomon's temple and the Passover of Hezekiah, the period of seven days was itself doubled on account of the enthusiasm of the occasion, 1 Kin. 8:65, 2 Chron. 30:23. That the feast of Unleavened Bread was in its origin limited to one day was maintained not only by Hitzig, who confined it to the day of the new moon, but also by others who conceived that the commemoration of the events of the exodus would naturally be at first restricted to one anniversary day. According to the uniform testimony of the Passover laws already reviewed, however, the spring feast from the first covered seven days. And the same was the case with the autumnal feast of Tabernacles.

A full festal period was thus a term of seven days, the week being the first denomination of time larger than a day. The adoption of the number seven into the festal cycle was intended to link it with the sabbatical series, of which seven was the regulative factor While the first and the third of the feasts lasted seven days each, the second had a similar association attached to it, though in a somewhat different manner, by being placed at seven times seven days remove from the preceding feast. The ordinary festal offering day by day likewise had, combined with other animals, the invariable number of seven lambs, or in Tabernacles of twice seven, while the total number of bullocks offered in a gradually diminishing scale throughout the seven days of the feast was seventy or ten times seven. And besides this septenary link of connection there was the sabbatical idea itself. One or more days were set apart in each feast for special religious devotion; labor was suspended and a holy convocation held, though the rigor of the abstinence from work was not so strict as upon the weekly Sabbath. On the latter the command was, Ye shall do no work; on the former, Ye shall do no servile work. All the sacred times were thus bound together into one common system, in their essence pervaded by the same idea, in their outward form marked by the prominence of the same sacred number.

The brevity of the feast of Weeks as compared with the other principal annual festivals naturally suggests the idea of its sustaining to one or the other some relation of subordination. And the fact of its time being determined by a fixed interval between it and its predecessor naturally raises the query whether they may not belong together. Accordingly Ewald devised an ingenious and remarkably symmetrical scheme on the hypothesis that the feast of Weeks was primarily and properly an appendage of the feast of Unleavened Bread. He considered it the formal close of that seven-day festival, standing in the same relation to it as the eighth day of Tabernacles to the preceding seven, not strictly a part of it, yet so attached to it as to bring the whole to a solemn and suitable termination. Only the feast of Weeks was separated from the body of the festival to which it belonged by the entire period of the intervening harvest season, which all received a consecration from being enclosed within hallowed and festive limits. And the parallel was pushed still further by observing that each of the two principal feasts was in turn preceded by a special service, and this of a nature which had its analogy in the ordinary method of the ceremonial and in the ideas which it customarily embodied. "Just as every great sacrifice may be initiated by an expiatory offering, and just as a suitable preparation and purification should form the commencement of every sacred action, so each of these two great annual festivals was preceded by a special festival of expiation, which was celebrated with great solemnity."[1] Tabernacles was thus preceded by the annual day of Atonement, on the tenth of the month, and Unleavened Bread by the Passover, which though slain on the fourteenth was, at its original institution, selected and set apart on the tenth.

The whole year was divided into two nearly equal portions. There was, first, the festal period, extend-

[1] Ewald's "Antiquities of Israel," translated (Boston, 1876), p 357.

ing from the middle of the first to the middle of the seventh month, within which all the festivals of the year were embraced. Then the remaining six months constituted a non-festal period, marked by the absence of any sacred festival. The festal portion of the year was again divided between the two great feasts, the vernal and the autumnal feast, the former occurring in the first month and thus opening the year; the latter forming its centre and culmination in the seventh, to which was accorded the dignity of the sacred or sabbatical month. In Tabernacles the festal idea rose to its maximum, as was shown by the duplication of sacrifices and by the fact that pilgrims were required to remain not one day, as at Passover, but the whole seven days, and one beyond. And each of these great festivals, which thus marked and, as it were, guarded the limits of the festal portion of the year, was composed alike of three constituents of similar character; first an expiation, then the main body of the feast lasting seven days, then one more day as a concluding festival at the end.

The striking correspondence thus exhibited certainly lends great attractiveness to this scheme, which has accordingly been extensively adopted. It is notwithstanding open to serious objections.

1. The virtual reduction of the feasts to two is an evident departure from the genuine Hebrew conception, as appears from the uniform triplicity of the festal laws, which from the beginning name three great feasts as so many distinct and separate festivals, the feast of Unleavened Bread, the feast of Weeks and the feast of Tabernacles.

THE FEAST OF WEEKS. 251

2. This scheme assumes that Unleavened Bread like the feast of Weeks is mainly and distinctively a harvest festival; that they are so entirely of the same tenor and design that one can be regarded as the continuation of the other; whereas the former was instituted in commemoration of the exodus, upon the anniversary of which it was observed. It, therefore, was historical in its intent and character, and properly speaking stood in no other relation to the harvest than that of conjunction in point of time; while the feast of Weeks was in the strict and proper sense a harvest festival. There was no such congruity between the two, therefore, as brought one into the intimate relation to the other which Ewald's scheme supposes.

3. This view also leads to the solecism, remarked upon in a former lecture, of celebrating the harvest feast before the harvest itself was reaped. George[1] indeed says: "In itself considered it appears to be a matter of indifference whether a harvest feast is celebrated at the beginning or end of harvest; and in our way of looking at the thing, it is more natural to observe the feast when the grain has been brought in from the field..... As, however, they were not content with the simple expression of thanks, but believed it to be incumbent on them to offer a part of the harvest unto God, and the first-fruits were selected for this purpose, the harvest feast must necessarily come at the beginning." The Jewish lawgiver judged differently; he put the ceremony of the sheaf of the first-fruits at the beginning of harvest,

[1] "Die älteren Jüdischen Feste," p. 260.

but the harvest festival itself at the end. And upon his own view of the case George finds himself puzzled to account for the observance of the feast of Weeks at all; but finally concludes that the Passover had special relation to the barley harvest and the feast of Weeks to the wheat harvest. But why the inferior grain should be emphasized by a feast of seven days, and that which was chiefly valued and furnished the principal staple of their subsistence, should call for a feast of but one day, he does not explain.

4. The historical association of the Passover likewise distinguishes it broadly from its assumed counterpart, the day of Atonement, which had no such association. The Passover was an initiatory expiation and an act of communion with God, in which the bitter herbs were suggestive of Egyptian bondage; but the whole service, so far from having the stern and severe aspect which has sometimes been attributed to it, was on the contrary calculated to enkindle thankful and joyous recollections of a great deliverance. The day of Atonement, on the other hand, was the one fast of the Jewish calendar, a day of humiliation and penitence, in which all were to afflict their souls, and by significant and striking symbols the sins of the past year were atoned for and removed.

5. The feast of Unleavened Bread was brought to a formal close by the services of its seventh day, which was observed as a Sabbath, Ex. 12 : 16, 13 : 6, and bears the same name עֲצֶרֶת Deut. 16 : 8, that is applied to the eighth day or concluding festival of Tabernacles. And not only was unleavened bread not

required to be eaten at the feast of Weeks, which was the special characteristic of the preceding festival, but leavened bread was actually directed to be offered to the LORD, which was not enjoined at any other feast or sacrifice.

The true relation of this feast is best set forth by Hupfeld,[1] and this is in fact the most valuable and satisfactory result of his discussion of this whole subject. While the Passover and feast of Unleavened Bread are distinctively commemorative of a great event in their national history, the divine deliverance from the bondage of Egypt, which brought them into being as a nation and as the LORD'S people, the two remaining feasts are agricultural and are designed to give expression to their joyful thanksgiving for the products of the ground. They obviously form a class by themselves, therefore, having the same general design and tendency. Besides these, and preceding them both, was the presentation of the sheaf of first-fruits at the Passover, which was the first formal act in public recognition of God's annual bounty. The acknowledgment of God's goodness in the year in supplying the means of subsistence accordingly advanced by three successive stages to its climax, in which Pentecost held the intermediate position.

There was first a barley sheaf,[2] brought at the be-

---

[1] "De primitiva et vera festorum ratione," Part 2.

[2] Wellhausen correctly infers from the special title, Lev. 23 : 9, 10, that in the plan of this chapter the oresentation of the barley sheaf, though occurring at Passover, is separated from it and attached to what follows because it is regarded as preliminary to Pentecost. " Jahrb. für Deutsche Theologie," XXII., p. 432.

ginning of harvest to be waved before the LORD, accompanied by a lamb as a burnt-offering and an appropriate meat-offering, significant of consecration. This act was to be performed upon one of the days of the feast of Unleavened Bread, a day, therefore, which in this general sense belonged to a sacred term, but not one specially hallowed as a festal Sabbath by abstinence from toil and a holy convocation. This gave its consecration to the harvest season then beginning, and no one was allowed to eat from the new grain bread or parched corn or green ears, until this offering had first been brought to God. Then came the feast of Weeks at the close of harvest, when the joy and thankfulness of the husbandman had been correspondingly heightened; this found its fit expression not merely in a sacred ceremony as before, performed on one of the ordinary days of a feast which was instituted for a different purpose, but in a feast specially appointed for this sole end, and upon a day which was sacredly observed as a Sabbath with its holy convocation. Then not merely a single sheaf of barley was presented and waved before the LORD, but two loaves of leavened wheat bread; the number was duplicated,[1] and instead of the crude material the final product prepared for human use was presented at the sanctuary, thus hallowing all the bread which they would use in their households

---

[1] The two loaves were to be made, Lev. 23 : 17, of two tenths of an ephah, or two omers, Ex. 16 : 36, of flour. As the word for sheaf, Lev. 23 : 10, 11, is also עֹמֶר *omer*, it is not improbable that it was of such a size as to yield an omer of grain; so that the quantity may have been precisely doubled.

THE FEAST OF WEEKS. 255

day by day. And to this was added not merely one lamb as before, but ten sacrificial animals for a burnt-offering denoting consecration; a kid of the goats for a sin-offering to make expiation for that sense of unworthiness which the reception of God's free gifts inspires, and with a fresh duplication of the former number two lambs as a peace-offering to represent and seal communion with God.

But with all the emphasis thus thrown upon this occasion, the feast was limited to a single day; this abbreviation of the full festal period showing that the climax was not yet reached. This came with the third and last member of the series at the close of the ingathering of fruits from the oliveyards and the vineyards, when all the products of the year had been stored, and the toil of the husbandman had received its full reward, in the feast of Tabernacles, which was not only prolonged to the complete festal term of seven days, but had an added day beyond it, and in which sacrifices were offered with a profusion unknown at any other festival. The feast of Weeks is the second stage in this ascending scale, linked both to the preceding ceremonial and to the succeeding feast, an appropriate termination to the harvest of grain, but when the husbandman was still looking forward to the ingathering of fruits.

The true position thus awarded by Hupfeld to this feast was unfortunately somewhat marred by his change of the calendar, which spoiled the symmetry of the festal period of the year, and disturbed the proper relation of the two great festivals. His idea that the feast of Unleavened Bread signified and sealed the priestly consecration of the people, led him to throw the chief emphasis upon it as marking the climax of the year, and consequently to invert the order of the feasts by adopting the reckoning of the civil instead of the ecclesiastical year, in which the seventh month became the first, and the first month the seventh. Tabernacles thus came to stand in his scheme at the beginning of the year, which was then opened by the feast of Trumpets on the first day of the same month as the formal proclamation of the new year. Passover then stood at the central or climactic point, in which the people reached their highest dignity in their elevation to sacerdotal communion with God, the Passover as a personal and domestic expiation, being likewise held to rank above the day of Atonement for the sins of the people *en masse*.

But this is plainly an inversion of Hebrew conceptions which Riehm[1] in reproducing Hupfeld's scheme has very properly corrected. The accumulation of festivals in the seventh month proclaims it to be the sacred culmination of the year, as the lengthened term of Tabernacles, and its multiplied sacrifices declare it to be the climactic festival, which it must in fact be upon Hupfeld's own showing of its relation to the sheaf of first-fruits and to the feast of Weeks.

The critics claim that there has been a development in the feast of Weeks like that which they essay to show in the other two great feasts, viz., a tendency at least to change its character from an agricultural feast to a historical commemoration; a

---

[1] "Handwörterbuch des Biblischen Alterthums." Art. Feste.

THE FEAST OF WEEKS. 257

change in the time of holding it which at first varied with the season, but came ultimately to be attached to a determinate date; a change in its ritual from voluntary gifts on individual account to public sacrifices regulated by statute, and a change in place from the various local sanctuaries to the temple at the capital of the nation.

The agricultural character and aim of this feast is undeniable; this is sufficiently indicated by the names applied to it, the added descriptions of its design, the peculiar ceremonial appointed for it, and the time of its occurrence at the end of harvest, which was estimated by a definite period of time from its beginning. And no other character is attributed to it or in the remotest way suggested for it in the laws of the Pentateuch. The admonition coupled with it, Deut. 16: 12, to remember that they were bondmen in the land of Egypt, does not suggest an additional reason for the institution of the feast, but is meant to enforce the kindly and generous use of the opportunity which it affords, to befriend the impoverished and dependent classes by the remembrance of their own late distressed condition. It is a motive which the legislator repeatedly employs, and has its value as an indication of the time when the laws were given. Such a reminder would be of great force in the mouth of Moses; it would have been absolutely ridiculous in the time of Josiah. But there is no suggestion in it that the occasion of the feast was in any way historical or connected with the exodus. The later Jews came indeed to associate it with the giving of the law, as the interval between it and the

THE FEAST OF WEEKS.

Passover corresponded in a general way at least with the recorded time between Israel's leaving Egypt and encamping at the base of Sinai. That was simply a deduction, however, made in post-biblical times, which is not alluded to even by Philo or Josephus, and to which there is no reference in Scripture, not even in the passages 2 Chron. 15 : 10, 12, John 5 : 1, 39, in which Vaihinger¹ professes to find it. It has no bearing, consequently, upon the question whether a development can be traced in the feast laws themselves, so that they must be assigned to different ages. It may, therefore, be dismissed.

The allegation that this was at first a movable feast lacks confirmation. The general and somewhat indefinite allusion to it, Ex. 23 : 16, merely establishes its relation to the harvest without in any way defining the time of its occurrence. The repetition of this law, however, in Ex. 34 : 22, by applying to it the designation 'feast of Weeks,' shows that it must have been observed a certain number of weeks after some given epoch from which it was calculated. What this was we learn more definitely from Deut. 16 : 9, 10. The feast is there placed at the end of seven weeks from the time of beginning to put the sickle to the corn. This, it is claimed, is making it dependent upon the state of the crop, not upon the phases of the moon or the day of the month.

[1] Herzog's "Encyklopädie," Art. Pfingstfest, p. 483. On the preceding page he quotes Maimonides ("More Nebochim," 3, 43) as saying, "The feast of Weeks was that day on which the law was given." To the question, When did God give the ten commandments? the Wurtemburg catechism answers, "On the fiftieth day after the exodus of the children of Israel out of Egypt."

But, 1. While this would fix it approximately at the end of harvest, it is observable that it is not stated in that form, as would have been most natural, if it had been intended to conform precisely to the season. The statement is not that the feast will be held as soon as they have finished reaping their corn, but a given number of weeks from the time of beginning, irrespective of any variations in the actual duration of the harvest in different years.

George[1] says on this point: "It would have been the most natural for it to have coincided with the end of work in harvest, and so have come earlier or later, according as this was accomplished more quickly or more slowly. We must, therefore, assume that there was originally an indefinite interval between the two feasts; but all authorities fail us in this matter, and so nothing definite can be established in regard to it. So far as we can follow it, we always find a fixed time between the two feasts, the injunction being that it should be celebrated seven full weeks after the Passover; and from this it even derived its name, 'the feast of Weeks.'" What the critic assumes, merely upon the strength of his own hypothesis and confessedly without evidence, is of no weight as an argument.

2. This mode of estimating the proper time for the celebration of the feast occurs in Deuteronomy, which steadfastly insists on all the feasts being observed at the common sanctuary. That being the case, its time must have been determined by some rule which all could apply alike. As the time of be-

[1] "Die älteren Jüdischen Feste," p. 259.

ginning to reap the harvest differed considerably in different parts of the land, some definite point of beginning for the seven weeks must be here referred to, which all could ascertain, or pilgrims would come straggling in at different times, and there would be no festival held by all in common.

3. We are consequently thrown upon the language of other laws to relieve if possible the vagueness of the expression when "thou beginnest to put the sickle to the corn." In Num. 28:26 it is also vaguely stated as 'in your weeks'; *i. e.*, in your feast of Weeks, implying some determinate mode of reckoning them, which was well known, and which it was not thought necessary here to repeat. The missing information is supplied, Lev. 23:15, that the seven weeks were to be reckoned from the day of bringing the sheaf of the wave-offering, which was upon a definite day of the Passover feast, "declared in the law to be on the morrow after the Sabbath." There is scarcely any point in the ritual that has been more disputed than the meaning of this expression.

George[1] contends that the whole passage respecting the sheaf of first-fruits and the feast of Weeks, vs. 9-22, is a fragment derived from some other source and inserted by the author of Lev. 23, because it suited his purpose. It is, he says, quite distinct in character from the rest of the chapter, and does not deal in the same phrases and expressions or ideas. It describes in minute detail the sacrifices to be offered, while the rest of the chapter is occupied with feasts and feast days and the mode of their ob-

---

[1] "Die älteren Jüdischen Feste," pp. 124 ff.

servance, specifying fixed dates in each case which are not given in this passage; moreover its closing verse relates to the care of the poor, which has nothing to do with the feasts. On these grounds he concludes that it had originally stood in quite a different connection; and that consequently it is out of all relation to the preceding part of the chapter and can not properly be explained by it, but must be interpreted by itself. He further argues that the word 'Sabbath' here employed can from its usage mean nothing but the weekly Sabbath; that counting seven Sabbaths can not be equivalent to seven weeks unless these be weeks ending in and limited by Sabbaths; and especially the phrase "the morrow after the seventh Sabbath," ver. 16, compels to the conclusion that 'Sabbath' is here used in its strict and only authorized sense.

He hence concludes that the Sabbath here spoken of is an ordinary weekly Sabbath, immediately preceding the harvest, which he thinks would naturally begin with the week. On this first day of harvest, then, which is likewise the first day of the week, and had nothing to do with the Passover, but is simply determined by the time when "ye shall reap the harvest," ver. 10, the sheaf of first-fruits was presented. From this seven Sabbaths more were to be numbered, and on the next day, which would again be the first day of the week, Pentecost was to be celebrated. It is obvious to remark that upon this showing no fixed date is assigned to Pentecost here¹ or anywhere else

---

¹ Unless it is claimed that the author of Lev. 23 intended that 'the Sabbath' should in the connection in which he placed it find its ex-

in the Pentateuch; and there is no development whatever in this respect in the Mosaic laws. The definite determination of the date, as we find it subsequently in Josephus and in the New Testament, arose from a misinterpretation of the law, and of course can not be cited to prove that the laws themselves represent the feasts at different stages of their growth and hence are to be attributed to distinct periods.

The passage, which George in common with Hupfeld and Wellhausen regards as a fragment inserted in this chapter from another quarter, is nevertheless a constituent part of it. For,

1. If this paragraph, vs. 9–22, were excluded from the chapter, it would give no account of the feast of Weeks whatever, which necessarily belongs in a complete conspectus of the feasts and is included in every other feast law.

2. The minute account given of the special services of this day and of the presentation of the sheaf at the beginning of harvest, which is urged as a reason for its belonging elsewhere, is, on the contrary, an indication of the consistent plan pursued by the writer. He had given full details of the mode of observing the Passover in Ex. 12, 13, and of the day of Atonement in Lev. 16. These consequently can be passed over in a few general sentences. But he had said nothing whatever of the ritual of the harvest-feast, nor of the mode of celebrating the feast of Taber-

planation in the Passover of the preceding paragraph; in which case the proof to be furnished that vs. 9–22 originally belong to this chapter nevertheless annuls the supposed evidence of a change in the time of the feast.

nacles. Upon these two points, therefore, he dwells at large. And the fact that he does so, instead of creating the suspicion that these passages are borrowed from another source, strengthens the conviction that there is but one and the same writer throughout.

3. The striking resemblance in phraseology and form of thought between this passage and ch. 25 which is plainly a continuation of ch. 23, and is by the critics referred to the same author, shows that they must be by one writer, and consequently that the passage in question belongs properly in the context in which it is found. Both begin in the same identical terms, 23 : 9, 10, 25 : 1, 2, "And the LORD spake unto Moses saying, Speak unto the children of Israel and say unto them," etc. And then the remarkable correspondence of the harvest term of fifty days, 23 : 15, 16, with the jubilee term of fifty years, 25 : 8, numbering seven Sabbaths until the morrow after the Sabbath in one case and seven Sabbaths of years unto the following year in the other; the one an acknowledgment of God's ownership of the harvest by presenting unto him first the sheaf and then the loaves of the first-fruits; the other an acknowledgment of God's ownership of the land by surrendering to him the whole of its produce in the Sabbatical year and the land itself for redistribution in the year of Jubilee. These must have sprung from the same mind and the same thought, and the very terms of expression are the same. All vouches for identity of authorship.

4. Num., ch. 28, 29, is evidently based on Lev. 23;

and Num. 28 : 26 plainly alludes to the contents of Lev. 23 : 15 ff. and would be unintelligible without it, thus freshly showing that it is in its proper place.

5. Lev. 23 : 22, which is specially objected to, is but a repetition of 19 : 9, 10, which is here introduced again by a very natural association.

This passage can not, therefore, with George be torn from its proper connection. The phrase which we are considering, "on the morrow after the Sabbath," must find its explanation in what had just before been said in relation to the Passover. Hitzig[1] proposes to explain it thus in his own peculiar way. He claims that according to Hebrew reckoning the first day of the year was not only the first day of the first month, but the first day of the week likewise, so that the seventh day of the first month was always a Sabbath. Accordingly Ezekiel 45 : 20 appoints a special sacrificial service for that day. The fourteenth day, on which the Passover was slain, would likewise be a Sabbath. And as the fifteenth or first day of Unleavened Bread was required to be hallowed by abstinence from labor and by a holy convocation, two Sabbaths here came together, a weekly Sabbath and a festive Sabbath, and this, in his opinion, was the reason why the paschal lamb was to be slain " between the evenings," in that doubtful interval which in strictness belonged to neither of these holy days, but lay between them. Deuteronomy, however, which does not attach the feasts to particular days of the month or week, drops this peculiar expression and directs the lamb to be slain "at even, at the go-

[1] "Ostern und Pfingsten," 1837.

THE FEAST OF WEEKS. 265

ing down of the sun." They were enjoined at the Passover feast to eat unleavened bread seven days; the seventh was a holy convocation, and servile work was forbidden; then on the "morrow after the Sabbath" they might eat bread, Lev. 23:14, *i.e.*, ordinary or leavened bread. This seventh day of the feast, which would be the twenty-first of the month, and the Sabbath referred to are, therefore, identical. From this the reckoning is made to Pentecost, which as the day after the seventh Sabbath, would invariably be the first day of the week. Josephus (Antiq. xiii., 8, 4) mentions that in the Parthian war Pentecost occurred the day after the Sabbath, and this accounted for a two days' rest of the army. How, he asks, could Josephus know this to be a fact or express himself about it as he does, unless Pentecost always occurred on the day after the Jewish Sabbath? On this basis he further undertakes to explain the puzzling expression in Luke 6:1, "the second-first Sabbath," by which he understands the first day of Unleavened Bread. By his hypothesis it always came after a weekly Sabbath, and thus was itself a second Sabbath; while at the same time in relation to the seventh day of the feast, which was also a Sabbath, it was the first. It was second in one respect, and first in another, and thus a second-first Sabbath.

Hitzig makes the sheaf of first-fruits to be presented on the twenty-second of the month, which is entirely outside of the limits of the sacred festival. And with him Kayser[1] agrees. Knobel and Kurtz[2] seek to

---
[1] "Das Vorexilische Buch," p. 74.
[2] "Alttestamentliche Opfercultus," p. 308 f.

correct this, while accepting the hypothesis in other respects, by placing it a week earlier. They suppose the Sabbath intended to be the fourteenth of the month, and that the sheaf was presented on the fifteenth or the first day of Unleavened Bread.

This hypothesis, however modified, is wrecked by its unsupported and untenable assumption that the first day of the year was invariably the first day of the week. This would always leave a broken week at the end of the year and be inconsistent with the fourth commandment. It is inconsistent also with Ex. 12 : 16, Lev. 23 : 8 ; for although the seventh day of Unleavened Bread by this hypothesis was a weekly Sabbath only servile work was forbidden and certain kinds of work were allowed.

According to the Baithusians [1] or Karaites the Sabbath in question is "the Sabbath of the creation," or the regular weekly Sabbath, occurring during the feast, on whichever day of Unleavened Bread it may fall; and to this Wellhausen [2] and Dillmann give their adhesion as most consistent with the language employed. But it is difficult to see why the presentation of the sheaf should be regulated by the weekly Sabbath, with which it has no obvious connection, while there would be a natural propriety in having the ceremony take place at one particular period in the festival. It is also liable to the objection that whenever the Sabbath occurred on the last day of Unleavened Bread the sheaf of first-fruits would not be presented until after the feast had ended.

[1] Lightfoot, "Hebrew and Talmudical Exercitations" on Luke 6 : 1 and Acts 2 : 1.

[2] "Zeitschrift für Deutsche Theologie," XXII., p. 433.

THE FEAST OF WEEKS. 267

The traditional interpretation, which is certainly as old as the Septuagint, and is besides vouched for by Josephus and Philo and the usage of the second temple, understands by the 'Sabbath' the first day of Unleavened Bread, which was observed as a festal Sabbath; according to this the sheaf was presented on the second day of the feast. And with this agrees Josh. 5:11, which informs us that the children of Israel after partaking of the Passover at Gilgal "did eat of the produce of the land on the morrow after the Passover, unleavened bread and parched corn on the self-same day." The reference to the Passover-law here is plain; and it is evident that the people governed themselves by its directions. They kept the Passover on the fourteenth day of the month at even, precisely as the law required, Lev. 23:5. They had previously circumcised all those who had not received this rite in the wilderness, in obedience to the statute, Ex. 12:48, that "no uncircumcised person shall eat thereof." The bread which they ate was unleavened agreeably to the command, Lev. 23:6. It was then "the time of harvest," Josh. 3:15, but they had refrained from eating of the productions of the country until "the morrow after the Passover," when they freely partook of them "on the self-same day." Clearly this is their interpretation of the law, Lev. 23:14, which forbade their eating "bread or parched corn or green ears until the self-same day" that they brought their offering of the sheaf "on the morrow after the Sabbath." "The morrow after the Sabbath" in the law is thus defined by the practice of the generation that entered Canaan under Joshua to mean "the morrow after the Passover."

But, say Kurtz and Knobel, they ate the Passover on the fourteenth day at even; the morrow after the Passover must, as in Num. 33 : 3, where the identical expression is employed, have been the fifteenth, or the first day of Unleavened Bread, which according to tradition is the Sabbath referred to in the law and not the morrow after the Sabbath, which was the following day, the sixteenth of the month. This difficulty appears to have embarrassed the translators of the Authorized Version,[1] who lest the children of Israel might here seem to have eaten of the new harvest a day sooner than the law allowed, have rendered "the old corn of the land," where the original has simply "produce," with evident allusion to the crop then just reaped.

But all the trouble arises from the ambiguity of the phrase. "Beyond Jordan" may denote either side of the river according as it is "beyond Jordan eastward," Josh. 1 : 15, or "beyond Jordan westward," 5 : 1. A person who shortly after midnight of Tuesday should speak of "to-morrow" might mean by it Wednesday, inasmuch as daylight had not yet broken, or he might mean Thursday, as by civil reckoning Wednesday had already begun. In certain portions of New England it was formerly the usage to regard the Sabbath as beginning at sunset of Saturday. All secular occupations and amusements terminated then, the holy day of rest continuing until the following sunset, which ushered in Monday and with it the transition to secular time. It is easy to

---

[1] The British Revisers have likewise retained 'old corn' in the text, for which the appendix substitutes 'produce.'

THE FEAST OF WEEKS.

perceive the ambiguity which might exist in the use of the word 'to-morrow' under these circumstances In the shades of evening after the Sabbath had begun, it might mean the day succeeding the Sabbath, *i. e.*, Monday, or the day succeeding the night upon which they had just entered, *i. e.*, Sunday. We are sensible of precisely the same ambiguity in the phrase "next week" uttered on Sunday morning; the secular portion of the week not having yet begun, the reference may be to the days which immediately follow; or as in strict reckoning the new week has commenced already, the period intended may be seven days later. So the Passover was celebrated on the evening of the fourteenth; but that evening was the beginning of another day which continued until the following evening, and 'the morrow after the Passover' may mean the fifteenth, as it does in Num. 33 : 3; but it may with equal propriety denote the sixteenth of the month, as it does in Josh. 5 : 11, which is in perfect consistency with the law as traditionally explained, and requires no forced interpretation or fanciful and unfounded hypothesis.

But can the first day of Unleavened Bread merely from the fact that all servile work is forbidden and a holy convocation required, be called a "Sabbath" as the term is here used without qualification? We are told that a festal day of rest might be called a *Sabbathōn* or a *Sabbath Sabbathōn*, but not simply a Sabbath. But in this very chapter, Lev. 23 : 32, we read of the day of Atonement : "It shall be unto you a *Sabbath Sabbathōn;* .... from even unto even shall ye celebrate your Sabbath." The Sabbatical year is called a *Sabbathōn*, Lev. 25 : 5, a *Sabbath Sabbathōn*, 25 : 4, and repeatedly a Sabbath, 25 : 2, 4, 6, 8, 26 : 34, 35, 43. The weekly Sabbath is called *Sabbathōn Sabbath*, Ex. 16 : 23, and *Sabbath. Sabbathōn*, Ex. 32 : 15, 35 : 2, Lev. 23 : 3, as well as Sabbath. The predominant application of *Sabbathōn* to festival days of rest, Lev. 16 : 31, 23 : 24, 39, is no bar, therefore, to giving them the denomination of Sabbath, with which it would seem to be convertible.

But as both the first and seventh days of Unleavened Bread were observed as Sabbaths, Kliefoth[1] contends that the latter, ver. 8, must be meant in Lev. 23 : 11, rather than the former, ver. 7, which is more remote. And Hupfeld[2] adds that on the traditional interpretation the harvest would fall within the term of the feast and the permission to eat of the new grain would conflict with the prohibition of leaven. But the superior prominence of the first day on which the whole festival was founded, makes it emphatically *the* Sabbath. The most obvious explanation of the permission to return home on the day after the Passover is the ripened harvest. Permitted absence from the ceremonial of the sheaf, which Kurtz thinks impossible, is as easily explicable as from the holy convocation; while the postponement of the ceremony till after the end of the feast would be incongruous. The prohibition to eat bread of the new harvest before the feast, which might be possible in some years, certainly gives no sanction to the use of leaven after the feast had begun, comp. Josh. 5 : 11.

[1] "Die ursprüngliche Gottesdienstordnung," I., p. 146.
[2] "De primitiva et vera festorum ratione," Part 2, p. 4.

That the Hebrew word 'Sabbath' may be used in the sense of 'week' may be argued apart from this passage, from its having this meaning in Chaldee, Syriac, and the Greek of the New Testament, Luke 18 : 12. 'I fast twice in the week' (δις τοῦ σαββάτου), and Mat. 28 : 1, where both meanings occur together in the same verse, "In the end of the Sabbath as it began to dawn toward the first day of the week." [1] And it may be further illustrated by the word חדש which, though primarily denoting 'new moon,' is used not only of the interval from one new moon to another, but of a month at whatever time it may begin. Counting seven Sabbaths is therefore equivalent to counting seven weeks; and the morrow after the seventh Sabbath is the same as the next day after the seventh week.

Lightfoot[2] explains the δευτεροπρώτῳ of Luke 6 : 1 as not 'the second Sabbath after the first,' but 'the first Sabbath after the second,' *i. e.*, the first of the seven Sabbaths following the second day of Unleavened Bread, from which the fifty days to Pentecost were counted.

The 'morrow after the Sabbath' on which the sheaf was waved before the LORD, Lev. 23 : 11, only defines more precisely what is stated in general terms in Deut. 16 : 9, as beginning to put the sickle to the corn. The very same time is intended in either case; no change had occurred in the period of the festival.

And no change took place in its duration. Mention is indeed made in later times in the period of

---

[1] 'Οψὲ δὲ σαββάτων, τῇ ἐπιφωσκούσῃ εἰς μίαν σαββάτων.

[2] "Exercitations" on Mat. 12 : 1.

the dispersion that Jews remote from Palestine observed two days instead of one, from their uncertainty which was the real day, the calendar being regulated by the appearance of the new moon at Jerusalem. This can not be adduced, therefore, in proof of a tendency to prolong festivals; besides it is foreign to the subject before us, as it belongs wholly to post-biblical times.

Nor can any change be shown to have taken place in the ritual. Ex. 23 : 19 and 34 : 26 connect with it the oblation of first-fruits. Deut. 16 : 10 f. directs the bringing of a free-will offering to the LORD accompanied by a joyful feast. Lev. 23 : 16 ff. prescribes the wave-offering of the two loaves with accompanying sacrifices,—not, as George interprets it, two loaves from every house, which, it has been well said, the priests would never have been able to consume, but two loaves such as were in ordinary use in their houses in the name of the whole people. Num. 28 : 26 f. ordains the proper festal offerings. But as has been seen already in the case of the Passover, these do not exclude, but supplement each other. There was no transition from private oblations in an earlier period to public sacrifices at a later time; but the day was characterized by both from the beginning. The one class is definitely prescribed as a matter of course, while the other is left to the pleasure of the offerer. But each held its appropriate place, and neither was permitted to override the other.

The discrepancy which has been alleged between the sacrifices enjoined upon this day in Lev. 23 and Num. 28 does not exist; for they are quite distinct in design and character, and both were offered. The one is a simple accompaniment of the loaves, and for that reason only is stated in Lev. 23, which does not in any case name the proper festal offerings. These latter are given in Num. 28, which prescribes the offering for this feast-day as such; and it is precisely identical with that which is enjoined for each day of Unleavened Bread.

Neither was there a transfer of this feast from local sanctuaries to one central place of worship. The same arguments are available here as in the case of the Passover. The very first reference to this feast implies its observance at one locality, and a centralized worship generally. Ex. 23 and 34 not only enjoin three pilgrimages in the year, in which all the males shall appear before the LORD God, but direct with specific reference to this feast: "The first of the firstfruits of thy land thou shalt bring into the house of the LORD thy God."

The appeal to history to sustain the critics' hypothesis is here particularly unsuccessful, for with the exception of Chronicles, which is not allowed to be an authority, except for the time when it was written, there is no mention of this feast in the entire Old Testament apart from the Pentateuch. We read in 2 Chron. 8: 12, 13, of Solomon's offering burnt-offerings unto the LORD, on the altar of the LORD which he had built, besides other occasions, "three times in the year, in the feast of Unleavened Bread, and in the feast of Weeks and in the feast of Tabernacles." This is confirmed by the parallel passage in 1 Kin. 9: 25, "Three times in a year did Solomon offer burnt-offerings and peace-offerings upon the altar which he built unto the LORD." Though the occasions of these offerings are not more particularly specified, their recurrence thrice in the year naturally suggests the three great festivals. To admit this, however, would be to confess that they were all celebrated at Jerusalem in the time of Solomon, which is contrary to the critical hypothesis. Even Ezekiel makes no allusion to the feast of Weeks, when prescribing a new ritual, ordaining sacrifices, and giving specific directions concerning the feasts of Passover and Tabernacles. This seemed so strange and unaccountable that the text has been altered to the complete destruction of the sense in order to introduce it. "The Passover, a feast of seven days," Ezek. 45 : 21, has by the insertion of a letter been made to read "the Passover, a feast of weeks of days"; and the attempt has been made to justify this reading on the assumption that the expression is meant to embrace both feasts as well as the interval that lay between them. The true correction is supplied by a comparison of Num. 28 : 16, 17, on which the verse in Ezekiel is manifestly based. Wellhausen admits without hesitation that the feast of Weeks can not be here referred to.

The fact, then, is that while the feast of Weeks is one of the three great annual festivals ordained in what the critics declare to be the very earliest codes, Ex. 23 and 34, it is nowhere mentioned in the history before the exile, nor by any prophet or psalmist, notwithstanding their allusions to the joy of harvest and the fruits of the earth and the first-fruits, which would have made such a mention natural. It is besides completely ignored by Ezekiel in his arrangements for the worship and the sanctuary. There is not even the slightest allusion to it in the writings after the exile, and no record of its observance by Ezra or the returned captives. The first and only reference to it is found in Chronicles, which the critics tell us could not have been written before the time of Alexander the Great.[1] The passage in Chronicles affirms its observance in Solomon's days; but the only conclusion that in the opinion of the critics is at all reliable is that this feast was observed at the time when this book was written. We may here see in a conspicuous instance the value of the argument from silence, which plays so important a part in modern critical reasoning. What becomes of the confident assertion that sin-offerings and trespass-offerings had no existence before the time of Ezekiel, who first proposed them, 40:39,[2] etc., and that the Pentateuchal laws, in which they are found, are thus shown to be post-exilic? Or that the annual day of Atonement was not even incorporated in the law so early as the days of Ezra? The feast of Weeks wrests their main weapon palpably from their hands.

And the law of development, on which they so strenuously insist, has, as we have seen, no application to it. Even George is compelled to acknowledge,

[1] Wellhausen's edition of Bleek's " Einleitung in das Alte Testament," p. 288.

[2] This is leaving out of the account or explaining away 2 Kin. 12: 16; 2 Chron. 29:21-24; Ps. 40:6; Hos. 4:8; Isa. 53:10.

"Of the Jewish feasts this is the one that has remained truest to its original mode of celebration, and has in the course of time experienced only a very trifling development." It would have been more accurate to say no development at all.

VIII.

THE FEAST OF TABERNACLES.

VIII.

THE FEAST OF TABERNACLES

THE last of the three great feasts, which closed the sacred cycle and terminated the festive portion of the year is, in Ex. 23 : 16, 34 : 22, denominated the feast of Ingathering, and elsewhere the feast of Tabernacles. This, as its name denoted, had special, though not exclusive relation to the ingathering of fruits from oliveyards and vineyards, the oil and the wine. Coming after the latest products of the year, it fitly commemorated God's goodness in the whole, who had plentifully rewarded all the labors of the husbandman, who, Ps. 104 : 14, 15, had brought forth food out of the earth, wine that maketh glad the heart of man, and oil to make his face to shine, and bread which strengtheneth man's heart. And hence, although the feast of Weeks was specially appointed to express the grateful joy of harvest, both the harvest and the vintage are joined together as giving occasion for the feast that followed. Deut. 16: 13, " Thou shalt observe the feast of Tabernacles after that thou hast gathered in thy corn and thy wine." Thus their occasions of exuberant joy and worldly gain and patriotic fervor were their sacred times, when they gathered at the sanctuary of God and poured out their thankful praise before him. Their secular life became thus a consecrated life; their secular joy a joy before the LORD. There was no severance between their daily occupation and their religious service. Both were firmly entwined together, and Jehovah was supreme and supremely honored in both.

Tabernacles, as it was the concluding, was likewise, as was stated in a preceding lecture, the culminating festival of the entire series. It occurred at the crown and apex of the year, in the seventh, which as such was the sabbatical or sacred month with its accumulation of festivals; and it was itself the climax of all that preceded. At this season, when grateful gladness reached its highest pitch in the experience of God's lavish bounty, came the most joyful festival of all, to which the sheaf of first-fruits and the feast of Weeks stood in the relation of preliminary antecedents, and in which Passover with its historical reminiscences was also, as it were, absorbed, since gratitude for the products of the land involved gratitude to him who had delivered them or their fathers from Egyptian bondage, and given them the land, Deut. 26:5-10. And it followed close upon the annual day of Atonement, when the sins and transgressions of the preceding year were all by a peculiar and striking ceremony expiated in the most solemn and impressive manner, and sent away into the desert, to a land not inhabited, never to be remembered or charged against them again. The people thus purged from their old sins could engage in this feast with the glad sense of pardon, reconciliation and communion with God, as well as the experience of his favor shown in the rich bounty of the year.

It was hence appropriately marked by the most elaborate and profuse sacrificial ritual of all the festivals. And while the feast of Weeks lasted but a single day, and while at the Passover pilgrims were permitted to return home after partaking of the paschal meal with which it began, at Tabernacles they remained not only through the full term of seven days, but an eighth day was added at the end, which in later times at least was reckoned 'the great day of the feast,' John 7:37. The people lifted to this rapturous and sacred height dispersed to their homes, abiding in the happy consciousness that they were the Israel of the LORD, blessed with his favor and happy in his service, until with the new year a fresh series of sacred festivals began, culminating as before, 2 Chron. 7:10.

As Tabernacles thus outranked all the other feasts, it is not surprising that it is oftenest mentioned in the history. Hupfeld appeals to Lev. 23:39, 41, 1 Kin. 8:2, 65, 12:32, Ezek. 45:25, Neh. 8:14, as showing that it is spoken of as 'the feast' by way of eminence. He even maintains that it was the one sole feast in the strict and proper sense; that the expiatory rites of the Passover were severe and stern, and the unleavened bread was unpalatable and forbidding, so that it could not fitly be called a feast; for this was of a joyous nature, as is shown by the combination, "eating and drinking and feasting," 1 Sam. 30:16. And the feast of Weeks is in Lev. 23:16, Num. 28:26, not called a feast at all, but only described as the time of offering a new meat-offering unto the LORD. He thence concludes that the latter is not entitled to rank as a separate feast, but only as a preliminary antecedent to the proper feast, that of Tabernacles. To this it is a sufficient reply that Ex. 23 and 34, and Deut. 16 expressly name three feasts; that if his view of the Passover and Unleavened Bread does not consist with its being a feast, this merely proves that view to be erroneous; the omission of the word 'feast' in connection with the second festival in Leviticus and Numbers is to be explained in the same way as the neglect of Num. 28 : 26 to define the period of its occurrence; it is assumed as known, having been spoken of sufficiently elsewhere. And the passages in which Tabernacles is referred to as 'the feast,' imply no exclusiveness or superiority, but simply denote it as the feast held at the time mentioned in the connection, or the feast which had before been spoken of.

The critics tell us that Tabernacles has passed through a like development to that which they claim for the Passover. Their arguments are similar to those which they employ in the case of the other feasts and involve the same fallacies. They convert the different aspects of the festival presented in different laws into successive stages belonging to distinct periods. They sunder laws which are entirely harmonious, but, as each has its own specific design, are needed to complete each other, and insist upon treating them as separate and independent statutes, void of all mutual relation. We first find in the Book of the Covenant, Ex. 23, and its subsequent reproduction, Ex. 34, the feasts briefly characterized and attendance upon them enjoined. Then in Lev. 23 the days of rest and the holy convocations belong ing to each are enumerated, and some peculiarities in the observance of the feasts that are not elsewhere mentioned. Num. 28, 29 detail the public sacrifices required at each. In Deut. 16 the great legislator, with an urgency and repetition natural in his farewell address to the people, enjoins it upon them to observe the feasts sacredly at the place that the LORD should choose, bearing their grateful offerings, and bringing their needy neighbors to share their festivities. Although these cohere perfectly together, the critics insist upon rending them apart, and making each dissevered portion stand for the whole; whereupon they urge that these are not identical, which was obvious enough from the first. They are of course distinct injunctions, but they all belong together and are needed to make up any proper view of the feast as observed at any one time.

And their treatment of the history is as arbitrary and unwarranted as their treatment of the statutes. It consists throughout in substituting their own imaginations for facts. Open and wilful violations of law are paraded as examples of what was reckoned lawful. Exceptional conduct under anomalous conditions is set forth as the normal course of procedure. And deviations are multiplied and exaggerated to an extent that has no existence but in the disordered fancy of the critic. Historical testimonies are credited or set aside at pleasure, and well-attested documents are freely manipulated. So with facts manufactured and authorities doctored to suit themselves they claim to have made out their point, when the whole thing is mere fancy from beginning to end.

Thus, in the first place, it is claimed that the character and design of the feast underwent serious changes. George[1] tells us that the vintage feast was adopted by Israel from the Canaanites, and was at first purely a sensuous feast with music and dancing, while the spirits were exhilarated with new wine. To this a religious element was soon added. As the Canaanites trode the grapes and went into the house of their god and did eat and drink, Judg. 9:27, so doubtless did the Israelites. The first of their oil and their new wine was brought to God, and served to enliven a joyful meal, of which the whole household partook along with the Levite, the stranger, the fatherless and the widow, Deut. 14:23; 16:14. Subsequently with the removal of its observance to a central sanctuary, it lost its original character, the first-fruits of oil and of wine became a perquisite of the priests, the joyful meals were abandoned and from a proper vintage feast it became one of general thanksgiving. Finally, it was changed still further by being dissociated from its agricultural meaning, and assuming a historical signification; the huts, which the whole population occupied during the vintage season, being separated from their original occasion, were supposed to commemorate the march through the wilderness, Lev. 23:43.

It is plain that all this is spun out of the critic's own brain. The vintage feasts of the ancient world generally were of a religious character; and that one ever existed in Israel destitute of any religious element is pure *a priori* theory. To assume that it was

[1] "Die älteren Jüdischen Feste," p. 276 f.

THE FEAST OF TABERNACLES. 285

borrowed by Israel from the Canaanites, is to assume without evidence and in the face of all the proof to the contrary, that Moses gave Israel no laws whatever relating to religious observances. For in both the most ancient codes, as the critics regard them, which are attributed to him and expressly declared to have been written by him, attendance upon the three annual feasts is almost the sole religious duty enjoined. Parallels are so numerous in the ancient world that sacrifices might as well be said to have been borrowed from the Canaanites as the feasts. And upon this ground alone the great body even of those critics who renounce the historical authority of the Pentateuch, and refuse to attribute the origin of the festal system to Moses, are disposed, as was shown at length in the second lecture, to consider these feasts pre-Mosaic. The assertion that the Hebrews first learned the cultivation of the soil after their occupancy of Canaan can not be proved. And if it could, it would not follow that Moses could not have framed laws adapted to the agricultural life which they were about to assume.

That Tabernacles ceased to be associated with the ingathering and came ultimately to have a historical meaning attached to it, is also a total misrepresentation. The Passover is adduced to illustrate a tendency in feasts which were originally agricultural to take on a historical character. But it has before been shown that the Passover was a commemorative festival from the beginning. And that the law of Tabernacles given while Israel was still camping in the desert should link the booths of the vintage in a subordinate way with the march through the wilderness to the goodly land of Canaan, involves no such gross misunderstanding as the critics affirm. So that we may dismiss without further remark the three counts in Hupfeld's indictment, that the children of Israel in the wilderness dwelt not in booths, but in tents; that carrying branches with leaves and fruit from the noblest trees stands in no relation to it; and that the most joyful feast of the year can not commemorate the penalty of living in the inhospitable desert. The law is not expounding the origin of the booths or their primary signification, but attaching to them an additional and not very remote association.

Again, the attempt is made to show that there were changes in the time of the celebration of this feast. It is alleged that, in the first instance, it varied with the time of the vintage; and George [1] conjectures that its duration was fixed at seven days, because of the imaginary habit of beginning to gather the fruits on the first day of the week and occupying a full week in the work. So, as he says, the seventh day should be a Sabbath as in the Passover; only there is no record of the fact. Dillmann [2] is not certain whether it originally lasted seven days; but this must early have become the custom, as appears from the feast in the time of Solomon, 1 Kin. 8:65. And he thinks it possible that in the first period of the settlement, in the general splitting up of the people, individual places and towns may have taken their own course as to the time of observing this feast.

[1] *Ubi supra*, p. 278.
[2] "Die Bücher Exodus und Leviticus," p. 582.

But as pilgrimages to a common sanctuary came into vogue, it was fixed at the period of the full moon. So that the only variation in different districts would be between the seventh and eighth months. But in Solomon's time, at least within the jurisdiction of the temple at Jerusalem, the decision was in favor of the seventh month, 1 Kin. 12 : 32 f. Further it is said, that this feast shared the general tendency to lengthen festivals; a day was accordingly added to it, not as in Passover at the beginning, but at the end of the proper seven days.

The feast of ingathering is said, Ex. 23 : 16, to be "in the end of the year, when thou hast gathered in thy labors out of the field." George[1] claims that no such statement could have been made prior to the Babylonish exile, as the Hebrew year originally began in the spring. It implies the reckoning after the exile, when the civil year had been introduced, beginning with the autumnal equinox; and as the vintage in Palestine was then finished, this feast could be held before the close of the year. In Ex. 34 : 22, the form of expression is slightly altered; "the feast of ingathering," not precisely "at the year's end," as our translators have it, but "at the return of the year." This according to George most probably indicates a still later period, when the feast had been fixed after the equinox in the seventh month of the ecclesiastical year, and consequently after the new civil year had begun. Hupfeld[2] finds in the expression "the end of the year" evidence of high an

---

[1] *Ubi supra*, p. 114.
[2] "De primitiva festorum ratione," p. 6.

tiquity and a trace of pre-Mosaic reckoning, which in Ex. 34 is changed to the more indefinite phrase "return of the year," for the sake of conforming to the Mosaic calendar. Wellhausen[1] maintains that these expressions are substantially identical, and both point to the year beginning in autumn, which in his estimation was the customary reckoning before the exile. The fact is, as has been mentioned on a former occasion, that there are clear indications prior to the exile of both modes of estimating the year as beginning in the spring and as beginning in the fall. It is the agricultural year that is here spoken of, which ended after the produce had all been stored and began with the ploughing and sowing for the new crop. This natural but somewhat indefinite style of reckoning did not correspond precisely with the calendar of the civil year, subsequently introduced, and hence the feast though occurring in Tisri is said to be " in the end of the year." In reference to this Dillmann truly observes, "It does not necessarily follow that the day was not fixed at the time of the author, but only that the general statement was sufficient for his purpose." " Such general statements were sufficient in law books of the laity; the more exact calculation of the times by the moon and lunar months was the affair of the priests."

Dr. Dillmann reaches his conclusions as to a possible variation in the length of this feast and the time of its occurrence by a careful and elaborate analysis of the laws, assigning each to its hypothetical writer, who is assumed to represent a distinct tradition, each

[1] "Geschichte," I., p. 111. Prolegomena (Eng. Tr.), p. 108.

valid for its own age, and the concurrence of two or more upon any given point creating a higher or lower probability as to the facts of a still earlier date. The ingenuity, the learning and the conscientiousness with which this process is conducted is beyond all praise. Nevertheless, everything rests on a primary assumption, which, to say the least, has not yet been proved. It is that the Pentateuchal laws are not at all what they profess to be, what they are uniformly by all the writers of both the Old and New Testaments represented to be, what they have always been believed to be, what the internal evidence upon any fair treatment shows that they must be, and what therefore they have every reasonable claim to be regarded as being, the genuine production of Moses.

If we really have no trustworthy account of the institutions of Moses, if there be nothing but uncertain traditions through anonymous sources, which are often conflicting and which were not recorded till many centuries after the Mosaic age, Dr. Dillmann has perhaps done as well as it was possible to do with such unsatisfactory and intractable materials. But his procedure and his results depend for their justification on his original assumption. He puts into the critical crucible at the beginning precisely what he brings out at the end. These institutions thus dealt with are but the plaything of the critic's fancy. He makes them to be not what they are in the record, but what he pleases to regard them. Ex. 23 and 34 speak in a general way of this feast, but do not mention its duration. Leviticus, Numbers and Deuteronomy assign to it a term of seven days.

THE FEAST OF TABERNACLES.

Now if the feast laws of Exodus antedate the others by centuries, then we have no certain evidence of the length of this feast for that interval of time; and Dr. Dillmann has some reason for expressing doubt on the subject. But until the contrary can be shown by irrefragable proof these laws must be accepted as holding to one another that intimate mutual relation which they claim, which has always been accorded to them, and which a fair examination of them abundantly justifies. If they be allowed to supplement and complete each other, all doubt vanishes at once, the whole intricacy of the subject is removed, and we are upon solid ground.

And there are no known facts in the history to invalidate this conclusion. In the earliest references to this feast, which afford any intimation of its duration or of the time at which it was held, the agreement with the Mosaic law is perfect. In the reign of Solomon it lasted seven days, and was held in the seventh month, 1 Kin. 8 : 2, 65, 66, so that although the temple was finished in the eighth month of the preceding year, 6 : 38, its dedication was delayed until the occurrence of this autumnal festival, the other annual feasts being less suitable on account of the brief stay of the pilgrims at the sanctuary apart from other considerations. From 1 Kin. 12 : 32, it appears that it was observed on the fifteenth day of the month. There is nothing anywhere to imply that there had ever been any fluctuation in the time. How far the distractions incident to the imperfect conquest of the land or the incursions of foreign foes may have interfered with the regular observance of the law in early periods we do not know, but this casts no doubt upon the existence of the statute, or of its appointment of a fixed time for the celebration of the feast. And it certainly does not justify the inference drawn from the arbitrary act of Jeroboam. The historian records that Jeroboam ordained a feast in the eighth month, on the fifteenth day of the month, even in the month which he had devised of his own heart. This innovation, as it is plainly declared to be, affords no ground even for the conjecture, much less for the assertion, which has no support from any other quarter, that the observance of the feast prior to this time, had varied in different sections of the country between the seventh and eighth months; much less is it any warrant for the opinion that there was no recognized statute on the subject.

Dr. Dillmann is likewise in doubt as to the antiquity of the *Atsereth*, or the day added after the seven days of Tabernacles, as a solemn termination to this feast or to all the festivals of the year. It is spoken of in Lev. 23 : 36, 39, and in Num. 29 : 35, but not in Exodus or Deuteronomy. But this suggests no doubt of its Mosaic origin, or of its being from the first a constituent of the festal cycle. For this eighth day is plainly shown in both passages not to belong to the feast of Tabernacles in its strict and proper sense. Lev. 23 : 34 ff. reiterates no less than six times that the feast of Tabernacles, its special offerings and its dwelling in booths, lasted seven days; but it adds that the eighth day was likewise to be kept holy and have offerings of its own. And Num. 29 : 12 ff. again declares that the feast lasts seven days, and proceeds to specify the sacrifices to be offered during these seven days in a regular gradation day by day. An eighth day is added, ver. 35, without a copulative as uniformly before, and its sacrifices stand in no relation to the preceding and do not continue the same graduated scale. Accordingly it was not to be expected that the laws of Exodus and Deuteronomy, which limit themselves to the three annual feasts, should speak of this day any more than of the feast of Trumpets or the day of Atonement. If Deuteronomy declares the feast of Tabernacles to be of seven days' duration, Leviticus and Numbers do the same with equal explicitness, so that no suspicion can arise of a change in the length of the feast in the interval.

Dr. Dillmann correctly remarks that it can not be certainly inferred from 1 Kin. 8:66, that this eighth day was not observed in Solomon's time. It is there stated that after the celebration of the feast, he sent the people away on the eighth day. According to the parallel passage, 2 Chron. 7:9, they had a solemn assembly on the 8th day and were sent away on the day following. The apparent discrepancy is, however, very easily reconciled. At the close of the solemn services held on the eighth day, Solomon formally dismissed the people, who thereupon returned home the day after. This eighth day is particularly mentioned in the observance of the feast by Ezra and Nehemiah, Neh. 8:18, and from the increasing concourse of pilgrims, it had risen to great consequence in the time of our Lord, John 7:37.

It is further claimed that a development can be traced in the mode of observing the feast and in its

sacrificial ritual. Thus the critics affirm that Lev.
23 : 39-43, which directs the people to take the boughs
of goodly trees and to dwell in booths, is plainly a
subsequent addition to the chapter, which came to a
formal close vs. 37, 38, and according to Neh. 8 : 17
this had not been observed prior to the time of Nehemiah. There is not a little divergence of critical
opinion about the proper treatment of this chapter of
Leviticus. Wellhausen[1] finds in it two distinct feast
laws, which have been combined into one by the Redactor. One consists of vs. 9-22, 39-44, the wave-
sheaf and wave-loaves and the supplementary statement respecting Tabernacles, all which depart from
the Elohistic style; on the contrary the remainder of
the chapter is purely Elohistic. Hupfeld[2] throws out
eleven more verses in addition to the preceding, viz.,
ver. 3, the law of the Sabbath, and vs. 23-32, the first
and tenth days of the seventh month, and declares
the verses thus sundered to be the ones which are
Elohistic and of the same style with Gen. 17 and Ex.
12. Knobel[3] thinks that all the chapter belongs to
the Elohist except vs. 2, 3, the Sabbath law, vs. 18,
19, 22, and vs. 39-44, the supplementary passage concerning Tabernacles, which were inserted by the Jehovist from some document closely approximating
that of the Elohist in style and language.

Kayser[4] makes a still more elaborate dissection of
the chapter. He agrees with Wellhausen in finding

[1] "Jahrbücher für Deutsche Theologie," XXII., p. 431 ff.
[2] "De vera festorum ratione," Part II., pp. 7, 13.
[3] "Die Bücher Exodus und Leviticus," p. 530.
[4] "Das vorexilische Buch," p. 73.

two distinct feast calendars in the chapter, though he differs from him in details. He assigns to the Elohist vs. 5–8, 14*b* the Passover, vs. 15*a*, 16*a*, 21 the feast of Weeks, and vs. 23–36 the festivals of the seventh month, together with the title and subscriptions vs. 4, 37, 38, 44. The remaining verses are from a different source and have special relation to the harvest, vs. 9–14*a* the sheaf of first-fruits at the beginning of harvest, vs. 15*b*, 16*b*–20 the new meat-offering of Pentecost at its close, ver. 22 the prohibition of gleaning, and vs. 39–43 Tabernacles as a thanksgiving for the harvest and vintage. He is not sure whether this latter calendar ever contained anything about the first day of the seventh month, or the day of Atonement; but he is persuaded that in its original form it must have stated the times of the several feasts, as the seven weeks' interval between Pentecost and its predecessor is given, and Tabernacles is put in the seventh month; it must, therefore, in consistency have mentioned the time of the Passover. It is obvious to suggest to him that the very thing he misses and which the calendar must plainly have contained, is here given as the chapter stands. It is only his critical hypothesis which has separated what by his own confession belongs together.

Reuss adopts substantially the same division; only he separates the supplementary paragraph itself, vs. 39–43, into two parts, assigning the last three verses to the Elohist, and attaching them to the preceding paragraph on the same subject, thus virtually giving up the whole dispute, so far at least as these verses are concerned. Kayser's dissection is so keen that he splits sentences in two, and splices the alternate halves together into new sentences, which are assigned to distinct writers, and thus he obtains a double law of the feast of Weeks. Dillmann, whose own critical knife has a very keen edge at times, pronounces his division and that of Knobel " arbitrary and impracticable." And he objects to Wellhausen that neither of his feast calendars are complete; one has no Pentecost, and the other no feast of Unleavened Bread, while expressions, which all critics affirm to be Elohistic, pervade those sections which he slices from the chapter to such an extent that no assumption of interpolations will meet the case. In Dr. Dillmann's judgment the chapter is a unit.

Where leading critics are so utterly at variance, it might be presumptuous in an onlooker to offer an opinion. But the chapter certainly has the appearance of being constructed on a uniform plan, with all its parts not only in close mutual relation, but in obvious relation likewise to other portions of the legislation of the Pentateuch. The formula, "And the LORD spake unto Moses, saying, Speak unto the children of Israel, and say unto them," is used four times, vs. 1, 9, 23, 33, to introduce the four principal sections of the chapter. There are two titles in ver. 2 and ver. 4 respectively, and two subscriptions, vs. 37, 38, and ver. 44, the last corresponding in form to the first title and the opening words, and thus marking the extreme limits of the entire chapter and of the calendar of sacred times which it contains. The first section of the chapter is divided into two parts by a second title, ver. 4, and the last section is also divided into two parts by the first of the two subscriptions, vs. 37, 38, which answers to the second title; and these embrace between them the core of the entire calendar, the annual festivals so far as they stand related to the services of the sanctuary.

Prior to this central portion and preceding the second title is the Sabbath law, ver. 2, which had its holy convocation, and could not be omitted from any complete calendar of the sacred times, and yet was not one of the annual festivals, nor did it stand in any exclusive relation to the sanctuary. It is described as "the Sabbath of the LORD in all your dwellings." It belonged appropriately to the chapter, therefore, and yet was distinct in character from the sacred times afterward to be described, which are accordingly preceded by a fresh title, ver. 4. In like manner the feast of Tabernacles, to which the last section of the chapter is devoted, had two aspects, one of which had to do with the sanctuary, and the other not. The former is first described with its holy convocations and daily offerings, and is immediately followed by the subscription, vs. 37, 38, summing up this portion of the chapter, "These are the feasts of the LORD, which ye shall proclaim to be holy convocations, to offer an offering made by fire unto the LORD," etc. Then follows the other aspect of the feast in a special paragraph, which could not properly have been included in the preceding, in which they are bidden to take boughs of goodly trees and dwell in booths during the celebration of the feast.

Wellhausen further complains that this second paragraph, relating to Tabernacles, has been interpolated from the first; and he claims that when these interpolations have been removed, the original contrariety of the two paragraphs plainly appears. He finds an interpolation in the opening words defining the time of the feast, "In the fifteenth day of the seventh month," which, he says, is inconsistent with what immediately follows, "when ye have gathered in the fruit of the land." According to the former the period of celebration was determined by the phase of the moon; according to the latter, by the housing of the fruit-crop. The former is, therefore, not an original part of the text; and this paragraph belongs to a time when the feast was held earlier or later according to the season; only, as is stated in ver. 41, it always fell somewhere within the limits of the seventh month.

But the alleged contrariety in the opening clauses of ver. 39 is only an invincible proof of the perversity of Wellhausen's mode of interpretation. This immediate conjunction of a fixed day of the month with the phrase "when ye have gathered in the fruit of the land," shows in the clearest possible manner that the two are perfectly consistent, that the relation of the feast to the ingathering is not disturbed by the assignment of a definite date; that the feast, to be agricultural, need not be movable; and that the hypothesis, that in consequence of their agricultural character they must at first have been movable, and afterward linked to determinate days, is altogether without foundation. The last clause of ver. 41, "Ye shall celebrate it in the seventh month," is not vaguely meant, as though it gave intimation that this should be done at some period in the month, but on no fixed day year by year; nor is it to be explained with Dillmann as in tacit contrast with the eighth month, conformably to his hypothesis that the usage varied in different parts of the land, but the legislator decides for the seventh. The real emphasis is on the number, the seventh, the sabbatical, the sacred month. The stress laid upon this number appears from the fact that within the brief compass of four verses, it is stated four times that the observance lasted seven days, and twice that it was in the seventh month.

Wellhausen finds another interpolation in the last clause of ver. 39, "on the first day shall be a *Shabbathōn* and on the eighth day shall be a *Shabbathōn*." He thinks it very extraordinary that the writer should announce that the feast was to be kept seven days, and then immediately proceed to speak of the eighth day of this seven days' feast. Throw out this clause and there will be at once perceived a discrepancy between this and the preceding paragraph. When this paragraph was written the eighth day had not yet been added to Tabernacles, which is nevertheless spoken of in ver. 36. But he only succeeds in showing that this paragraph presupposes the preceding, is built upon it, and can only be understood in connection with it.

And the same thing appears in other respects likewise. In ver. 34 this is called the feast of Tabernacles; no reason is given for the name that is here used for the first time. The feast has a different appellation in Ex. 23 and 34. This name does not recur in Num. 29:12. It is found again in Deut. 16:13, but with no hint why it is so called. The only explanation is furnished by the direction to "dwell in booths" or tabernacles, ver. 42. Further, the phrase, ver. 39, "when ye have gathered in the fruit of the land," is a plain allusion to the denomination in Exodus "feast of ingathering," and marks it clearly as an agrarian festival, an aspect which had not been brought out in the preceding paragraph; hence the occasion for supplementing it in this particular here. Wellhausen thinks that the change of name from feast of Ingathering to feast of Tabernacles was the initial alteration which paved the way for subsequently attributing to it a historical instead of an agricultural meaning. But this unlucky paragraph stands in his way once more; for here we have the agricultural and the historical sense combined together, vs. 39, 43, showing that both were held at the same time and that no interval was needed to pass from one to the other.

The further explanation of the mode of observing Tabernacles contained in this supplementary paragraph was, moreover, to be expected from the plan of the chapter. As was shown in a former lecture, it passes lightly over those sacred times as the Passover and the day of Atonement, whose peculiar services had been fully explained elsewhere; it only alludes in a general way to the festal sacrifices, whose details were reserved for Num. 28, 29; and it enters into particulars respecting the feast of Weeks and the accompanying and preceding presentation of firstfruits, which had not been explained before. This method of treatment obviously required that in dealing with the third and greatest feast of the year regarding which no particulars are given elsewhere, the general observations of vs. 34-36 should be supplemented by some fuller and more characteristic account of its celebration, such as is to be found in the concluding verses of this chapter.

Hupfeld maintains that the boughs spoken of in ver. 40 were intended to be carried in festive procession, and that Neh. 8 : 15 quite misunderstands the purport of the injunction when it speaks of using them to make booths for the people to lodge in. But the directions to take the branches and to dwell in booths stand in very obvious relation; and it is difficult to see why the branches might not be, as in actual fact they were, used for both purposes.

That Neh. 8 : 17 does not oblige us to suppose that the feast of Tabernacles had never been observed before the time of Nehemiah is plain, not only from previous mention of it at earlier periods of the history, but from Ezra 3 : 4, where it is expressly said, that they kept the "feast of Tabernacles as it is written"; where this brief formula is only an abridgment of that which is used two verses before, "as it is written in the law of Moses, the man of God." Neither can the passage in Nehemiah mean that booths were then for the first time used in the celebration of this feast; for the express reference to the time of Joshua implies that it had certainly been kept, as the children of Israel then kept it, in Joshua's days,—not Joshua the high priest, the contemporary and coadjutor of Zerubbabel, as J. D. Michaelis strangely fancied, but Joshua the son of Nun, the successor of Moses.

THE FEAST OF TABERNACLES. 301

The primitive character of this mode of celebrating has a further voucher in the name of the feast, Tabernacles (סכות *booths*), which here finds its only explanation; also in the usage of the vintagers to lodge in booths while gathering the fruit from which it is derived; and in Hos. 12:9, which makes special allusion both to the manner of observing the feast and the historical association connected with it: "I that am the LORD thy God from the land of Egypt will yet make thee to dwell in tabernacles as in the days of the solemn feasts."

The point of this passage in Nehemiah lies not so much in the thing done as in the manner of doing it. It is not that this action had not been performed before since the time of Joshua, but they had not done *so*. The universality with which it was done, and the gladness, as is added immediately after, with which it was done, had no parallel since the days of Joshua, when all Israel were in tents and were rejoicing in the manifest presence of Jehovah among them and in their recently acquired possession of the land flowing with milk and honey. So the exiles who had lately returned from captivity and were now settled in the land of their fathers, assured of Jehovah's almighty protection and help, engaged with alacrity and unanimity in every requirement of the law, now freshly expounded to them, and felt as though those early days of triumph and of joy had once again returned.

The same allegation is also made in regard to Tabernacles as the other feasts, and with as little reason that there was a transition from the voluntary private thank-offerings customary in the early periods to public sacrifices rigidly prescribed, and which were an affair of the priests rather than of the people ; that the tithes and first-fruits of their oil and their wine became the legal due to the priests instead of a grateful gift to God, and hence no longer supplied material for a joyous meal of the offerer and his friends at the sanctuary. Thus religion, it is said, became more and more separated from the affairs of daily life and from the occasions of pious gratitude which the changing seasons and the bountiful productions of the soil afforded. It lost its native warmth, its naturalness and spontaneous character, and became formal and cold, a mere matter of statute and rigid requirement. It was symptomatic of the transition from ancient Israel to modern Pharisaic Judaism.

How unfounded all this is we have already seen. The Priest Code of Leviticus and Numbers, which ordains the sacrifices to be offered day by day throughout each feast on behalf of the people, makes explicit provision at the same time for all the gifts and vows and free-will offerings, which the pious zeal of the people prompted them to present, Lev. 23 : 38, Num. 29 : 39. And it bids them rejoice before the LORD their God throughout the feast, Lev. 23 : 40, in terms very similar to those employed in Deut. 16. And that this combination of national and individual worship, of public sacrifice and private festivity and glad rejoicing before the LORD characterized these feasts down to the time of Solomon, and so on to the close of the Old Testament, is abundantly apparent from 1 Kin. 8 : 5, 62–64, Ezra 3 : 4, 5, Neh. 3 : 10–12.

And in fact the common sanctuary of Israel, God's dwelling-place in Zion and the worship there maintained, and the confidence there reposed, and the help thence experienced, so far from chilling the fervor of devotion and leading to a cheerless and spiritless formality, was the very spring and fountain of warm religious life and elevated aspirations and ardent devotion, as is apparent in the entire book of Psalms from first to last, which clusters about the one earthly habitation of the Most High, and places there all hope and draws thence every inspiration and stimulus.[1] "How amiable are thy tabernacles, O LORD of hosts; my soul longeth, yea, even fainteth for the courts of the LORD; my heart and my flesh crieth out for the living God." "As the hart panteth after the waterbrooks, so panteth my soul after thee, O God. My soul thirsteth for God, for the living God; when shall I come and appear before God?" "LORD, who shall abide in thy tabernacle? who shall dwell in thy holy hill? He that walketh uprightly and worketh righteousness, and speaketh the truth in his heart." "Who shall ascend into the hill of the LORD? and who shall stand in his holy place? He that hath clean hands and a pure heart; who hath not lifted up his soul unto vanity nor sworn deceitfully. He shall receive the blessing from the LORD and righteousness from the God of his salvation. . . . . Lift up your heads, O ye gates; even lift them up, ye everlasting doors; and the king of glory shall come in. Who is

---

[1] See the noteworthy article by Smend, "Ueber die Bedeutung des Jerusalemischen Tempels in der alttestamentlichen Religion," in the "Studien und Kritiken," for 1884, pp. 718 ff.

this king of glory? the LORD of hosts, he is the king of glory." "I was glad when they said unto me, Let us go into the house of the LORD. Our feet shall stand within thy gates, O Jerusalem, ... whither the tribes go up, the tribes of the LORD unto the testimony of Israel to give thanks unto the name of the LORD." "O send out thy light and thy truth; let them lead me; let them bring me unto thy holy hill and to thy tabernacles. Then will I go unto the altar of God, unto God my exceeding joy; yea, upon the harp will I praise thee, O God, my God." "I cried unto the LORD with my voice and he heard me out of his holy hill."

We hear a great deal from the critics about the centralization of worship proving the death-blow to the old religion of Israel and substituting a round of external formalities in place of true inward devotion. Let them explain then the book of Psalms, and trace the fervor of its enthusiasm, its pure, rapturous devotion, its elevated and enlightened piety, to its source. It was the sanctuary on Zion which kindled it to a glow. What was there corresponding to it, that was ever produced in those local sanctuaries and that popular religion, of which we hear so much? I do not now call attention to any argument derived from the Davidic origin of any of the Psalms, and the proof thus afforded of the unity of the sanctuary in the age of David. But dismissing all questions of date and authorship, look at the book as a whole, as the utterance of pious hearts in Israel, as the flower and the crown of Old Testament devotion. Accept, if you please, the critical conclusion, that the Psalms are almost without exception post-exilic, and that all that we really know about them is that they formed the hymn-book of the second temple. This book, then, is not only contemporaneous with Ezra's alleged issue of the Priest Code, which we are told deadened and formalized the piety of Israel; but it derives all its spring, gathers all its fervor, draws all its lofty and pure devotion from that centralized sanctuary and that centralized worship, which, as they tell us, this formal and stiffened code was the means of establishing.

Finally, it is claimed in regard to the feast of Tabernacles as to the others, that its observance at one central place of worship was unknown both to the older laws and to the earlier period of the history; that it was at first celebrated in local sanctuaries in various parts of the land, and only in the course of time came to be observed by all the people at one common centre. We have seen that this allegation is quite unfounded so far as concerns the Passover and the feast of Weeks. It is equally so in the case of the feast now before us. There is no implication in the law that it was ever to be observed in a variety of places; there is no statement in the history that it ever was observed anywhere but at the common sanctuary; and there is no recorded fact from which a different practice can with any reason be inferred. The injunction in Ex. 23 and 34 is the same in regard to all three of the annual feasts. Three times in the year all thy males shall appear before the LORD God; and this not in various sanctuaries, in different houses of God, but in "the house of the LORD thy God." This house of God must have been where his altar was; and his altar was to be where God would record his name, Ex. 20 : 24. So that this is coincident with the requirement in Deut. 16 : 16: " Three times in the year shall all thy males appear before the LORD thy God in the place which he shall choose." There is entire unanimity in all the laws upon this point. It is at the one house of God that all Israelites are annually to appear and keep these sacred feasts. Or if a distinction is to be found in these commands, and the critical principle is to be pressed that each law is to be interpreted absolutely by itself and out of relation to every other law, the conclusion which would follow would be precisely the reverse of that which Wellhausen actually draws. In the Book of the Covenant and in Deuteronomy pilgrimages to the sanctuary are required at each of the annual feasts. In the Priest Code, in Leviticus and Numbers this requirement is not repeated; it is simply taken for granted as already known. But if no law is to be allowed to supplement another, the inevitable conclusion will be upon Wellhausen's own principles that originally the people kept the feasts at one common sanctuary, but after the exile this ceased to be the case.

Wellhausen[1] undertakes to expound to us the course of things with regard to the autumnal feast of ingathering. The earliest notice of such a festival he finds in Judg. 9 : 27, where the idolatrous inhabitants of Shechem celebrate the completed vintage in the house of their god Baal-berith, and it is further

[1] "Geschichte Israels," pp. 96 ff. Prolegomena (Eng. Tr.), p. 94 ff.

alluded to in Jotham's parable, vs. 9, 13, which speaks of the fatness of the olive, "wherewith they honor God and man," and the "wine which cheereth God and man." Then in Judg. 21 : 19 ff., mention is made of a like annual festival in the vineyards of Shiloh, which though occurring in a narrative, that he thinks to be in the highest degree incredible, is nevertheless confirmed, 1 Sam. 1 : 3, by the yearly visit of Samuel's father to Shiloh. This occurred "at the return of days," ver. 20, an expression almost identical with that which is rendered "at the year's end," Ex. 34 : 22, the time of the autumnal festival. His inference is that instead of continuing to observe the feast in every different locality throughout the land, particular centres began to form in the latter part of the period of the Judges, like Shechem and Shiloh, whose sanctuaries were rising into prominence, and drew pilgrims from the surrounding district. When Shechem became an Israelitish city, its new occupants neither abolished the sanctuary nor the Hillulim or vintage feast, which was habitually celebrated there. The great royal temples of a later time were still more widely influential. So that from the reign of Solomon this feast was held at Jerusalem in the seventh month, and at Bethel since Jeroboam probably somewhat later in the season. This was then the only Panegyris or assembly of the whole people. The harvest feast may have been observed already, but only in small local circles. This distinction is reflected in Deuteronomy, according to which Tabernacles, although it theoretically had no precedence, was the only feast which was observed for the full week

Pilgrims had to remain but one day at the sanctuary at Passover, and even this brief demand is more emphatically inculcated than the other, showing that it was an innovation.

But the idolatrous worship of Baal-berith has nothing to do with the feasts of Jehovah. There is nothing in the passage cited, nor in any other, to suggest that these latter were ever celebrated at Shechem. On the contrary express mention is made of the feast of the LORD in Shiloh. And although this is found in the last chapter of Judges, the fact there recorded belongs early in the history of this book, for Phinehas the grandson of Aaron was priest at the time, 20:28. Shiloh was the place where Joshua had set up the Mosaic tabernacle, Josh. 18:1, and where the house of God continued through the period of the Judges, Judg. 18:31, 19:18, down to the time of Samuel, when it still bore the name "tabernacle of the congregation," 1 Sam. 2:22, a term never applied to any building but the sacred tent of Moses. To this worshippers gathered not from the surrounding region of Ephraim merely, but from all Israel, 1 Sam. 2:14; and it was God's habitation, the one divinely commanded place of sacrifice for the entire people, where the one priesthood ministered that was chosen of God out of all the tribes of Israel to this service, vs. 27–29. The critics tell us that the passage last cited is an insertion by the Deuteronomic reviser, the only proof of which is that it flatly contradicts their whole hypothesis. We can not accommodate them in their very natural wish to rid themselves of its unwelcome testimony. They have appealed to the history, and by the facts of the history they must abide.

THE FEAST OF TABERNACLES.

The mention of 'the daughters of Shiloh' in particular, Judg. 21:21, as dancing at the time of the festival, does not prove that it was only locally observed; for apart from the fact that the representatives of the people there encamped would naturally plan to absolve their own daughters, which they had pledged themselves not to give in marriage to Benjamin, women were not required by law to come to the feasts, and they would be less likely to do so voluntarily at this time of war than in ordinary years. It is observable, however, that the entire camp of Israel left the seat of war, came to Shiloh, 21:12, and remained there until after the feast, ver. 24.

The next allusion to one of the religious feasts is at the dedication of Solomon's temple, which, in order that it might be a truly national celebration, was appointed at the time of the feast of Tabernacles in the seventh month. The vastness of the assemblage on that occasion appears from the provision made for them by Solomon's sacrifice of two and twenty thousand oxen and an hundred and twenty thousand sheep, 1 Kin. 8:63, comp. ver. 5. The ark of the LORD and the tabernacle of the congregation and all the holy vessels that were in the tabernacle were deposited in the temple, which thus became heir of the exclusive sanctity that before had been vested in them. The 'tabernacle of the congregation,' or more exactly rendered, 'tent of meeting,' is of course not the tent which David had pitched on Mount Zion for the temporary reception of the ark, which never bears this name, but the old Mosaic tabernacle of which this was a standing designation, and which, since the loss of its divine significance by the capture of the ark, had remained an empty shell at Nob and at Gibeon until now.

All the meaning and impressiveness of the dedication centred in the removal of the ark. "The elders of Israel, and all the heads of the tribes, the chief of the fathers of the children of Israel, assembled unto king Solomon in Jerusalem," not to gaze upon and admire or even worship in the superb structure that he had reared, but "that they might bring up the ark of the covenant of the LORD out of the city of David, which is Zion," 1 Kin. 8:1. Before this ark on its sacred passage to its new abode " King Solomon and all the congregation of Israel that were assembled unto him were sacrificing sheep and oxen that could not be told nor numbered for multitude," ver. 5. This ark, the symbol and pledge of the divine presence, contained "the two tables of stone, which Moses put there at Horeb, when the LORD made a covenant with the children of Israel, when they came out of the land of Egypt," ver. 9. And when this ark had been set in its proper place, "the cloud filled the house of the LORD, so that the priests could not stand to minister because of the cloud; for the glory of the LORD had filled the house of the LORD," vs. 10, 11, as it had previously filled the tabernacle of Moses on its erection. Then spake Solomon, The LORD said that he would dwell in the thick darkness. I have surely built thee an house to dwell in, a settled place for thee to abide in forever, vs. 12, 13. Since the day that God brought forth his people Israel out of Egypt, he chose no city out of all the tribes of Israel to build an house that his name might be therein, ver. 16. And God had not dwelt in any house since the time that he brought up the children of Israel out of Egypt, but had walked in a tent and a tabernacle, 2 Sam. 7:6. But now that he had given rest to his people on every side, 1 Kin. 5:3-5, Solomon had, in accordance with the promise divinely made to his father David, been permitted to build the house to the name of the LORD God of Israel, and he had set there a place for the ark. He expresses his amazement that the God, whom the heaven and heaven of heavens could not contain, should condescend to dwell in this house which he had builded. And yet he prays, Let thine eyes "be open toward this house night and day, even toward the place of which thou hast said, My name shall be there, ... and hearken thou unto the supplication of thy servant and of thy people Israel, when they shall pray toward this place; and hear thou in heaven thy dwelling-place," 1 Kin. 8:20 ff.

Nothing can be plainer from the record than that this was to Solomon and to all Israel not one sanctuary among many, but the one sole sanctuary of the Most High; and that its superior sacredness was not due to the greater magnificence of the structure, or its being at the royal residence, but to the presence of the ark and the consequent indwelling of the LORD of hosts. Of course the critics make free use of their knife upon this most damaging recital. The postexilic writer of the book, they tell us, has transferred the superstitious reverence with which the temple came to be regarded in later days to the time of Solomon, when no such view was entertained. We challenge them for their proof. There is absolutely none forthcoming, but that the plain letter of the history is at utter variance with their hypothesis. All the testimony that can be gathered from every source within reach tends one way and to one result, viz., that the temple was the one only legitimate sanctuary in Israel after Shiloh. There is not a syllable of contradiction or rebutting evidence from any quarter. But all must be discredited and set at nought because, forsooth, it does not please the critics.

Ah! they say, but the high places were not done away even after the temple was built. Solomon's heart was in his old age turned away after other gods, 1 Kin. 11:4, 7, and he built an high place for Chemosh the abomination of Moab, and for Molech the abomination of the children of Ammon. And in the reign of Rehoboam, 14:23, Judah built high places and stocked them with the various emblems of idolatry on every high hill and under every green tree. And so Aaron and Israel made a golden calf at the foot of Sinai. And so Judas betrayed his Lord. There have been shameful apostasies and departures from truth and duty in every age. What does this prove except the corruption of human nature and the innate tendency of man to turn away from the holy God and the purity of his worship and service, which breaks out in the most unexpected quarters and the most humiliating manner? Or will it be claimed that Solomon did not know but that Chemosh and Molech were as much entitled to his service as Jehovah? If his transgression is to disprove the existence of the law which he so grossly violated, it is not the unity of Jehovah's sanctuary, but whether Jehovah was the God of Israel that is thus brought into question.

Again we are reminded that the ten tribes kept their autumnal feast at Bethel. But this does not prove that Bethel was an equally legitimate sanctuary. We have a historical account of the establishment of this schismatical and idolatrous worship by Jeroboam, whose aim was to terminate the worship at a common sanctuary which had previously prevailed, lest a continuance of religious unity should cement again the lately ruptured political unity. With this view he set up the golden calves at Bethel and at Dan, and ordained a feast in the eighth month at Bethel, 1 Kin. 12 : 26 ff. This account Wellhausen considers unreliable. Very naturally; he is in the habit of bowing every witness out of court whose testimony is not to his mind. The critics tell us this was an ancestral sanctuary, where it had been the custom to worship Jehovah under the image of a young bull. We have the express statement of the historian on the one side, and the unsupported word of the critics on the other; which is to be believed? There is not a trace of this calf-worship in Israel from Aaron to Jeroboam; not only no proof that such worship was considered lawful, but even their apostasies from God never took that form. It came from Egypt and was one of the fruits of Jeroboam's long sojourn in that country.

If Bethel was a true sanctuary and the worship there lawful, why did Elijah offer his sacrifice designed to reclaim the people from the worship of Baal not at Bethel, but at Carmel, which had no sacred association? and upon an altar whose twelve stones were a protest against the schism and at an hour which corresponded with the worship in the temple? And why, when his life was in peril from the rage of Jezebel, did he seek the LORD at Horeb, from whose summit the law had been proclaimed, not only, Thou shalt have no other gods before me, but, Thou shalt not make unto thee any graven image? Why did not only Elijah denounce Ahab, who introduced the worship of Baal, but Elisha likewise repel Jehoram, who had abandoned Baal and clave to the golden calves, 2 Kin. 3:2 f., 13? and proceed to anoint Hazael to be a scourge to Israel, 1 Kin. 19:15, 2 Kin. 8:13? And why did Hosea speak with such contempt and abhorrence of the worship of the calves, 8:5 f., 10:5 f., 13:2, denounce their feasts as feasts of Baal, 2:13, point to Bethel as the very fountainhead of corruption and ruin, 10:8, 15, declare their kings to be self-appointed and void of divine sanction, 8:4, and link all the hope of Israel's future to their return from both their false government and their false worship to seek the LORD their God and David their king, 3:5? Neither Bethel nor the calves find sanction anywhere.

But it is claimed that while Tabernacles was observed at one common sanctuary at an early period, there is no evidence that this was the case with the other feasts likewise. Only one feast is spoken of at Shiloh, Judg. 21:19. Elkanah went up but once in the year, 1 Sam. 1:3 ff., and the same feast is mentioned at the dedication of Solomon's temple, 1 Kin. 8:2, and contrasted with the feast of Jeroboam, 12: 32 ff. There could have been, it is argued, but one pilgrimage feast throughout this period; the others must have been observed as yet at local sanctuaries throughout the land. But with the exception of Joshua's Passover the silence respecting it and the feast of Weeks in all this period is total. There is no record of their local observance, and no intimation of any such thing. Yet the most ancient laws, as the critics regard them, those which, we are told, govern the practice of this period, ordain three feasts and enjoin pilgrimages alike to each. Clearly, then, either the law existed without being observed, or the silence of the history does not disprove their observance. Either admission deprives the hypothesis of one of its main props.

The Psalms of David recognize throughout but one sanctuary, that in Zion. Of their genuineness we have the proof drawn from their titles, corroborated in certain cases at least by strong internal evidence, as well as by general references to him as the "sweet Psalmist of Israel," 2 Sam. 23:1, and to his musical skill, 1 Sam. 16:16 ff. Amos 6:5, by the repetition of Ps. 18, in 2 Sam. 22, by his other poetic compositions, 2 Sam. 1:17, ch. 23, and the association of music with public worship, Am. 5:23, Isa. 30:29, Jer. 33: 11, not to speak of the explicit testimony of the books of Chronicles. But it does not agree with the hypothesis to admit that any extant psalm can be referred to David. All are consigned to the period after the exile.

What then do the prophets say? Hosea and Amos denounce the sanctuaries of Israel in unmeasured terms, Hos. 4 : 13, 15, 10 : 8, 15, Am. 3 : 14, 4 : 4, 5 : 4, 5, 8 : 14. The former calls the feasts celebrated there feasts of Baal, Hos. 2 : 11, 13, and connects their true seeking of the LORD with a return to David their king, 3 : 5. Amos, 1 : 2, appeals to God's loud voice of judgment which was resounding from Zion and Jerusalem. Isaiah 29 : 1 (Heb.) speaks of the feasts as running their annual round in the city where David dwelt; of glad processions to celebrate the Passover in the mountain of the LORD, 30 : 29; of the LORD as coming down to fight for Mount Zion and defending Jerusalem, where are his altar fires, 31 : 4, 5, 9 ; of Zion the city of our solemnities, which no foe can successfully assail, 33 : 20, 26 : 1, 10 : 32, where Jehovah dwells, 8 : 18, and reigns, 24 : 23, and is worshipped, 27 : 13, and presents brought from foreign lands to the place of the name of the LORD of hosts, the Mount Zion, 18 : 7, to which all nations shall one day flock in eager submission, 2 : 3, where he shall make to all people a feast of fat things, 25 : 6, and shall renew the pillar of cloud and smoke as the symbol of his presence and protection, 4 : 5, and whose courts he claims as his own though trampled and profaned by unworthy worshippers, 1 : 12.

The fact that Jerusalem, and not the high places of Israel, was to the very earliest prophets the true sanctuary of Jehovah, is undeniable ; and the critics have recourse to every evasion to break its force. They say it was not a preference of one sanctuary over others as such, but because of the corruptions that had gained a foothold in the latter. Dr. Robertson Smith says it was not because the temple was in Jerusalem, but this was the capital of the kingdom, the seat of Jehovah's empire. But how entirely the ideas of a sanctuary and a royal residence were dissociated, appears from the fact that in the ten tribes these were never combined in the same locality. Smend[1] confesses that it is the sanctuary in Jerusalem which the prophets exalt, but it is because they anticipate the overthrow of the ten tribes and the preservation of Judah. They stand or fall with their temples. And then the actual overthrow and desolation of the northern kingdom freed Jerusalem from its rivals; while the disastrous defeat of Sennacherib heightened the prestige of Jerusalem. But Smend precisely inverts the order of cause and effect. It was not the protection accorded to Jerusalem which made it Jehovah's dwelling; but because it was his chosen seat, his holy arm was made bare for its defence. Isaiah and Micah and Jeremiah and Ezekiel foretell the desolation of Jerusalem and its temple; this does not in their eyes obscure the fact that it was the divine abode. Jehovah forsook Israel and he forsook Zion because of the iniquities practiced there, but this did not annul the divine choice in the one case nor in the other.

But Smend maintains that we can not infer from the predominance of the temple in the time of Isaiah and Amos that it possessed the same predominance in the period preceding, because the Jehovistic

[1] "Studien und Kritiken," for 1884, "Ueber die Bedeutung des Jerusalemischen Tempels," p. 703.

narratives of Genesis which belong to that time, are framed with the view of exalting the sanctuaries at Bethel, Beersheba and elsewhere by mythical accounts of these spots being hallowed by divine manifestations to the patriarchs or their offering worship there. They presuppose a period, therefore, in which these sanctuaries were held in honor and were resorted to and venerated by the pious. But how does it appear that these narratives belong to that period? Because these sanctuaries were venerated then, and this would give rise to the stories. How does it appear that the sanctuaries were venerated at that time? Because that is when these stories originated. And thus they prove the stories by the sanctuaries and the sanctuaries by the stories in a perpetual circle. Why, then, does Hosea, who denounces the sanctuaries, admit the truth of these patriarchal narratives, and even point his condemnation by it, 12:4? The Bethel of Jacob has become a Bethaven, 10:5, 8; the house of God is converted into a house of iniquity.

The allegation that the patriarchal histories are sheer inventions is gratuitous and without the semblance of a foundation. It was the sanctity given to these places by patriarchal reminiscences, which led to their selection by idolaters for their unauthorized worship. The history determined their choice of sanctuaries; the sanctuaries did not produce the histories any more than Bunker Hill monument originated the story of the battle which opened the American Revolution.

The ark, Smend tells us, lost its prestige after its

capture by the Philistines; and hence its long seclusion until the victories of David brought it once more into notice and restored it to popular favor. The ease with which the critics create their facts is amazing. The history knows of no such loss of prestige. It was not that the ark had ceased to be regarded as a power, that it suffered this long neglect; but because its power spread only consternation and dismay. The inflictions upon the Philistines compelled its return to Bethshemesh. The infliction upon the men of Bethshemesh compelled them to send it away. It was armed with terror and destruction, and their despairing cry was, Who is able to stand before this holy LORD God? and to whom shall he go up from us? 1 Sam. 6:20. It may be said that this is all legend and superstition. Nevertheless it shows in what esteem the ark was held in Israel; and that the reason of its long seclusion was not contempt, but apprehension.

The withdrawal of the ark from the tabernacle deprived Israel for a season of the manifested presence of Jehovah. It was a time of the affliction of God's habitation and the curtailing of the blessings which it brought to Israel, 1 Sam. 2:32 marg. The law of the unity of the sanctuary necessarily lapsed with the cessation of the sanctuary itself. Samuel as God's accredited messenger assumed the functions of the degenerate priesthood, built an altar at his own house in Ramah, 6:17, and offered sacrifices at Mizpeh, 7:9, Gilgal, 10:8, 11:15, and Bethlehem, 16:2. The people went up to God at Bethel, 10:3, where he had met with Jacob, and sought him elsewhere as they were able, just as the pious in the ten tribes did at a later period under a like necessity when debarred from attendance at the legitimate sanctuary, 1 Kin. 18 : 30, 19 : 14. The persuasion that the breach between Jehovah and his people was at length at an end and that Jehovah's dwelling was once again to be established in the midst of his people, was the secret of that enthusiastic joy with which the entire nation hailed the advent of the ark to Zion, 2 Sam. 6 : 15.

And here it may be remarked, by the way, that the ark affords a fresh indication of the weakness of the argument from silence, which figures so largely in critical reasoning. The ark is not once mentioned or referred to by any of the prophets with the exception of a single passage in Jeremiah, 3 : 16. Hosea nowhere alludes to it, nor Amos, nor Isaiah, nor any of their contemporaries. It is not spoken of by Ezekiel nor by any of the prophets after the exile. It is nowhere spoken of in the Psalms with the single exception of Ps. 132 : 8 ; comp. 2 Chron. 6 : 41 ff. How natural the inference on critical principles that the ark was first made in Jeremiah's days or that it was never made at all. And yet, even though the statements of the books of Joshua and Chronicles respecting it were discredited, its existence, its supreme and awful sanctity and its Mosaic origin are attested by Judges, Samuel and Kings. And as there never was more than one ark, this is of itself a demonstration that there was but one legitimate sanctuary from the days of Moses. And how can the Priest Code, which so exalts the ark and makes it the central and most venerated object in the sanctuary, that in fact which constitutes it the dwelling-place of Jehovah, be attributed to the period after the exile when the ark was no longer in existence and the sanctuary of Israel was destitute of any such symbol of the divine presence? If this was the invention of Ezra, what design can he have had in it but that of bringing the second temple into disrepute from its lack of that which constituted the glory of the Mosaic sanctuary, and thus degrading the ritual which he was so bent upon exalting?

But even after the ark was restored and the temple was built, the critics tell us that there is no trace of its exclusive sanctity in the Books of Kings, except in the passages which simply reflect the opinions of the post-exilic writer. And how are we to distinguish these passages? They are those which declare the temple's exclusive sanctity; so that here we have the same vicious circle infecting the reasoning again. And so it is constantly. The hypothesis is always and evermore proved by the hypothesis; and it has no other basis.

GENTLEMEN OF NEWTON THEOLOGICAL INSTITUTION: The task which you assigned to me is accomplished. The long and weary road over which we have been travelling together is now ended. I thank you for the patience with which you have listened to this often tedious discussion. We have not knowingly shunned any point that our antagonists have raised. I think that we may say after a fair examination that the hypothesis of Wellhausen finds no support in the sacred feasts. It is one of its main defences; but it is worth nothing. No gradual growth of these institutions is attested by the laws. The alleged corroboration from the history is altogether illusive. The entire ritual legislation bristles with points which have been in like manner perverted to the defence of this hypothesis and with just as little reason. Critical studies should not be shunned nor despised because of this perversion. The serpent before which Moses fled in alarm, became a rod of power in his hand, when he boldly seized it by the tail. The cloud may be black with tempest, and vivid flashes leaping from its bosom awaken consternation in the timid; but the electrical discharges will prove harmless if the cloud be pierced by a suitable conductor, and that which seemed so threatening will but yield a copious and refreshing shower.

INDEX.

PASSAGES OF SCRIPTURE QUOTED OR REFERRED TO.

GENESIS.

	PAGE
1 : 14	172
2 : 4	151
2 : 7	134
6 : 22	137 note
7 : 5	137 note, 138
7 : 9	137 note, 138
7 : 13	135 note, 136
7 : 16	137 note
14 : 19, 20	170
14 : 21	134
15 : 18	109
ch. 17	293
17 : 7	131
17 : 12	213
17 : 12, 13, 23, 27	132
17 : 12, 27	132
17 : 14	131
17 : 23, 26	135 note, 136
18 : 6	199
18 : 19	161
19 : 3	199
21 : 4	137 note
21 : 22, 32	135
23 : 17	146
24 : 32	170
26 : 26	135
30 : 33	145
43 : 28	146
45 : 18	183 note
47 : 12	133, 134

EXODUS.

3 : 21, 22	119
4 : 23	112
4 : 29-31	97 note
6 : 1	147
6 : 6	134 note
6 : 10-12	119
6 : 26	135
6 : 28-30	119
7 : 2	113 bis
7 : 4	113, 134 note, 135

	PAGE
7 : 4, 5	113
7 : 6	137 note, 138
7 : 10, 20	137 note
7 : 14	113
7 : 16	113
8 : 1	113
8 : 2	113
9 : 1	113
9 : 2	113
9 : 25	135
9 : 35	140
10 : 2	161
10 : 20	140
10 : 28, 29	112
ch. 11	112
11 : 2, 3	119
11 : 4	112, 113
11 : 4 ff	107, 110
11 : 4, 5	110
11 : 4-8	96
11 : 5	147 bis
11 : 9, 10	116
11 : 10	113
ch. 12	90, 92, 94, 103 bis, 116, 181, 185, 228, 236, 293
ch. 12, 13	86, 89, 158, 159, 165, 183, 195, 207, 238, 262
12 : 1	95, 144, 156
12 : 1-13	88, 90 note
12 : 1-28	45, 117
12 : 2	117, 142, 159
12 : 3	110
12 : 4	95, 133 bis, 133 note
12 : 4, 15, 16, 19	134
12 : 6	131
12 : 7, 12, 13	97
12 : 8	53, 90, 108
12 : 8-11	117
12 : 9	218
12 : 10	110, 114, 183
12 : 11	53, 107, 120, 192, 195
12 : 11-13	114

(323)

INDEX OF SCRIPTURE PASSAGES.

Reference	Page
12:12.... 110, 112 bis, 134, 134 note, 135,	160
12:12 f............. 122,	147
12:12, 23.............	120
12:12, 29.............	113
12:13............. 114, 145,	192
12:14..... 114, 115, 120,	133
12:14, 17.............	131
12:14-20....88, 90, 90 note, 109, 114, 115, 117,	140
12:15......... 94, 108, 114, 120,	200
12:15-20.............	103
12:16.... 104 bis, 131, 217, 226, 252,	266
12:17... 109, 110, 111, 114, 120, 135 bis,	160
12:18.... 94, 103, 144, 210, 211,	213
12:19... 106, 114, 120, 131, 132, 160,	200
12:20............. 96, 114,	131
12:21............. 97, 146,	195
12:21-23.............	96
12:21-27........ 88, 96,	117
12:22.... 108,	110
12:22 b, 23.............	97
12:23........ 96, 113, 145,	192
12:23, 27, 29.............	147
12:24........... 133,	218
12:24-27.............	95
12:25, 26.............	145
12:25 ff.............	160
12:27............. 97, 144, 146,	192
12:28.. 88, 96 bis, 118, 120, 135, 137 note, 139 bis,	141
12:29............. 96, 110, 144,	147
12:29 ff.............	122
12:29, 30.............	118
12:29-42.............	88
12:31.............	112
12:31-33............. 113,	118
12:31, 42.............	110
12:31-36.............	118
12:34, 39........ 96, 107, 108,	115
12:35, 36.............	119
12:37............. 120,	146
12:37 a............. 118,	120
12:37 b, 38.............	118
12:38.............	146
12:39............. 53, 118,	120
12:40.............	144
12:40, 41.............	118
12:41-42.............	90 note
12:41.. 114, 115, 119, 135 bis, 160,	206
12:41, 51.............	110
12:42..... 90, 92, 114 bis, 118,	227
12:43.............	131
12:43-49..... 90 note, 95, 106,	118
12:43-50.............	117
12:43-51............. 45,	89
12:44.............	132
12:46.............	95
12:48............. 228,	267
12:48, 49......... 95, 132,	160
12:50...... 135, 137 note, 139,	140
12:50, 51.............	90 note
12:51............. 119, 135 bis,	160
ch. 13..... 92, 94, 95, 103, 171,	217
13:1, 2.............	89
13:1-16............. 90, 90 note
13:2............. 95,	135
13:3.............	144
13:3, 4.............	209
13:3-6.............	98
13:3-10....... 45, 89, 103, 181,	184
13:3, 14.............	145
13:3, 14, 16.............	147
13:3-16............. 117,	161
13:4............. 94, 110, 144,	206
13:5............. 145 (4 times),	160
13:6........ 91, 104, 215, 216,	252
13:7.............	146
13:9............. 147,	161
13:9, 10.............	161
13:11.............	145
13:11-16.............	89
13:12.............	160
13:12, 13.............	95
13:14.............	145
13:15............. 135, 144,	160
13:17.............	120
13:18.............	135
14:19, 20.............	135
16:16, 18......... 133 note,	134
16:23.............	270
16:23 ff.............	104
16:34............. 137 note
16:36............. 254 note
17:1.............	131
ch. 19-24.............	66
19:7, 8.............	97 note
ch. 20............. 168,	169
ch. 20-24.............	17
20:2............. 145,	197
20:24............. 223,	306
20:24, 25............. 18,	33
20:25.............	34
ch. 21-23......... 165,	168
21:13, 14.............	18
21:14.............	33
22:5, 6.............	18
22:29.............	18
22:29 f.............	104

INDEX OF SCRIPTURE PASSAGES. 325

	PAGE
22 : 30	19, 24, 180, 188
ch. 23	165-168, 170, 182, 196, 205, 207, 209, 231, 232, 247, 273, 274, 282, 287, 289, 298, 305
23 : 10, 11	18
23 : 14	144, 182
23 : 14-19	46
23 : 15	91, 104, 157, 167, 180, 182, 195, 206, 244
23 : 15, 16	244
23 : 16	18, 66, 74, 160 *note*, 182, 186, 243, 245, 246, 258, 279
23 : 17	182
23 : 17-19	167, 182, 184
23 : 18	91, 115, 182, 219
23 : 19	33, 182, 223, 272
24 : 4	158
ch. 25-40	17
ch. 32-34	17
32 : 15	270
ch. 34	18, 165-170, 182, 196, 205, 207, 209, 231 f, 247, 273 f, 282, 288 f, 298, 305
34 : 1	169
34 : 4	137 *note*
34 : 9, 10	170
34 : 11 ff	167
34 : 14-26	168 *note*
34 : 18	91, 144, 157, 167, 181, 183, 195, 206, 244 *bis*, 245
34 : 18-20	104
34 : 18-26	46
34 : 19-21	244 *bis*
34 : 22	160 *note*, 243-245, 258, 279, 287, 307
34 : 25	91, 98, 115, 181, 183
34 : 26	223, 272
34 : 27	158, 169
34 : 28	169
35 : 2	270
35 : 2 f	104
35 : 3	131
38 : 22	137 *note*
39 : 1, 5, etc.	137 *note*
39 : 32	138
39 : 32, 43	137 *note*
39 : 42	137 *note*
39 : 42, 43	139
40 : 16	137 *note*, 138, 139
40 : 19, 21, etc.	137 *note*

LEVITICUS.

ch. 1-7	174
2 : 11	199
2 : 12	199
2 : 14	199

	PAGE
3 : 17	131
4 : 15	146
7 : 26	131
7 : 38	16
ch. 8-10	174
8 : 4	137 *note*
8 : 9, 13, etc.	137 *note*
8 : 22 ff	200
8 : 36	137 *note*
9 : 1	146
9 : 10	137 *note*
ch. 11-16	174
12 : 3	213
ch. 16	158, 262
16 : 31	270
16 : 34	137 *note*
ch. 17-20	176
ch. 17-26	176
ch. 18-20	176
ch. 18-23, 25, 26	176
19 : 2	174
19 : 9, 10	264
22 : 25	132
ch. 23	46, 144, 158, 165, 171, 174, 181, 185, 226 f, 236, 260 f, 263, 272 f, 283
ch. 23, 24, 25, 26	176
23 : 1, 9, 23, 33	295
23 : 2	295
23 : 2, 3	293
23 : 3	270, 293
23 : 3, 14, 21, 31	131
23 : 4, 37, 38, 44	294, 295
23 : 5	267
23 : 5, 6	211
23 : 5-8, 14 *b*	294
23 : 6	211, 267
23 : 7	104, 270
23 : 7, 8	217
23 : 8	266, 2 0
23 : 9 ff	186
23 : 9, 10	253 *note*, 263
23 : 9-14 *a*	294
23 : 9-14	201
23 : 9-22	260, 262, 293
23 : 10	199, 246, 261
23 : 10, 11	254 *note*
23 : 11	104, 270, 271
23 : 14	199, 265, 267
23 : 14, 21, 28-30	135 *note*, 136
23 : 15	260
23 : 15 ff	264
23 : 15, 16	263
23 : 15 *a*, 16 *a*, 21	294
23 : 15 *b*, 16 *b*, 20	294
23 : 16	261, 272, 281

INDEX OF SCRIPTURE PASSAGES.

	PAGE
23:17	199, 246, 254 note
23:18, 19, 22	293
23:22	264, 294
23:23-32	293
23:23-36	294
23:24, 39	270
23:32	269
23:34	298
23:34 ff.	291
23:34-36	300
23:36	214, 226, 298
23:36, 39	291
23:37, 38	293
23:38	220, 302
23:39	297, 298, 299
23:39, 41	73, 281
23:39, 43	299
23:39-43	293, 294 bis
23:39-44	293 bis
23:40	300, 302
23:41	297
23:42	299
23:43	284
24:23	137 note
ch. 25	263
25:1	156
25:1, 2	263
25:2, 4, 6, 8	270
25:5	270
25:8	263
25:9, 10, 22	160 note
25:16	133
ch. 26	175
26:34, 35, 43	270
26:46	156
27:16	133
27:23	133
27:34	156

NUMBERS.

ch. 1-10	17
1:19	137 note
1:54	137 note, 139
2:33	137 note
2:34	137 note, 139
3:13	104, 110, 120, 160
3:42, 51	137 note
4:49	137 note
5:4	137 note, 139
8:3	137 note
8:17	104, 110, 120, 160
8:20	137 note, 139
8:22	137 note
ch. 9	181, 185
9:1 ff	158, 178
9:1-14	165

	PAGE
9:5	137 note
9:5-14	46
9:11	232
9:11, 12, 14	158
9:17	133
10:11	185
11:21	146
14:8	145
14:28	145
ch. 15-19	17
15:36	137 note
17:11	137 note, 139
18:17, 18	202
20:9	137 note
20:27	137 note
ch. 25-36	17
26:54	133
27:7, 8	161
27:22	137 note
ch. 28	172, 181, 185, 220, 226, 235 f, 272 f
ch. 28, 29	46, 144, 165, 177, 207, 263, 283, 299
28:16, 17	211, 274
28:17	211
28:18, 25	217
28:19 ff	190
28:26	243, 260, 264, 272, 281, 282
28:35	214
29:12 ff.	291, 298
29:35	226, 291, 292
29:39	199, 220, 302
31:7, 41, 47	137 note
31:28, 37-41	133
31:31	137 note
33:3	110, 268, 269
33:4	120, 134 note
33:5	120
33:17	131
33:44	146
ch. 34, 35	146
35:1	156
35:29	131
36:10	137 note
36:13	156

DEUTERONOMY.

ch. 5	168
5:15	47
5:23	97 note
12:1-8	20
12:5	34
12:8 f	179
12:9 f	34
12:15, 21	23
12:19	23

INDEX OF SCRIPTURE PASSAGES. 327

	PAGE
14:23	284
14:23-26	24
15:19, 20	24, 104, 202
15:20	184
ch. 16	54, 178, 209, 217, 232, 247, 282 f, 302
16:1	104, 115, 143 f, 206, 228
16:1, 2	185
16:1, 3, 8	106
16:1-8	159, 181
16:1-17	46
16:2	103, 190
16:2 ff	213
16:3	195, 200
16:4, 8	211
16:7	94, 212, 214 f, 219
16:7, 8	105
16:8	226, 252
16:9	186, 201, 271
16:9, 10	246, 258
16:10	243, 272
16:12	257
16:13	279, 299
16:14	284
16:16	306
18:6-8	23
24:8	179
26:5-10	280
26:8-10	197
27:5, 6	34
31:9, 24	159
32:14	183 note
32:48	135 note, 136
34:9	137 note

JOSHUA.

1:15	268
3:15	267
5:1	268
5:10	230
5:11	135 f, 199, 267, 269 f
10:27	136
10:28 ff	134
10:40	137 note
11:11	134
11:15	137 note
14:5	137 note
18:1	35, 308
19:51	35
21:8	137 note
ch. 22	35
24:5 ff	197
24:17	145

JUDGES.

2:1	197
6:8 ff	197

	PAGE
6:19	199
9:9, 13	307
9:27	225, 284, 306
18:31	35, 308
19:18	35, 308
20:28	38
21:12, 24	309
21:19	35, 65, 307, 314
21:21	39

RUTH.

2:14	199

I SAMUEL.

1:3	36, 65, 307
1:3 ff	314
1:4 ff	219
1:20	307
1:24	36
2:14	36, 230, 308
2:15	218
2:22	36, 308
2:27-29	308
2:28, 29	36
2:32	319
4:4	36
6:17	319
6:20	319
7:9	319
8:4, 7	97
10:3	319
10:8	319
11:15	319
16:2	319
16:16 ff	315
30:16	281

2 SAMUEL.

1:17	315
3:10	161
5:1, 3	97 note
6:15	320
7:6	311
11:1	160 note
17:4, 14, 15	97 note
19:11, 14	97 note
ch. 22	315
ch. 23	315
23:1	315

I KINGS.

3:2	37
5:3-5	311
6:1, 38	142
6:38	290
8:1, 5, 9, etc	310
8:2	73, 142, 232, 281, 290, 315

328 INDEX OF SCRIPTURE PASSAGES.

	PAGE
8 : 5	302, 309
8 : 16–21	37
8 : 20 ff	311
8 : 62–64	302
8 : 63	309
8 : 65	73, 247, 281, 286, 290
8 : 66	292
9 : 25	273
11 : 4, 7	312
11 : 7, 8	37
12 : 16	215
12 : 26 ff	313
12 : 28	197
12 : 32	73, 225, 281, 287, 290, 315
12 : 32, 33	232
14 : 23	37, 312
18 : 26	191
18 : 30	320
19 : 10, 14	37
19 : 14	320
19 : 15	314
20 : 22, 26	160 note
21 : 11	97 note

2 KINGS.

3 : 2 f, 13	314
4 : 23	65
8 : 13	314
10 : 20	227
12 : 16	275 note
16 : 3	161
22 : 3	160
ch. 23	232
23 : 1, 2	97 note
23 : 9	54 bis
23 : 21, 22	228, 232
23 : 21–23	231
23 : 22	54, 229
23 : 23	160

1 CHRONICLES.

11 : 1, 3	97 note
16 : 7	232
23 : 31	65

2 CHRONICLES.

5 : 3	73
6 : 41 ff	320
7 : 8, 9	73
7 : 9	292
7 : 10	281
8 : 12, 13	273
8 : 13	230
10 : 16	215
15 : 10, 12	258
29 : 21–24	275 note

	PAGE
29 : 30	232
ch. 30	229, 230
30 : 10	230
30 : 15	232
30 : 16 f	217
30 : 23	247
30 : 26	230
35 : 1	232
35 : 7–9	185, 190
35 : 11	217
35 : 13	218
35 : 18	230

EZRA.

3 : 4	300
3 : 4, 5	302
6 : 19 ff	231

NEHEMIAH.

3 : 10–12	302
8 : 14	73, 281
8 : 15	300
8 : 17	293, 300
8 : 18	292

PSALMS.

18	315
40 : 6	275 note
42 : 4	227
63 : 5	183 note
81	232
81 : 3	73
81 : 3–5	233
81 : 16	183 note
95 : 11	47
104 : 14, 15	279
132	37
132 : 8	320

ISAIAH.

1 : 12	316
1 : 13	226
2 : 3	316
4 : 5	226, 316
8 : 18	316
10 : 32	316
11 : 15, 16	197
18 : 7	316
24 : 23	316
25 : 6	316
26 : 1	316
27 : 13	316
29 : 1	65, 226, 316
30 : 29	65, 115, 227, 315 f
31 : 4, 5, 9	316
31 : 5	192, 228

INDEX OF SCRIPTURE PASSAGES.

	PAGE
33:20	227, 316
37:30	160 *note*
53:10	275 *note*

JEREMIAH.

31:38–40	237
33:11	315
36:22	160 *note*

EZEKIEL.

2:3	135 *note*
24:2	135 *note*
34:3	183 *note*
40:1	135 *note*
40:39	275
45:18 ff.	234
45:20	264
45:21	211, 274
45:21–24	231
45:25	73, 281

HOSEA.

2:11	65, 316
2:13	314, 316
3:5	314, 316
4:8	275 *note*
4:13, 15	316
8:4	314
8:5 f.	314
9:1	210
10:5 f.	314
10.5, 8	318
10:8, 15	314, 316
11:1	197
12:4	318
12:9	301
12:9, 13	197
13:2	314
13:4	197

JOEL.

1:14	227
2:15	227

AMOS.

1:2	316
2:10	197
3:1	197
3:14	316
4:4	316
5:4, 5	316
5:21	227
5:23	315
6:5	315
8:14	316

ZECHARIAH.

2:4	237

MATTHEW.

17:1	213
26:17	212
28:1	271

MARK.

9:2	213

LUKE.

6:1	265, 271
9:28	213
18:12	271

JOHN.

5:1, 39	258
7:37	281, 292
11:49 ff.	60
18:39	61
20:26	213

ACTS.

12:2	60

I CORINTHIANS.

5:8	200

JOSEPHUS.

Antiq. iii. 10, 6	243
Antiq. xiii. 8, 4	265

www.ingramcontent.com/pod-product-compliance
Lightning Source LLC
Chambersburg PA
CBHW021158230426
43667CB00006B/450